The Student Dancer

For the dance community,

with affection and respect

The Student Dancer

*Emotional Aspects of the
Teaching and Learning of Dance*

Julia Buckroyd

DANCE BOOKS
Cecil Court London

Published in 2000 by
Dance Books Ltd
15 Cecil Court
London WC2N 4EZ

ISBN 1 85273 074 9

A CIP catalogue record for this book is
available from the British Library

Design: Sanjoy Roy
Cover photo: Chris Nash

Printed in Great Britain by
H. Charlesworth & Co., Huddersfield

Contents

Preface

This book has been a good number of years in the making and is the fruit of a range of experience and developments in my thinking which have been facilitated by many people. I would like to take the opportunity of acknowledging at least some of them.

I owe thanks first of all to Ellen Noonan who ran the Certificate in Student Counselling at Birkbeck College, University of London, when I attended it from 1982 to 1984. It was in that environment that I first became aware of the possibility of applying psychodynamic ideas to educational settings, and thus acquired the basic tools for understanding the emotional processes involved in teaching and learning. The effect that the course had on me at the time was revelatory; for the first time I could begin to make sense of my own educational history and the responses of the students that I taught.

My first contact with professional dance training came in my time as Student Counsellor at London Contemporary Dance School, from 1984 to 1989. I was fortunate to have that role in a dance training institution which was unconventional and alive to emotional processes within students. I am grateful to the former Principal, Richard Ralph, and to the staff of LCDS for their concern with difficult issues of student welfare. I learned a lot from my colleagues, especially from Sonia Noonan, the Body Conditioning Tutor, about dance training and the pressures it exerts upon students. More recently I have benefited from conversations with Louise Donald, Director of Student Services, and from the current Student Counsellor, Elizabeth Nabarro. Ronald Emblen, Peter Connell and Lyndon Branaugh were also kind enough to allow me to interview them. As quotations from the current student handbook in this book will reveal, LCDS is in the forefront of developments within professional dance training towards a more humanistic model.

Since I left LCDS I have worked as a psychotherapist with a good many dancers. Their honesty about themselves and their lives as dance students and dancers has been invaluable in helping me to understand more about the psychological issues involved in dance training.

Over the past ten years I have also worked as a consultant in many dance training organisations with both staff and students, mostly in relation to my interest in eating disorders. These contacts have been important in extending the range of my experience of dance training institutions, and in giving me the opportunity to see a wide range of different attitudes to dance training. I am particularly grateful to Anne Stannard at the Central School of Ballet, to John MacNamara at Elmhurst and to Jane Billington and Rachel Rist at Arts Educational School, Tring, for their interest in my ideas and their willingness to discuss them with me and share their own views.

The research for the chapter on male trainees was done in three training organisations. I am particularly grateful to the boys who participated and who were willing to be pioneers in an attempt to record and understand their experience of dance training. Thanks therefore to the following students: James Dobb, Phil Williams, Damian North, Adam Galbraith and Tommy Snell at LCDS; Martin Collyer, Kenneth Tindall, Benjamin Whitson, Blake Clayfield, Jake Nwogu, Eliot Rudolph, Toby Smith, Isaac Mullins, Vincente Bustamante, Joel Morris, Christopher Smith, Andrew Blackman, Simon Kidd, Chris James, Ian Burdon and James Dodd at Central School of Ballet; and James Barton, Richard Leavey, Patrick Shipman, Silas Stubbs, Thomas Forster, Jack Tobin, Rhys George, Luke Rabbito, Paul Rooney, James Skilton, Charles Tamburin, Graham Tigwell, Ben Warren, Matthew Bond, David Higgs, Michael Lee, Jamie Beeson, Philip Catchpole, Alexander Durrant, Nathaniel Yelton, Angus Barnetson and Aaron Piper at Elmhurst School.

A good number of people from the dance community have encouraged and supported this work. I would like particularly to mention Joysanne Sidimus, a former Balanchine dancer and now Director of Dancer Transition in Canada; Fiona Dick, whose concern for dancers resulted in her involvement in the Healthier Dancer Project and who has willingly provided advice and references; Jessica Shenton at Dance UK, whose support and interest have been valuable; Charlotte Kirkpatrick, former dancer with London Contemporary Dance Theatre and now concerned with how dancers are trained, who has encouraged me over a good number of years and was an early supporter of my writing when I was still at The Place; Maja Delak from Slovenia, whose passionate belief in what I have to say has been a great strength; Mary Evelyn at LCDS, whose interests closely parallel my own; Sara Matthews at Central School.

The work of the late and sadly missed Peter Brinson has been a great inspiration to me throughout this project. His two conferences, The Healthier Dancer, in 1990, and Tomorrow's Dancers, in 1993, together with the book which he wrote with Fiona Dick, *Fit To Dance* (1996), provide a foundation for the 'climate of change' in dance teaching to which he was so committed. I hope that my work, like his, will capture the imagination of those responsible for the training of professional dancers, and lead to new attitudes and developments.

Students from the University of Hertfordshire have been aware of some parts of the work and have encouraged and supported me with their interest and appreciation. I would like to mention in particular Ray Weedon and Carol Smith, whose paper on counselling values in the classroom I have used.

I am grateful to colleagues who have read parts of the book in draft and have discussed the issues involved, or who have offered me their particular expertise. They have helped me to continue with what has at times felt like an unending task. I would particularly like to acknowledge the help of Maggie Turp, who as a Researcher at the University of Hertfordshire has helped me a great deal with the project, and whose own work on psychosomatics and related issues has been a valuable resource. Helen Payne, Senior Lecturer at the University of Hertfordshire, has helped me greatly through her knowledge both of dance and of research methods. Brian Thomas has generously shared his work on the psychology of dancers and dance teaching. Steve Seaton has given me his expertise on mainstream education. Jim Miller, Anne Gray and Michael Philps have also been a great support. Dorothy de Longchamps has drawn my attention to a number of articles in the media.

I count myself fortunate that I work at the University of Hertfordshire, which has been unfailingly supportive of my research and professional interests. My Head of Department during the writing of this book, Helen Cosis Brown, has translated that support into study leave and a personal concern that I have valued enormously. David Leonard, the publisher at Dance Books, has been steadfastly patient and positive over the years it has taken to generate this book and has sustained me to complete the task by his belief in it.

Finally, let me thank those close and dear to me, especially Hilary Harwood and Bernardine Bishop who have, in their different ways, generously accompanied me on the journey, and without whom this book would never have been written.

I have found while I have been writing that many of the issues I discuss overlap and are interrelated. I have referred the reader to other parts of the book throughout the text, but, in the interests of dealing with each issue in a fairly complete way, I have also included some repetition of key ideas and issues. In the course of my researches for the book, I have come across many examples of good practice, some of which I have shared with the reader in what follows. These contributions are printed in shaded boxes. I am indebted to the institutions and individuals concerned for permission to reproduce this material for the benefit of others. Throughout the text I have used the female pronoun to refer to dance trainees and their teachers, except where exclusively male trainees or teachers are referred to. I have adopted this usage because the overwhelming majority of trainees and their teachers in Western Europe and the USA are in fact female.

Julia Buckroyd
University of Hertfordshire, 1999

1

Introduction

> The education offered by dance teachers is no different, except in subject matter, from the rest of education. It has to communicate, inspire, be practical and be valued by its consumers. It has to come to terms with the changing attitudes and priorities of a new century. Unless it does this it will become irrelevant to the needs and interests of young people in that century. It will be a marooned curiosity. Investment in change, therefore, is urgent if dance is to be part of the mainstream of British cultural education.
>
> (Brinson, 1993: ix)

This book seeks to explore emotional and psychological aspects of the teaching and learning of dance at a professional level. It is therefore directed primarily at dance teachers in vocational schools and colleges, and at those who teach such courses in larger institutions, such as universities. My aim is to review what is known about the emotional needs of young people and to discuss the relevance of that information for the dance training environment. In this way I hope to offer dance teachers a way of thinking about their dance teaching in the light of current understanding of how to facilitate learning and development in young people.

The book will also be useful to the parents of young dancers who may wish to think about the emotional implications of learning to dance for their developing son or daughter, and who would like to be better informed of the issues involved in the choice of a dance training at an elite level. As elite physical trainings of all kinds (including even instrumental music education) become more and more physically demanding for ever younger participants, so there is mounting concern at the cost, both physical and psychological, of the relentless pressure to achieve. Parents, as some commentators have observed, do not have adequate criteria for judging the effect on their children's physical and emotional health of vocational training in any field which makes such strenuous demands (Skrinar and Moses in Clarkson and Skrinar, 1988). I am not qualified to comment on the physical aspects of dance training, but I hope what I have to say about the emotional needs of developing young people will help parents to discriminate between training that is beneficial to the emotional health and general level of functioning of their children, and training that is damaging.

I hope that my ideas will also find a wider audience within the dance community. Choreographers, artistic directors, rehearsal directors, and school and company administrators may find it useful in reflecting upon the psychological environment they create in their work with dancers. In addition, those who teach the very many dance classes for young people that are an introduction to the art of dancing and may perhaps be the stepping stones to further study, may similarly wish to use these ideas for thinking about the psychological complexities of working with and on the bodies of young people.

Furthermore, I believe that the ideas in this book can be applied to any mode of physical training for young people. They are particularly relevant for those training at a vocational or elite level. I hope those who coach youngsters in athletics or in sports that recruit very young competitors, such as tennis, gymnastics and swimming will find the ideas useful for their work with adolescents. They can easily be applied to physical trainings which have an artistic component, such as ice-skating. I hope that those who coach and train youngsters in these events will find something to stimulate reflection.

I also think that those who provide elite training for young people in any of the arts, such as music or drama, might be able to find something useful in this exploration of how technical skill and creativity can be nurtured while at the same time young people are supported in their emotional and adolescent development.

A central premise in what I have to say is that young people, by definition, do not have a fully developed sense of self. Because of their age and developmental stage, both children and adolescents have fragile self-esteem. Self-esteem for adults is supported and increased by adult accomplishments such as work, sexual partnerships and property owner-ship. The child and adolescent has no such accomplishments to bolster identity. At that stage of life, identity is strongly invested in the body and the developing sense of mastery of it. For teenage girls particularly, the sense of self is near identical to their sense of their bodies and physical selves. Physical training for young people, therefore, has the potential either to enhance and develop their confidence and self-esteem, or to undermine and damage it. The results in either case are likely to be long-lasting. This book therefore seeks to explore the ways in which dance training can enhance confidence and self-esteem and to identify those modes of dance training which run the risk of being damaging.

I have two principal motives for engaging in this study. The first is to make available to the dance community an up-to-date synopsis of current ideas about the emotional needs and development of young people so that those who preside over the teaching environment for dance training are fully equipped to provide optimum conditions for training. More attention to psychological issues would enable more effective learning for students and prove less demanding for teachers. With renewed attention to these matters, I am sure that the quality of work and level of achieve-ment of young dancers would improve. Just as there have been develop-ments in our knowledge of how to make dance training more effective physically, (e.g. Koutedakis in Brinson, 1993; Brinson and Dick, 1996), so I am sure that knowledge of psychological issues could also make the learning process more effective.

Secondly, I am aware of the large numbers of youngsters who embark on vocational dance training but for one reason or another do not com-plete it, or, even if they do, never continue to a dance career. I think it vital that this experience is not seen as wasted or as a failure, but as a useful part of a young person's education and experience. Potentially, dance training at every level has a huge contribution to make to the development of confidence and competence in young people, with a resulting improvement in all aspects of their functioning. I am concerned to explore how that may most effectively be done in the context of vocational training.

I have no personal experience of either learning or teaching dance (unless I include the compulsory ballroom dancing lessons that were part of the curriculum of the very traditional girls' school I attended). I was, however, interested in athletics as a teenager and young adult and derived considerable pleasure from those activities. I have therefore some small personal understanding of the charm and excitement of developing physical prowess and refining physical skills. This history has some part to play in my interest in dancers.

What is probably much more significant is that I have never been out of an educational environment. Throughout my life I have been either learning or teaching, or both at the same time, in some kind of educational institution. Over the years I have become very interested in how people learn and in the factors both personal and environmental that seem to affect their capacity to learn. My own teaching has been very much influenced by my reflection on these issues.

A further ingredient in my interest in dancers has been my training as a student counsellor and then as a psychotherapist. This training has provided me with a number of concepts and a vocabulary which have helped me to think about the emotional meanings to the individual of the experiences of learning and teaching.

However, what has been by far the most powerful factor in the development of my interest in dance training and the welfare of dancers was the five years I spent as the Student Counsellor at London Contemporary Dance School. My role during those years was to offer individual students an opportunity to discuss in confidence issues that troubled them. I saw a very large number of students, something approaching a third of the student body of approximately 180 during any one academic year. Some were referred by teachers; the vast majority were self-referred. Some came for a single meeting; some met me weekly for two years or very occasionally even longer. I learned an enormous amount about adolescents and their preoccupations and about the experience of vocational dance training. I heard a lot from these troubled youngsters about the emotional distress the training caused them, despite the deserved reputation that LCDS enjoyed for enlightened concern, compared with many similar dance training institutions, and about their struggles and longings. My hope is that what I have to say may go some way to reducing the avoidable distress of dance training for students. Because I was also a member of staff at the dance school, I had a great deal of interaction with my colleagues. From them I learned how hard and unfulfilling their task could sometimes be and I saw at first hand their devotion to dance and their exhaustion and frustration when the results of their teaching were not all they would have hoped. My conviction is that what I have to say also has the potential to make their interactions with students less stressful and to liberate them from some of the burdens that they carry.

This book, therefore, is to a very large extent the fruit of those five years, modified and expanded by my continuing experience as a therapist with dancers, interest in the issues which preoccupy them, and my work as a consultant to a number of dance schools. Most important of student concerns is the subject of creativity. The vast majority of the dancers I have talked to have had a sense of their own creative potential and a frustration about their inability to reach it. My wish is, therefore, to consider how dance training may best support and develop the creative potential of student dancers and, in that process, strengthen them and develop them as people and as artists.

Throughout this book the principal emphasis is on the psychological and emotional needs of girls and young women. This is not because the needs of boys are not equally complex and deserving of attention, but because dance, along with gymnastics, ice-skating and swimming, recruits girls at an early age. The technical demands of these activities favour the pre-pubescent female body. As these technical demands escalate, as they have done relentlessly over the past twenty years, the age of participants becomes ever younger. The same is not true for boys, where the demands for power favour the post-pubertal boy. Cultural imperatives may be changing so that boys will be made as unconfident about their bodies as girls. Men's 'health' magazines seem to be beginning to preach a doctrine of how the male body should look, which promises to place an equivalent and equally unrealistic demand on them. However, a boy, at least at the moment, is culturally less vulnerable than a girl to poor self-esteem, and by beginning training later, as he often does, has a better chance of having a reasonably strong sense of self by the time the training becomes intensive. It is also a simple truth that fewer boys than girls engage in vocational dance training. Dance training, and dancing at a professional or elite level, is largely (if not entirely) for females (Burt, 1995). However, the fact that boys are so exceptional within the dance world creates its own problems; there are also issues, for instance of sexual identity, which are raised for boys but not for girls by the very fact of undergoing dance training. For these reasons I have devoted one chapter to the particular issues and concerns of male dance trainees.

I would now like to describe in more detail the focus of this book and the intellectual origins from which it has evolved.

The Concept of Adolescence

The first idea which informs what follows, as a kind of backcloth, is the cultural conviction of Western society in the twentieth century that adolescence is a crucial developmental stage in the formation of the personality. This idea is in turn part of a Western tradition of individualism which has shaped our society for hundreds of years, at least since the Renaissance.

It is a cultural reality, whether we like it or not, that our society regards the development of the individual, of oneself, as the highest responsibility, capable of being expressed even in terms of religious duty, as in the parable of the talents. It is often seen as a responsibility greater than loyalty to family, kinship group, community, class and sometimes even nation. These ideas are expressed clearly in the American cultural myth: 'anyone can be president'; 'a man's got to do what a man's got to do'. They are deeply embedded in Western society and have received an extra fillip in the past two decades from the Thatcherite anti-society, and anti-collectivist, individualist drift of European politics.

To some extent, women have in the past been excluded from this cultural imperative, it being assumed that their personal realisation lay in facilitating the development and achievements of their husbands and sons. However, the women's movement has made significant inroads into that assumption. At the beginning of the twenty-first century it is increasingly seen as necessary and desirable for women, in Western society at least, to strive to realise their personal potential in individual terms. Moreover, the cultural rewards for responding to this imperative are high. Our society loves and benefits winners, celebrities, achievers, stars; 'just do your best' must be an injunction familiar to every child in the Western world. The fact that not everyone can be a 'winner' has, however, contributed to the environment of envy which is the less attractive side of the individualist society. Those who succeed are likely to be fêted and envied in equal measure.

There have been countervailing voices which have urged more attention to 'Eastern' values and have pointed to the need for a balance between 'being' and 'doing'. Some have urged the adoption of what are seen as more spiritual or feminine values in the face of so much that emphasises competition and striving. However, in the world of elite performance (whether of dance, music, gymnastics, sport, and so on) the emphasis has overwhelmingly been on effort, achievement and individual success. There seems little point in pretending or hoping that professional dance can in the immediate future stand outside these current cultural imperatives. We can value the enormous accomplishments and successes of our individualist society, not least in dance, but we should also remember what dangers and destructiveness are inherent in individualism and consider how the competitiveness it fuels can be addressed and moderated.

Adolescence is a crucial stage in terms of the individual's capacity to make the development necessary for self-realisation. How it is negotiated will also determine whether individualism is experienced as damaging or creative. In the decade from twelve to twenty-two years old, a young person is expected to make an enormous transition: the transition from the relative dependence of the child beginning secondary education to the relative independence of the young adult with some kind of training or preparation for the adult world of work. The transition encompasses the acquisition of numerous social and personal skills, but also a degree of separation from the family of origin. Young people in their early twenties in our society will have moved from a stage where their parents are the most important people in their lives, to a stage of attachment to their peer group and will have formed significant relationships within that group. It is assumed that most will also have developed sexual partnerships within the peer group. Most of all, and most crucially for our purposes, it is expected that a young adult will have developed sufficient sense of self to make relatively autonomous life choices. We expect youngsters in their late teens and early twenties to have a sense of who they are, what they want and how to go about getting it.

These cultural requirements for self-realisation are very considerable. It is doubtful if many people of twenty-two or so can accomplish all of them. They are probably particularly hard for young women to accomplish since our culture makes it exceptionally difficult for young women to grow up with a strong sense of self (Pipher, 1994). Moreover, adverse economic and employment circumstances have prolonged adolescence and financial dependence for many young people in the past decade or so. Nevertheless it is expected, and indeed required, that to the best of their ability adolescents should make steps towards the goals of autonomy. Those who do not or cannot are not likely to function easily in adult society.

It is this development towards autonomy which concerns me in much of what follows. There is a problem, which the dance community needs to address, in facilitating this transition from childhood dependence to adult independence. It is a problem faced by any discipline that requires young people to devote unusually long hours and abnormal concentration to a single external focus. The problem is the same for young swimmers, musicians, gymnasts and dancers. They are required to complete a basic education, just like every other child, but at the same time to pour huge amounts of time and effort into the acquisition of further skills. In this process, the emotional tasks of adolescence may well remain hopelessly incomplete. Some influential voices within these elite environments argue that adolescence, for their unusually gifted charges, is a luxury that cannot be afforded. I strongly disagree. There are too many stories of those who emerge from their lives as performers to find themselves cast adrift in the real world. There are even more accounts of adolescents who could no longer square the circle of training for elite performance with accomplishing normal adolescent goals (such as having a social life) and who resolved the dilemma by dropping out of training.

The issue, therefore, that I am concerned to address in much of what follows is how professional dance training can change and adapt to enable adolescents, especially the adolescent girls, who form the large majority of trainees, to achieve the vital emotional growth necessary to their becoming mature adults, without sacrificing the development of their specific physical and artistic talent. I consider this to be an important and exceptionally difficult task for the dance world to address; talent is rare and we can ill afford to squander it.

Psychoanalytic Concepts

A second strand in my thinking for this book arises from psychoanalytic theory. There are two concepts from this body of theory that I think might be particularly useful for reflecting on emotional aspects of dance teaching. The first, most often associated with Melanie Klein (e.g. 1959), is that as human beings, from our earliest days, we are capable of feeling a wide range of emotions in relation to others. These include those emotions that we all prefer and are proud to own, such as pleasure, satisfaction, love, admiration and gratitude; and they also include those much less easy feelings of hate, anger, envy, jealousy, rivalry, aggression and the wish to hurt. Klein's position was that there seems little point in denying the existence of these less amiable feelings in each one of us. Indeed, the failure to acknowledge and accept the existence of those feelings in ourselves and others condemns us to find more damaging ways of expressing them by acting them out.

How can we transpose this way of thinking to the dance class? If rivalry, envy and competition, for example, can be openly acknowledged by teacher and students as a fact of life and the source of painful and unwelcome feelings, then there will be less incentive to act them out, for example by vicious gossip (Skynner and Cleese, 1983). In practice it seems to me that dance classes in vocational schools are hotbeds of unacknowledged hostile and difficult feelings between students and between student and teacher, which are never openly admitted, far less managed. Most often they are left unmentioned and unspeakable (Schnitt, 1990), and find expression in the many small acts of hostility that can make dance schools such emotionally poisonous places. Sometimes rivalry, envy and competition are even encouraged and worked up by teachers in the mistaken view that this will improve the students' motivation. Instead the inevitable, ordinary rivalries are compounded and disrupt the students' capacity to work creatively (Kirkland, 1987; de Mille, 1952). The attack on Nancy Kerrigan, the American skater, by the ex-husband of her rival Tanya Harding, is perhaps the best known and most shocking example of the lengths to which acted-out rivalry and hostility can go (Ryan, 1996: 111–9). Rivalries within the dance world can certainly be as destructive emotionally, if not physically.

The second concept brought into service from object-relations theory, especially from the work of Wilfred Bion (e.g. 1967), is the concept of containment. This is the idea that the safe management of strong feelings, bad or good, is difficult and rests upon a capacity developed gradually during the process of growing up. At the beginning we all need someone else, usually the mother or maternal figure, to help us learn to manage or contain feelings. For example, the arrival of a new baby frequently provokes great jealousy, rivalry and aggression in older siblings. If a mother can say to a three-year-old, when he hangs over the baby in a threatening way, 'I think you must feel very jealous of your baby brother. I bet you wish he would go away,' and can show the child at the same time, perhaps by cuddling him, that even having such feelings he is a loved and valuable person, then she enables him to accept and contain within himself those feelings. The mother's capacity to *think* in the face of the child's feelings, contains the situation. In this way she makes the pressure within the child to act the feelings out, for example by tipping baby brother out of his carry-cot, much less urgent. So, in this example, the mother, by acknowledging and accepting the child's feelings, rather than punishing him for having them ('What a horrid little boy you are to be so nasty to your baby brother; if you do that again I'll smack you'), does not allow them to get out of hand, and contains them. She puts the feelings into words and by doing so enables them to be managed. This capacity on the part of the mother in turn enables the child in due course to think about his feelings, to learn to put them into words and so to contain them. As he develops and as the experience of having his feelings named, accepted and acknowledged is repeated over and over again, throughout his development, so gradually he internalises this function and learns how to do it for himself.

This containing function, however, does take many years to internalise. Adolescents in any educational setting are unlikely to have yet come to the point where they no longer need it demonstrated by the responsible adult. It is highly likely to be a continuing developmental need, especially since adolescence is a time of very strong feelings (for example, sexual desire, aggression or conversely depression and despair) which the adolescent finds alarming and needs help to manage.

What is particular to the dance class is its physicality, underlined by the revealing clothing worn by students, and its focus on the body, its shape and its capacities, at a point in development where feelings about one's body, one's sexuality and that of others are in any case very powerful and difficult to manage. In this environment it is more than ever necessary that the dance teacher can become aware of, acknowledge and contain these feelings. How in practice this might be done will be explored later. The results would not only be useful for the emotional development of students, but by moderating the force of feelings, would enable them to be less distracted by them and to focus better.

Humanistic Educational Theory

A third major theme in this book is the significance for dance training of the ideas of Carl Rogers. Rogers' central conviction was that human beings have an innate tendency to growth and development in all aspects of their being: physical, emotional, intellectual and spiritual. This growth, he believed, depended on the provision of an enabling environment which he described in terms of the 'core conditions' of empathy, acceptance and genuineness. These necessary but sufficient conditions would, he believed, enable human beings to develop into the people they were capable of becoming, with whatever talents, capacities and accomplishments that implied.

These ideas were originally developed in the 1950s in the USA for a therapeutic setting. Although they have some similarities and areas of overlap with psychoanalytic ideas, their emphasis was rather different. Rogers focused on the client's perception of his own world. The role of the therapist, he proposed, was to provide the emotional environment of empathy, acceptance and congruence which would provide a safe enough setting for the client to address his hopes, fears, anxieties, feelings – in short, himself. The therapist's task was to enter as fully as possible into the client's world and convey his compassionate understanding of the client's life and experience. The therapist's function was to be the companion on the client's journey of self-discovery. The resources for growth, development and cure resided in the client, and it was the client's responsibility to bring them into play.

Rogers applied his ideas to many areas of human functioning – not just to therapy, but also to teaching and learning. He proposed a radical alteration to traditional ideas of the relative roles of teacher and student. 'Client-centred therapy' translated into 'student-centred learning'. Rogers' vision was that instead of the hierarchical power relationship between the 'teacher who knows best' and the student who is ignorant and dependent on the teacher for knowledge and understanding, there should develop a relationship where the teacher provides a learning environment characterised by the core conditions of empathy, acceptance and genuineness. Within this environment, he believed, the student would be safe enough to confront his own 'not knowing' and to use the teacher as a resource in his search for knowledge and understanding (Rogers, 1969, 1994).

These ideas have had their equivalents in pure educational theory, but they are particularly interesting and coherent because they derive from a well-articulated theory of the human being. Rogers' ideas have had their critics, some particularly savage (Cohen, 1997), as have the ideas of those, such as A.S. Neill, who have developed radical educational alternatives in Britain. Over the life of the last Conservative government in Britain especially, there were many attacks on the supposed idiocies of 'progressive education'. However, when compared with teaching methods and educational theory of fifty years ago, it is evident that many of those radical ideas have percolated into mainstream education and become ordinary. Teachers in state schools are no longer seen as remote, terrifying figures; pupils are encouraged to learn, discover and find out for themselves and to use the teacher as a learning resource. Even if there is something of a backlash against 'student-centred learning', it is unlikely that there will be a return to the old authoritarianism. Our society has become much more egalitarian and less hierarchical over the past half-century, and mainstream education has absorbed and reflected those trends.

When we turn to the education of the elite professionals who are the subject of this study, however, we are faced with a model of teaching and learning that survives nowhere else. It is rare to find a studio/gym where the teacher/coach is not an absolute authority with a very clear hierarchical control over the students. In Rogerian terms, this not only inhibits the development of the person, but is directly counterproductive to the maximum realisation of the talents of the students in question.

In what follows I am concerned to consider how this state of affairs has come about, whether it can be understood as having any positive value and whether Rogers' ideas might be incorporated more widely into the teaching and learning of dance at a professional level. I am particularly interested in how the relationship between teacher and student in that setting might become less confrontational and more collaborative. Rogers' ideas seem to me to have the potential to offer a model of teaching dance that develops the autonomy of the student without sacrificing her training, and as such are well worth considering (Buckroyd, 1988, 1997, 1998).

The Body Self

A fourth strand in the ideas that inform this book is work that has attempted to link the sense of self in a person to the quality of 'indwelling', a concept developed by Winnicott and expanded further in current work by Turp (1997, 1998, 1999a, 1999b). Turp is especially concerned to draw attention to the inseparability of the mental and physical senses of self and to emphasise that the optimal functioning of the person depends on the integration of these various aspects of one embodied self.

How do I know that my body is mine, that my body is me? This may seem a foolish question, but it seems clear that we come into the world without any such certainty. (This is demonstrated by the small miracle that takes place when a baby for the first time discovers its own toes.) It seems certain from the work done in infant observation, both by psycho-analysts such as Bick (1968) and by developmental psychologists such as Stern (1985), that our sense of inhabiting our body is built up in two principal ways, involving our own use and movement of the body on the one hand and responsive handling of the child's body on the other. Thus we consolidate our sense of ourselves as embodied via our gradually increasing capacity to use and control our bodies, but at the same time are crucially dependent on the concerned and appropriate physical handling of our care-givers as well.

On this basic sense of inhabiting our bodies is built a sense of recognition of ourselves by the mirroring function of those around us ('Who's got lovely blue eyes, then?'). When babies and children copy and are copied in their movements, or hear comments on their physical appearance, they learn to identify with and take ownership of their bodies, as those external perceptions are fed back to them.

This ownership is strengthened by a developing sense of agency: the baby's and then the child's and then the adolescent's sense of being able to control and manipulate its own body to achieve its own purposes (to walk, to put on clothes, to get something out of the cupboard, to write, to do a *pirouette*). This agency is supported, enabled and encouraged by those around so that the developing person is helped to continue and persevere with the process of acquiring and extending physical skills.

As a young person develops he will be progressively more able to discriminate between different physical sensations which he will be taught to identify with words denoting emotions and feelings: pain, hunger, tiredness, anger, fear, anxiety, excitement, contentment and so on. In this way his increasing capacity to be aware of sensations in his body will add to his capacity to identify himself in terms of his feelings (I am hungry; I have a pain in my left foot; I feel disappointed).

Finally, this sense of self and identification with the body will be consolidated and furthered by systematic and regular physical exercise. It has been conclusively shown, as will be described in the next chapter, that exercise can contribute to self-confidence and improve functioning in all aspects of living: physical, intellectual, social and emotional.

Clearly, then, dance training should have a very major role to play in establishing and furthering the sense of self. Ideally, the young dancer in training is a confident young person with high self-esteem and an excellent sense of self. She is aware of her body and its messages to her, and has learned to respect and take care of herself physically and emotionally as a result of attending to them. We should expect that dance training develops these capacities in tandem with its development of physical skills to an unusually high degree. How can it be ensured that dance training does in fact promote and support these desirable ends?

One of my goals in what follows is to identify aspects of current practice in dance training that are likely to have those positive effects. It is a sad fact that many dance trainees have a very poor sense of self-esteem; they have a confused or disturbed sense of body shape and size (not knowing whether they are fat or thin, for example); they have learned to override the signals from their bodies so that they are unable to identify consistently such sensations as pain, tiredness or hunger; they feel alienated from their bodies and talk about parts of their bodies as though they had no identification with them ('I hate my boobs'; 'Is my bum that big?'); they have little sense of their bodies' capacities and are often engaged in a frantic struggle for 'control' of a body that seems to belong to someone else. Thus they show a particular tendency to treat themselves abusively via eating disorders, inadequate rest, cigarettes, drugs, and carelessness towards hurt or injury. These problems are not confined to dancers – and indeed seem endemic in the young female population, if the evidence of such popular books as Helen Fielding's *Bridget Jones's Diary* (1996) or Arabella Weir's *Does My Bum Look Big in This?* (1997) is to be believed. This is a truly disastrous state of affairs, and there are many casualties in the ranks of vocational dancers in training. In this book, therefore, I have tried to use current research and ideas on these subjects to identify good practice and to help those who care about dance and dancers ensure that dance training is a positive and life-enhancing experience which can offer a more creative way of living to young women especially, rather than imprisoning them even more tightly in the current cultural anguish of female adolescents in the Western world.

Holistic Theory

Finally, in exploring these issues I have been influenced by ideas, ultimately deriving from an existentialist and humanistic view of the person (Bandy in Kleinman, 1987), which emphasise a holistic understanding of the human being. They have much in common with Eastern traditions of thought (Kleinman, 1987) and with current complementary medicine in the West, such as naturopathy (Mitchell, 1998). They contrast with a long tradition in European thought, generally referred to as dualism. In this tradition, which arose in the context of Christianity, the mind or soul is understood to be separate and distinct from the body. In this understanding there is a hierarchy of separate elements of the human being in which the body is at the bottom of the pile. The body is seen as distinct from the person and in need of discipline and control. In the Pauline tradition, the undisciplined desires of the body will take over from the higher functions of mind and spirit and lead the soul to destruction. So the female body is seen as particularly dangerous, sinful and deserving of repression. Dancers probably do not think in these quasi-religious terms, but there is undoubtedly a powerful tradition within dance that thinks in terms of the dancer subduing or conquering her body, her appetites and her physical needs, especially for food or rest; ignoring pain or discomfort as messages from a part of her that should be tamed and disciplined. Attention to physical need in this construction is seen as a kind of indulgence to which the dancer cannot afford to surrender for fear of imperilling her identity and capacity as a dancer. (Thus it is possible for a choreographer to say, as was reported to me, 'You have 364 other days of the year on which to have lunch; today you are rehearsing.') These splits in identity are revealed in that most famous of clichés, 'Your body is your instrument.' What the phrase implicitly assumes is that 'you' and 'your body' can be separated. The way is then clear for 'you' to misuse or abuse 'your' body or to allow someone else to do so, if that seems to serve 'your' interests as a dancer.

Recent neurophysical research (Damasio, 1996; Goleman, 1996) demonstrates that such dualism has no basis in brain chemistry or neurology. It shows conclusively that the physical, the emotional and the mental are

---

'The body as instrument' . . . dehumanises the whole person to a thing to be designed, tempered, refined and sharpened to perform particular skills. It suggests an unfeeling precious thing to be handled with care and used only for a specific purpose . . . This concept reinforces the body-mind split so prevalent in Judeo-Christian culture . . . We are gradually moving towards a more holistic culture. Perhaps we should be moving towards holistic dance teaching as well.'

(Geeves, in Brinson, 1993: 11)

inextricably interrelated to the point that attempts to disentangle them make no sense. There is no 'me' as opposed to 'my body'. I have no mind that can be separated from my body. These different aspects of myself are entirely intertwined and interdependent. This understanding has the capacity to transform the mind-set that will allow the bodies of dancers to be objectified and abused by themselves and others. Peter Brinson could even speak of a future in which dancers would be seen as 'prophets of a different future and better humanity in which body, mind and emotions equally are balanced and valued' (Brinson in Brinson, 1993). At the least, a holistic view of the self will have precisely the same protective functions as an embodied sense of the self. The holistic vision will permit the dancer to remain in contact with the signals that her neuropsychological and chemical transmitters are conveying, and prevent the split which disowns, despises and objectifies the body. Dance teaching informed by these holistic ideas can go a long way to providing a model of understanding that can protect trainee dancers from the abusive behaviours in which they so often indulge and make them less vulnerable to those teachers (choreographers, rehearsal directors, ballet masters, company directors, and so on) who subscribe to older, dualistic modes of thinking and teaching.

Sports Psychology

Over the past twenty years or so, exercise psychology and sports psychology have developed as distinct disciplines. Both employ cognitive behavioural techniques to enhance motivation and performance for those participating in exercise and sports. These techniques are now very commonly used at every level of organised physical activity, from participation in a local gym to Olympic athletics. Methods such as target setting and visualisation have been convincingly demonstrated to enhance satisfaction and performance.

The principles of sports psychology have begun to be applied to dance, especially dance performance, and have been used to help dancers recovering from injury, to deal with performance anxiety and to assist with concentration and motivation. Tajet-Foxell (1997), Gallagher (1993), Hamilton (1997) and Taylor and Taylor (1995), for example, have made valuable recent contributions to dance psychology to which the reader is referred.

There are points at which my interest in dance training and the ideas and principles of dance psychology overlap and where I have used concepts drawn from it; for example, in talking about a trainee's responsibility for her training, I have used the concept of target setting. In general, however, my concern in what follows has been to discuss dance training from a point of view that is primarily concerned with emotional development, relationship and emotional meaning. In a training environment respectful of these values, dance psychology will certainly be an additional tool for focusing and enhancing the trainee's achievement.

These themes and ideas, then, form the basis of much of what will follow in this book. The ideas themselves are fairly familiar to those who work in the fields of psychology, education and psychotherapy. So far, however, there has been little work that links them to dance or enables dance professionals to use them to reflect upon what they are doing when they train young people (Schnitt and Schnitt in Clarkson and Skrinar, 1988). I feel there is much to be done in attempting to elucidate a philosophical and educational theory for dance training that takes account of understanding developed in mainstream developmental psychology and education. I am glad to be able to offer the dance community, from whom I have learned so much and whose work has given me so much pleasure, the opportunity to consider dance training in the light of these concepts and their possible applications.

2

Physicality, Dance Training and the Sense of Self

The sheer pleasure that comes from physical movement in dance . . . is the existential discovery that the body is made for movement. Movement – swift, graceful, strong, elegantly controlled movement is the end . . . of our skeletons and musculatures. The pleasure we derive . . . comes from the inarticulate realization that this is what we are for, that bodily, we were made for this . . . In this exuberance of movement we know ourselves . . . The exercise of the body results in joy or happiness, the proper fulfilment of the soul. (Balkam in Kleinman, 1986: 37)

[Dance] is the most physically expressive of all the arts disciplines and is thus particularly valuable in helping young people to develop a pride in their bodies, their capacity for creative movement and ultimately in themselves. (Richey in Davies, 1997: 9)

There can be few parents or teachers who do not hope that young people will emerge from dance training, of whatever kind and at whatever level, stronger, fitter, better co-ordinated, more confident and more assured, with a better sense of self. There is considerable evidence to suggest that regular exercise of any kind has these beneficial effects (e.g. work reviewed by Turp, 1997; Sime in Van Raalte and Brewer, 1996; Rejeski and Thompson in Seraganian, 1993; Willis and Campbell, 1992; although see Tuson and Sinyor in Seraganian, 1993, for a more cautious opinion).

These benefits also result from participation in non-professional dance classes, which, it has been claimed in a number of studies (reviewed by Schnitt and Schnitt, 1988; see also Davies, 1997; Allen and Coley, 1995), may be particularly effective in enhancing self-concept and other positive psychological states. However, it is not clear that professional dance training will have these positive benefits. Research suggests that rates of injury (Brinson and Dick, 1996; Bowling in Brinson, 1991; Ryan and Stephens, 1987; Stephens, in Ryan and Stephens, 1987), smoking and substance abuse (Brinson and Dick, 1996; Schnitt, 1990; Schnitt and Schnitt, 1991) and eating disorders (Vincent, 1979; Loosli et al. in Ryan and Stephens, 1987; Lowenkopf and Vincent, 1982; Garner et al., 1987; Schnitt and Schnitt, 1986; Greben, 1989; Schnitt and Schnitt, 1991) are alarmingly high among trainees and professional dancers, which at the very least suggests that dance training is not preparing professionals in such a way that they can care for themselves appropriately (Gallagher in Brinson, 1993). A number of autobiographical accounts of the training and professional careers of dancers (e.g. Kirkland, 1986; Belair, 1993; Brady, 1994; Gordon, 1983) paint a dismaying picture of a world in which the welfare of trainees and dancers is far from a priority and where dancers' own sense of themselves is so damaged that they are capable of extremely self-destructive behaviour. We are thus presented with a paradox: there is research evidence that non-professional dance training has a tendency to strengthen the sense of self, with all the positive consequences for living creatively that implies; however, professional training, which might potentially deliver these same positive benefits, is plainly also capable of damaging self-esteem (Bakker quoted by Schnitt and Schnitt in Satalott et al., 1991; Smith, 1997, 1998; Wilson, 1994) and of failing to protect young people from destructive and self-destructive ways of functioning whether as trainees or as professional dancers.

In this chapter I want to explore the subject of developing a sense of self. How is that achieved for any of us, and what particular relevance does it have for dance training? What aspects of dance training can promote self-esteem and positive functioning, and where are the danger points at which it is possible for damage to occur?

The subject of the development of a sense of self is enormous; it would be impossible to address it with any degree of completeness in a work of this kind. Much that contributes to the adult's sense of self is outside the parameters of the concerns of this book: work, with its demands, satisfactions and rewards, belongs to a later life-stage than the one with which this book is primarily concerned. Yet work, together with the establishment of sexual relationships of an enduring kind, the creation of a supportive range of kinship and friendship relationships, the creation of a domestic base, the acquisition of the range of material goods that in our society spell an ordinary degree of comfort and, for a substantial number of people, the raising of children, constitute powerful elements in the adult's identity and self-esteem. Nevertheless, the roots of the ability to use adult accomplishment to consolidate a sense of self lie in something more fundamental: the sense of 'bodily indwelling', the sense that I am my body and that my body is mine. This is the fundamental feeling that enables each of us to feel real and to feel substantial. In the following section, therefore, I want to explore how that sense of being a person develops in the normal child and adolescent, and is consolidated by the experience of mirroring, agency and the symbolisation of feelings in words. I will also begin to consider the relevance of these ideas for the psychological environment of dance training.

Physical Indwelling

Over his forty years of practising as a paediatrician and analyst, Donald Winnicott often described the importance for babies of achieving a sense of 'indwelling' (Winnicott, 1960, 1962, 1966, 1967, 1970). His consultations with literally thousands of mother–baby pairs convinced him that babies arrive in the world without clear notions of 'me' and 'not me', without a firm idea of the boundaries between internal and external environments and events. He came to understand that an infant's gradual establishment of such boundaries, and thus the beginnings of a sense of a separate self, depended on 'good enough mothering'. The good enough mother was normally the biological mother, but might also be a substitute caring figure who provided reliable physical care ('handling') alongside emotional responsiveness ('holding'), tuning in to the baby's needs and communicative gestures in a way that helped it to manage both physical and emotional experiences that would otherwise be overwhelming.

> Last week I saw a baby a year old in a pram. The pram had been carried down some steps, swaying and bumping a bit. The baby became alarmed and started to cry and then was rapidly less able to control her panic. She began to scream in real earnest. Her

mother picked her out of the pram and held her. She stopped screaming as she was being lifted out . . .What happened then was that the mother conveyed a feeling, an attitude of love and support and reassurance, *physically*. There is no other way to do it for a baby; they don't understand talk.   (Buckroyd, 1986)

Esther Bick, also a psychoanalyst, writes about the infant's first psychological need as one of being held together physically, and describes how this gives the baby a feeling of being all of a piece within his skin. His own skin does not offer a sufficient sense of containment in the early months, and he feels in danger of falling apart. In the following extract from a psychoanalytically-informed infant observation, 'Eric', aged six weeks, is seen being given a bath. He cries when he is undressed, but then calms down in the warm bathwater.

When mother removes the baby from the tub, he begins shrieking again. He reddens, kicks in lightning quick movements and his lower lip trembles. He keeps moving his head in a backward thrusting motion . . .Mother needs to pick him up and hold him firmly and absorb his distress before he can be calm. By holding him physically, nurturing him in a pleasurable way and emotionally responding to his distress, mother enables Eric to internalise capacities to struggle with his anxieties.   (Miller et al., 1989)

Mollie Davies, who spent a lifetime studying movement and dance for young children, describes a very similar incident in terms of 'expressive interaction'. This is interesting evidence that these dynamics, as one would expect, have been noticed within the dance community, even if the vocabulary in which they are described is slightly different.

In responding to a young infant who is fractious and ill at ease, a quiet soothing tone, accompanied by a rocking or stroking action (involving the movement elements of sustainment and gentleness) may often have a positive effect. The success of this expressive exercise on the part of the handler is seen first in the sharing, by the infant, in the newly created mood of calm and, second, in the retention of that mood.   (Davies, 1995, 33)

Turp (1997) argues that there is compelling evidence that quality of handling in infancy has far-reaching emotional and physical effects. She quotes the work of Hopkins (1990) who has shown that a child's muscle tone and physical liveliness depend on handling. Turp goes on to refer to the work of Terry Brazelton (1975), a developmental psychologist, who has described and captured on video the extraordinary range and nuance of movement, gesture, facial expression and vocalisation whereby the baby indicates its changing experiences to the mother. He has drawn attention to the ways in which an infant's movements are transformed by human contact from jerky and uncoordinated to smooth, rhythmic and circular. Turp suggests that similar smooth and rhythmic movements in adult life, of which dance movement is an example, have the potential to call to mind the loving attentions of the mother that first gave rise to them. Movement and feeling are intimately related (Turp, 1997).

What this work describes, then, is how the basic building block in the sense of being a separate person, of having a sense of self and of being able to manage the innumerable anxieties that we will face as humans, is laid by the physical processes of handling and holding that are the practical manifestation of the care-giver's physical and emotional responsiveness to the baby's need. A similar responsiveness throughout childhood and adolescence will continue to be necessary in an age-appropriate form, if the capacity to contain and self-soothe is to be thoroughly established and integrated. Indeed it is probable that these needs remain in modified form throughout the life of the ordinary healthy person (and in a less modified form in the lives of those who are physically or mentally unwell) (Skynner and Cleese, 1983). When a person feels as if she is 'falling apart' as a result of feelings and experiences that are overpowering, then what may well be enormously therapeutic is physical holding and/or the symbolic equivalent, words which contain, shape and order experience. It is interesting that the metaphors to describe acute emotional distress are those which describe a collapse of physical integrity; thus in addition to 'falling apart' our language supplies us with a whole range of similar expressions: 'collapsing', 'having a breakdown', 'disintegrating', 'going to pieces'.

Mirroring

More than this basic requirement of containment is, however, needed in the process of developing a sense of self; a further process, often known as 'mirroring', is certainly also crucial. In order to have a sense of myself I must be able to conceive of myself as existing in the mind of the other.

> In order satisfactorily to function, we depend throughout our lives on the presence of others who will accord us validity, identity and reality. You cannot be anything if you are not recognised as something; in this way your being becomes dependent on the regard of someone else. You may be confirmed, or you may be disconfirmed, and if the latter is the case, often enough and pervasively enough, you simply cease to exist as a person.   (Smail, 1984: 18)

The sense of existing, then, is born of the experience of being seen and of having what is seen reflected back. This dynamic is seen in the imitation of a baby's movements which is such a part of the earliest dialogue with infants, and in the baby's capacity, evident within hours of birth, to mimic the movements of others.

> The importance of imitation for origins of self, is that consciousness of mutual human relations provides the most direct feedback about one's own personhood.
> (Butterworth in Bermudez et al., 1995: 99)

It appears that the baby itself is innately programmed to respond to such mirroring, and indeed in case of need, to initiate it (Skynner and Cleese, 1983). The first basic mirroring is that of one's physical existence. It is known that when depressed mothers fail to show by eye contact or facial responsiveness their awareness of the baby, the baby will become more and more energetic in an attempt to establish contact. If it fails in this endeavour it will become obviously depressed (Murray, 1988). We are dependent on mirroring for physical self-awareness as basic as that of gender identity. I can only know that I am a girl if my environment gives me that feedback. Much of the baby talk that seems to serve no useful purpose, conveys by its tone that sense of recognition; 'Who's Mummy's lovely boy, then?' is a question that presumes the delighted answer, 'I am', even from a baby of a few weeks or months. The 'good enough mother', that benign construction of Winnicott's (1962), will continue that creative and positive recognition throughout childhood and adolescence. The mirroring of the child's physical existence and appearance

('Your hair looks nice today'; 'I think you've grown taller while you were at camp'; 'You're a strong girl, can you carry this upstairs for me?') will be accompanied by a recognition of qualities ('What a good/clever/happy/busy/helpful/sad/disappointed/cross/funny girl you are') and also of achievements, until the young person has internalised a sense of her own goodness and value. Out of such a sense of her own value ('I am worth looking after') a young dancer will be able to take care of herself and be patient with the mistakes and inadequacies that she will undoubtedly have to tolerate within herself as part of the process of training.

Heinz Kohut, one of the most important figures in the development of therapy that focuses on the development of the self (self psychology), came to similar conclusions about the need for the child to experience itself as 'the gleam in the parent's eye' (Kahn, 1991). The delighted recognition of the child and young person's accomplishments enables her to develop a sense of herself as 'grand' which will in turn give her the confidence to attempt further tasks and goals. These will of course be age-appropriate and will range from delight in the toddler's capacity to clap hands and sort shapes, to pleasure in a child's learning to skip or recite tables, to satisfaction with a teenager's capacity to cook his own scrambled eggs or struggle with his maths homework. All of these experiences of positive recognition permit a cumulative conviction within the young person of her value. Moreover, says Kohut, if this process has been well enough carried on by the primary care-givers and significant others, the young person will be able to value herself even in the temporary absence of such external validation. Indeed the internalisation of this capacity is necessary for all of us as adults.

However, it is unfortunately true that the primary care-givers may not offer the kind of mirroring described so far. Depression and other emotional difficulties will limit the parents' capacity to offer what is needed. There are also cultural traditions common in Britain which can mean that a child is diminished, criticised and corrected, far more than he/she is positively mirrored. The clear research evidence from behavioural studies, that learning is best supported when mistakes are ignored and success is rewarded, is insufficiently followed in our society. Indeed there are some who feel that positive recognition makes children 'big-headed' or 'conceited'. Certainly, positive mirroring will make children confident. Moreover, just as positive feedback will be internalised, so will negative. The child's fragile sense of self will be vulnerable to criticism. What is more, since our society values males more highly than females, girls will have a particularly difficult task of constructing a positive self-image (Pipher, 1994).

These considerations are of importance for dance training. Traditionally, dance training has emphasised a different kind of 'mirroring'. This may be in the literal sense of observation of oneself in the mirror, or in the sense of imitating the mirror image of the class that the demonstrating teacher presents, or in the sense of the teacher giving feedback to the student. What is more, there is a very strong tradition within dance training of negative mirroring: the mirror itself is frequently experienced as a hostile force to the point where students will identify particular mirrors in particular studios that are 'good' or 'bad'; a teacher–student communication within the world of professional dance training is known as a 'correction' and is almost certain to indicate errors and inadequacies. While the youngster who has come from a background of positive reinforcement may be able to tolerate some of this, the girl who comes to dance training with a sense of self that is already shaky and self-critical is likely to feel herself to be worthless when criticised. The fact that the criticism is of her *body*, her essential self, will make that criticism all the more unbearable. Throughout this book we will explore how dance training might address these tricky problems.

Being Capable

> The infant no sooner moves its limbs, and feels that they are moved at its will, than it begins to enjoy itself in the use of its own power . . . It is the love of power, or rather the pleasure of self-consciousness in the use of means, by which we obtain outward evidence of our own inward life, in relation to ourselves.
>
> (Dr George Moore (1848), *Man and his Motives*, quoted *London Review of Books*, 9 February 1995: 13).

Part of the process of developing a sense of self lies in the development of physical capacities that enable us to control our bodies and use them to achieve our own ends. The fundamental and innate sense which enables this sense of 'agency' is that of proprioception. Proprioception refers to the numerous information systems that provide us with information about 'the state and performance of the body' (Eilan et al. in Bermudez et al., 1995). It corresponds closely to what dancers mean by kinaesthetic awareness, a sense of the body in space and in relation to the environment and itself. As the infant builds upon the information provided by these systems, it comes to have a sense of itself doing and effecting: 'In learning skilled, goal-directed activity, the infant can discover more about the agency of the self' (Butterworth in Bermudez et al., 1995).

Agency is initially expressed in the mastery of basic movement capacities. The achievement of walking has huge psychological significance, as may be gauged by the excitement with which it is usually received. As Davies implies in the following description, walking is a landmark on the long road to independent living and, as such, a crucial element in the development of the person.

> The day in which young children make the transition, albeit only momentarily, from dependence on people or furniture to taking first steps without support, is hailed as a red letter day in the family circle.   (Davies, 1995: 35)

Soon, however, the child will proceed to more complex motor skills. Their importance to the child will be indicated by the sense of triumph with which a young child will report that she jumped with both feet together, or learned to hop. Davies (1995) comments on 'the pleasure and sense of well-being which is experienced [by children] as they are helped to realise their bodily potential'. (It will become ever clearer to the reader what an enormous task faces the handicapped child, who also needs to develop a strong sense of self.) The process of developing more and more sophisticated and complex gross and fine motor skills continues throughout childhood and adolescence. Learning to drive in the late teens or early twenties can often be seen as the culmination of the acquisition of all the skills of control and co-ordination, and as a rite of passage into adult life. The capacity to drive a car can be seen symbolically as the ultimate answer to the total dependence of the newborn child. Little wonder that it is an accomplishment of enormous significance for many youngsters.

In this context it is clear why the acquisition of an unusual degree of physical skill is valued by peer groups among children and adolescents and is strengthening to the individual's sense of self. It means that the young person 'can do'. Academic success, although valued by adults, is often not so prized either by the child/adolescent, or by the peer group.

The words for an academically successful child used by young people themselves (swot, boffin) are often not very complimentary.

It follows, then, that competence as a dancer should enhance the sense of agency ('I can do it!') and therefore the sense of self. As we have already seen, there is evidence that at a non-professional level dance does have this effect. How can professional dance training use the evidence of the undoubted skill and competence of trainees to enhance the sense of self, rather than damage or diminish it, as, alarmingly, it often seems to do. The answer to that question will be considered throughout the rest of this book. However, a preliminary answer may be indicated by the repeated evidence of an increase in competence consolidating a sense of self when it is met by approval, delight, encouragement, validation, and other positive and reinforcing responses (Hamilton, 1997). When the levels of competence displayed routinely are very high, as they are in professional training, it can be easy for teachers to forget to celebrate accomplishment, or delight in competence. Similarly students can learn to dismiss their achievements, rather than enjoy them. It has seemed to me that students who arrive on their course in the first year full of passionate enthusiasm for dance and delight in movement, can have that pleasure so reduced by an environment that focuses only on what is done badly, or what has not yet been accomplished, that their self-esteem is much lower at the end of the year than it was at the beginning. (See also Bakker, quoted Schnitt and Schnitt in Satalott et al., 1991.) Dance teachers and dancers often conceptualise it as their task to identify what is wrong in order that the student can improve. However, the ideas that I am discussing here suggest that in order to maximise the creative possibilities of the training for the dancer, it may be at least as important to recognise what is right (Thomas, 1993; Coryndon, 1999). It takes psychological strength to accept and correct mistakes; that strength, current theories about the development of the self seem to suggest, is nurtured and developed by a positive and supportive environment (Hamilton, 1997).

Words for Feelings

So far, then, in this chapter we have considered how a sense of self develops in a young person via a sense of physical indwelling, an identification with one's body and a sense of it as good and competent. We have considered briefly that dance training needs to focus on responding positively to young people if the experience of the training is not to be damaging. In the final part of the chapter, I want to explore how the capacity to identify feelings and name them in words is part of the process of developing a strong sense of physical indwelling, and therefore of self-esteem.

Over the last twenty years or so, in the study of psychosomatic illness, it has become steadily clearer that it is vital for us all to be able to know what it is that we feel (e.g. McDougall, 1989). This capacity involves the ability to decode the information provided for us via the body and its complex systems, both external and internal. The feelings thus identified are our only reliable guides to action. Without knowledge of our feelings we are condemned to act on the basis of thought alone, which is a poor basis for decision-making (Damasio, 1996; Goleman, 1996). Without the capacity to identify feelings and act on the basis of them, we are vulnerable to somatic expression such as illness and addiction. However, the process of learning to identify and name feelings is a long one and lasts well into adult life. It is also vulnerable to distortion and error.

The infant, who has no power of speech and limited physical expressive power, nevertheless experiences physical sensations via the information-giving systems of the body. These signal physical states, such as hunger, tiredness, pain, and a range of psychological states, such as anger, fear, happiness, loneliness, satisfaction, grief. (The separation of feelings into physical and psychological is almost certainly mistaken since all feelings are signalled physically and have emotional meaning. In what follows no such distinction will be maintained.) The baby expresses these varying states via smiling, kicking, crying and screaming. The infant, therefore, depends heavily on its care-givers for the interpretation of these expressions. This is a difficult task, as parents of a first-born frequently comment when they are faced with caring for their child. It can be hard to know what a baby needs, and to distinguish between, for example, cries which may signal hunger or tiredness or pain.

In a relatively short time the baby/toddler's expressive range widens and refines and it becomes somewhat easier for care-givers to identify distinct feeling-states. Two-year-olds' tantrums, for example, fairly clearly signal anger or frustration, even if they do not indicate the reason for those feelings. As the child develops, parents begin to teach an emotional vocabulary: sad, happy, cross, tired, hungry, thirsty, disappointed, jealous, and so on. Even before a child has secure use of this language, it is being taught to name feeling states by the parents' identification of them in the child ('Oh, what a tired boy!'). Words, as opposed to somatic expressions, have the enormous advantage of precision and agreed meaning. Consequently, the child who, by the age of seven or so, has acquired a fundamental vocabulary of this kind will have learned to identify a number of feeling-states for itself in his/her own body and be able to convey them to others ('I was really sad when Granny went home again'; 'Don't do that, it hurts'; 'I'm too tired to play football'; 'It makes me angry when you do that'). This capacity then has the enormous advantage that it identifies the child to him/herself ('I am a child who feels this when that happens') and thus is a powerful element in building an identity and sense of self. It has the further advantage that it relieves at least some of the need to 'act' the feelings, for example by hitting, sulking, and so on. As the reader will be well aware, the acquisition of such skills is by no means universal in our society. There are many adults who lack such an emotional vocabulary and who conduct their emotional lives via somatic expressions that would be ordinary in a preschool child, for example, shouting, hitting, losing their temper, sulking, slamming doors. There are also a number of socially permitted ways of acting out feelings, of which getting drunk is one and becoming unwell is another.

The fact is that we live in a society where there are many ways in which the process of learning to identify feeling-states in words can go wrong (Skynner and Cleese, 1983; Bakal, 1999). Let us consider some examples. In the first place there are many families where certain feelings are prohibited. Most commonly, anger will be a taboo feeling. This does not mean that miraculously in those families no one feels angry. It means that direct, straightforward identification of the feeling-state of anger and its expression is forbidden. But since, like water, feelings find their way, it will mean that anger in that family turns into something else, often depression, or is expressed somatically, perhaps by tiredness or eczema or compulsive working. Sometimes feelings have to be taken outside the family and expressed somewhere else, for example at school or at work. We have feelings, whether we like it or not – it is only a question of how skilful we are in identifying them and expressing them appropriately.

It is common for some feelings to be permitted only to some members of the family, for example parents are frequently the only ones allowed to be angry, and pain or sadness that is expressed by crying is frequently forbidden to males. Sibling rivalry may be repressed ('You know you love your sister'). Again, such prohibitions do not magic away the feelings;

they merely force the feelings into less straightforward forms. There are some families in which *any* expression of feelings, good or bad, is strongly discouraged. So, then, crying for a hurt knee or a broken heart, or talking about it, will be powerfully discouraged, often by contempt or ridicule (cry-baby, making a fuss, whining, belly-aching, wimp, sissy). Laughing or celebrating may be equally repressed ('Stop making such a noise'); anger will be instantly repressed ('Go to your room at once'). Not surprisingly, relationships in such families are likely to be distant and inexpressive.

Families often muddle feelings. This can be done by processes which make it very unclear who is feeling what: 'If you don't stop that I'll tell Daddy not to take you out tomorrow'; 'Don't upset your sister or I'll smack you'; 'Daddy will be tired when he comes in, so I want you to play quietly upstairs for a while'; 'Granny's coming to stay so I want you to be a kind girl and share your sister's room so Granny will be more comfort-able'. In these examples, neither the feelings of the speaker nor those of the one who is spoken to are identified. In each example, a third person is involved whose feelings are assumed and who has no voice of his or her own. It is extremely difficult for a child in such an environment (common enough) to identify and name his or her own feelings. Rather, the family is living in a kind of emotional soup where the feelings of any member are seen as the property of all.

A variation on this theme occurs in the family where feelings (often the child's) are misidentified: 'You must be tired'; 'You can't be hungry'; 'You knew I didn't want you to do that'. If we all find it hard to identify and name what we feel, how much harder that task is when someone else is telling us what it is that we feel, whether we like it or not.

The result of such dynamics can be that a young person does not develop the kind of accurate emotional language that was described above and is therefore at the mercy of all kinds of distortions and acting out, which conceal and deny the authentic self. Winnicott (1960) de-scribed the reaction of a person who has been unable to identify and live by his own feelings as the development of a false, or caretaker, self which protects and conceals the authentic person and his potential. Unfortu-nately the false self also prevents authentic growth and development and ultimately stunts the entire development of the person if the true self is not offered the opportunity and acceptance that will enable that more fundamental part of the individual to grow. Recent commentators have also stressed that our sexist and 'lookist' culture is inimical to the development of the true self of the adolescent girl and that its requirements for behaviour and appearance stunt and reverse the maturity that the pre-pubescent girl (the successful child) has accomplished: 'When girls fail to acknowledge their own feelings, they further the development of a false self. Only by staying connected to their emotions and by slowly working through the turbulence can young women emerge from adolescence strong and whole' (Pipher, 1994: 58).

In this context, creative and expressive dance has an enormous amount to offer. It can enable the young person to find a positive means of expressing feelings that have not been identified in words, but yet are desperate for expression. When I was involved in auditioning young people for London Contemporary Dance School (Buckroyd, 1986a; 1987a) their passion for dance was frequently described to me in terms of the opportunity it offered for expressing feelings. As one student memorably said to me, 'I feel most like myself when I'm dancing.' Even though the movement vocabulary of ballet is so much more formalised than that of contemporary dance or jazz, for example, yet I am certain that it too offers the opportunity for the focused expression of feeling. However, dance is not just a means of symbolising feelings for those who have not yet identified them in words – a kindergarten symbolism, so to speak. Most authorities think that as much as 70 per cent of meaning may be conveyed by 'body language'. Dance is a universal and powerful instrument for the enhanced expression of feeling. When the feeling is named and clear, dance becomes that much more focused. Dance performance is devoted to precisely these ends but in my view dance training can also be used to embody feeling. Dance class offers the opportunity for the exploration of the movement qualities of whatever the student might be feeling that day, whether those feelings are ones the student has with her, or are elicited by the class or the music. Students can be encouraged to imbue the movement of the class with whatever feeling is most present to them at that time, and thus to use their training to explore and enhance their awareness of their inner world. By this means, dance training, no less than informal and non-professional dance, can be an element in the growth of the person in self-awareness.

To think of dance training in this way may, however, require a further change in the way that both teacher and student conceptualise the work. There is a tradition in dance training that suggests that in order to be fully available for the training, the student must empty herself of everything but a focus on the dance class: 'Leave your troubles at the studio door'. I do not believe this to be possible in a dance class any more than it is in a family situation. What is possible is an act of repression of feelings which itself takes energy from the dance. But if feelings – troubles, even – cannot be named, acknowledged, accepted and used for dancing, the activity itself is weakened and diminished. Anna Halprin, one of the most distinguished of the post-modern choreographers, was described as having become 'convinced that each performer could only essentially perform himself. Each person is his own art. Whatever was being suppressed in the individual would become a severe limitation to an artist' (Luger and Laine, quoted in Adair, 1992). In order to develop into expressive artists of the highest quality, students need to have refined and developed their awareness of feeling to an unusually high degree, and to be capable of using their bodies expressively with an unusual freedom. This facility cannot develop solely in the performance arena but needs to be cultivated energetically at all stages of training. Rather than encouraging students to 'leave their troubles at the studio door', teachers might encourage students to bring them in with them, name, acknowledge and accept them, and use them as much as possible to inform and deepen their movement. Again, it may be necessary to rethink a teaching environment where the teacher is the unchallenged authority and the student is not permitted to enter into dialogue; when students are forbidden to express opinions or feelings in relation to the teaching, then those feelings have to be repressed and the learning is therefore damaged. I am thinking, for example, of those situations where a teacher says something insulting to a student (I have heard name-calling of the most cruel kind). The student is expected to take such behaviour from the teacher without responding (Schnitt and Schnitt in Ryan and Stevens, 1987; Smith, 1997, 1998); how can she possibly do this without a Herculean attempt at repression? I am sure that most teachers are not wilfully hurtful and insulting but have perhaps lacked a way of thinking about their interactions with students. Behaviour from the teacher such as I describe will probably have been intended to spur the student on to greater effort; teachers need to be aware that forcing a student to repress her justifiable protest is unlikely to have that effect.

If the goal of acknowledging and accepting the feelings of students within a class situation is considered worth pursuing, then there are other aspects that are often present in professional dance training that may also require revision. Dance training involves a willingness to tolerate a considerable amount of discomfort, even pain, tiredness and probably hunger. It is one thing to be aware of these feelings and to tolerate them in so far as they are not harmful or damaging: to stretch a little further, to do the exercise one more time, to choose an apple rather than apple pie. It is another to desensitise oneself to feelings so that awareness of pain, tiredness and hunger is lost. Yet some dance training can seem as if student, teacher and institution engage in a systematic collaboration to ignore and desensitise dancers to what is going on in their bodies. A study by Tajet-Foxell and Rose concluded 'The meaning of pain, the importance of acknowledging pain and of learning how to respond to it should be targeted as early as possible in a dancer's training' (1995: 34). This subject will be explored further throughout the following chapters, especially in relation to injury and eating disorders, but, for example, dance training institutions might consider the effect of timetabling on students' levels of fatigue and on their need to eat appropriately during the day.

Teachers perhaps need to consider whether their demands on students – delivered, as they often are, with huge authority – override students' own sense of their limitations. Students themselves need to be more aware of their responsibility for themselves and their training and their needs for food and rest. Sometimes it can seem that dance audiences have been taught to admire the skeletal dancer, smiling as she performs with two broken toes. The dance community, if it allowed itself an appropriate pride and self-esteem, would abhor such an abusive attitude to elite athlete performers and insist that professional dance should not be damaging to participants, either physically or emotionally. The more dance trainees are encouraged to be in close contact with their feelings, the more such a change is likely to come about.

3

The Emotional Uses of Dance Training

In the last chapter I described some of the processes by which a young person comes to have a sense of themselves through body awareness, and briefly discussed how dance training can enhance that sense of self by appropriate acknowledgement of the student's needs. The assumption was made in that chapter that the student's use of movement and of dance was likely to be creative so long as the dance training did not exert a damaging influence. I would now like to add a discussion of what the student is bringing to the training, because of course she does not arrive in the dance school without a history. In this chapter I want to explore more thoroughly the different ways in which students may use the training to meet their emotional needs (Buckroyd, 1986b, 1986c) and how the institution can respond to students to try and ensure that their use of it is creative rather than destructive.

As I described in the last chapter, research has demonstrated that exercise, and perhaps especially dance classes, taken by the ordinary person, improve the psychological welfare of the participants. Yet there is some doubt whether professional dance training – that is, a life focused on dance movement – necessarily has a beneficial effect. Indeed for some people it seems plain that it does not. Certainly, the training itself has a large part to play in whether a student experiences her training as helpful or damaging to her development; much of what follows will be taken up with an analysis of how the training can be as creative and as unharmful as possible. Nevertheless, I do also want to explore the different meanings that a student may bring to the training. In order to do that, I would like to describe the spectrum of attitudes to the training that I can identify and the range of emotional uses to which it can be put.

At the most creative end of the spectrum there is a group of young people for whom dance is a mode of being that permits them to use their bodies to express feelings, fantasies, desires and their inner world of imagination and creativity in a way that makes them feel most alive (Buckroyd, 1986a). Probably most of the great dancers and choreographers have used dance in this way; Martha Graham's work, for example, was saturated with imagery and emotional meaning. It was for her 'an exploration, a celebration of life' (de Mille, 1991). Because such a dancer uses dance to express (aspects of) herself, she can communicate feeling with her body and thus has emotional and dramatic force as a dancer. A dancer of this kind may have technical or physical limitations but these can be transcended by vitality and presence.

> For many, Rudolf Nureyev will remain the greatest male dancer in the history of classical ballet. His critics, however, accuse him of being a 'mediocre technician', whose performances were sustained throughout his sixties heyday only by force of personality, sexual charisma and hype . . . but his legacy – an extraordinary expressiveness despite technical limitations – keeps on dancing.
>
> (*Guardian*, 11 November 1998, preview of 'Dance on Four: Nureyev Unzipped')

It is this quality that is often described as the power to make an onlooker or audience watch. Dancers like this use dance as a means of expression and communication. Many of them want to choreograph as well as dance because dance for them is the vehicle for their creativity. Pina Bausch comes to mind, also Kenneth MacMillan, and of younger artists, Matthew Bourne. Sometimes those who have this way of using dance cannot dance (well enough) themselves, but want to use the bodies of others to embody their creative imagination.

It would be rash to claim that dancers of this kind are by definition well-rounded, mature personalities. Artistically very gifted people often seem to find it very difficult to develop into mature adults (Storr, 1972). However, dancers in the group of people that I am trying to describe seem to have the capacity to use dance to enhance their own lives and to help them manage both inner and outer reality.

> Dancing is generally a form of escapism as much as a vehicle for achieving a certain balance between outer reality and the inner world of a dancer. The more Makarova is hurt or disturbed by reality, the more passionately she becomes involved in her dancing.
>
> (Makarova, 1979: 172)

Makarova's use of dance enables her to embody her inner world in such a way that it becomes less troublesome. Her use of dance seems to me not 'escapism' but enactment of what moves or affects her. Her feelings do not limit or restrict her dancing but are the source and strength of it (Storr, 1972).

But let us now return to dance trainees. In the dance trainee who can use dance in the way that I am trying to describe, is the embryonic possibility of development into an artist whose creative imagination can be embodied in dance. She will be hungry for feedback and encouragement, for ideas, information and images. She will take whatever her teachers have to give and make it her own. She will bring colour and feeling and interest to whatever movement is asked for. She will be eager to experiment, to develop and to move on. This is the student who will want to see dance performances, who will be open to stimuli from other art forms and so will take up suggestions that she might visit art exhibitions or attend musical events. This is the student who will make use of the supportive curriculum and will demonstrate the effects of what she has learned in dance and choreography. Even if technically she has limitations, she is the student with presence and the power to project herself. If, in the end, her physical limitations prevent her from becoming a professional dancer in the conventional way, she will find a route and a vehicle for her creative and expressive talents. Above all, this is the student who uses the training in positive and creative ways for her own development. It will be evident to her teachers that, whatever her limitations, she is changing and growing in positive and life-enhancing ways. Socially, she is likely to get on well with her peers and to be able to collaborate and participate with them and in the work of the class. She will develop as a dancer technically and artistically. Her own ideas and qualities will become progressively clearer as she grows. Nobody needs to worry much about her.

Let us now turn to the dancer at the other end of the spectrum of attitudes to the training and of the emotional uses to which it can be put. There is a kind of dance student who is admitted to professional dance training schools without much of a problem. She is the student who, by all the standard modes of assessment such as turn-out, posture, weight, physical suitability and level of technical achievement, appears to be ideally suited for further training. She probably will not have much to say for herself, but then in many audition processes she will not be asked to say much. She may very well look the part of the dancer to perfection in terms of her dance equipment, her hair and her deference to authority. Reports from her earlier training may well indicate that she is a particularly diligent student who works hard and has made good progress with technique. She may seem young and shy for her age and if she is asked what she brings to dance and what contribution she can make to the school she will find it hard to reply. Similarly, if asked what dance performance she has seen recently and what she thought of it, she is unlikely to be able to give much of an answer. However, many girls (and such a student is likely to be a girl) of her age are quiet and shy and self-conscious, so perhaps her difficulties are unremarkable. If she is asked at audition to dance something she has choreographed herself, it will almost certainly be very derivative – but then so are many audition pieces. In other words, there is very little at audition to suggest that this student will be other than suitable for the training.

The problems begin to become apparent about half way through the first year of the training. It becomes clear that this student is not developing as she should. She will probably manage the technique satisfactorily, but it is the *way* she dances that starts to cause concern. There is no feeling in her dancing. She works hard, she puts plenty of effort in, but she does nothing with the movement herself. She fails to make it hers. If her teachers try to talk to her about this difficulty, she will generally respond in a compliant way, but it will become clear over time that she does not really understand what is meant by 'making the movement hers'. The more traditional the dance school, the less these problems will give cause for concern because, above all, this student does what she is told. On a scale of watchability she is off the bottom; her failure to project means that she has no presence in the room and consequently is all but invisible. It becomes gradually clearer that she is using dance and the training for some secret purpose of her own which has very little to do with performance art. If she is asked to leave at the end of the first year she will very likely audition and be accepted elsewhere, for much the same reasons that she was accepted in the first place: she is physically suitable and technically competent. However, since she seems young for her age and causes no trouble, she may be allowed to continue with the training in the hope that she will gradually develop.

Instead, as time goes on, her limitations will become more obvious. Although she is unlikely to skip classes in the supportive curriculum, she will derive no benefit from them as far as her dancing is concerned and may well be contemptuous and dismissive of them as irrelevant to the task of learning to dance. Her interest, indeed her obsession, is with technique classes. She is unlikely to be interested in watching dance performance and will appear to get nothing from other artistic or aesthetic experiences, although she will probably continue to conform by attending as required. As time goes on and she gets more familiar with the institution, she will absent herself from all but technique classes if she senses that will be tacitly condoned. Socially, she is almost certainly isolated, a loner (Wilson, 1995). She may become anorexic; she will give the impression of someone who does not inhabit her body and consequently may not take adequate care of herself. She may appear not to notice pain, discomfort, tiredness or hunger, although she may look pale and depressed. Alternatively, she may seem rather manic and obsessed. It is possible to find her practising technique on her own in a studio and she may have a very strong interest in body conditioning, but she is likely to pursue that on her own rather than under the direction of a coach. She has no wish to perform, although that may not become evident for a long time since in many trainings, performing is deferred until the later stages. She finds it almost impossible to improvise or choreograph, especially if this requires collaboration with other students, and will minimise her participation. This may pass unnoticed since so many students are eager to take part. She may be allowed to finish the training, but her achievement in relation to her peer group will steadily decline.

Clearly this student has not been able to use the training to enable her growth and development, yet equally clearly she wants to continue with it. Whatever purposes she is putting it to, they have nothing to do with becoming a professional dancer. When she leaves the school she may audition but is very unlikely to get a job. What she may do is find a job in some quite other field, probably something that demands relatively little of her, but which permits her to continue the daily ritual of the dance technique class. She leaves behind a baffled and rather uneasy institution that cannot understand what on earth she was all about and wonders whether there was something that should have been known or understood that would have made sense of her behaviour. Most likely she will simply be characterised as someone who just didn't have what it takes to become a professional dancer.

Such adolescents are quite well known to therapists, who understand them as being in retreat from a world whose demands they find terrifying and as creating a protected space for themselves which they desperately defend (Wilson, 1995). The openness and vulnerability that learning to dance requires is impossible for them, but at the same time the technique can be used to create the safe place. Dance becomes a ritual of survival rather than a creative opportunity (Storr, 1972). To coax a youngster like this into the real world is probably beyond the competence or the remit of the dance school.

Although these portraits are very strong, I do not believe them to be extreme or caricatures. There are dance students of both these kinds in every dance school from time to time. However, it is certainly true that the vast majority of dance students fall somewhere in between. I have drawn these portraits to illustrate my point that the dance student comes to the school with an unconscious emotional use for the training already in mind, a use that has nothing to do with the institution she is entering and that has not been determined by it. For the students I have described, the dance school can probably do very little, for good or for ill, to alter this emotional purpose or to affect the likely course of events, but for the majority in the middle I think the school can use its influence creatively or destructively and can alter considerably the uses to which the student puts the training. In order to explore the meaning of these unconscious emotional purposes, with a view to thinking about how students can best be enabled to use the training creatively, I would like to review some of the literature on the relationship between feelings, the body and movement.

It has been understood for a very long time that feelings affect movement and, as a result, the development of the body. Alexander Lowen, the founder of bioenergetics, was one of the first to explore exactly what results feelings could produce on physical development.

> The living organism expresses itself in movement more clearly than in words. But not alone in movement! In pose in posture, in attitude and every gesture, the organism speaks a language which antedates and transcends its verbal expression. Further there are a number of specific studies which correlate the body structure and physique with emotional attitudes.   (Lowen, 1958: xi)

More recently Keleman (1985) has produced an alternative schema in his book *Emotional Anatomy* which, like Lowen's work, attempts to relate physical development (size, shape, muscle development, flexibility, and so on) to emotional expression. In parallel, dance movement therapy has developed which uses as its primary tool the concept that our bodies in movement can and do tell the emotional stories of our lives (e.g. Stanton-Jones, 1992).

However, for the purposes of this book I am interested in a related but slightly different line of thought which has developed from the under-standing of the interrelatedness of feelings and movement. It is the idea that we all use our bodies and movement to help us cope with what life sends our way, and that coping can be creative and useful or sterile and restricting. The two examples that I have given above show in the first case how movement maximises the student's energy and creativity, and in the second case how it diminishes and restricts creative functioning. In what follows I will try and explore some ways of understanding these differences. Why does one student use dance for growth and develop-ment and another use it only for survival and escape? The answers to these questions will I hope point the way to how dance teachers can encourage their students to use their training creatively and try and discourage destructive use of it.

In the last chapter we saw how crucial it is for a child's sense of self and capacity to survive emotional and physical upsets that it has respon-sive and sympathetic handling and holding, both physical and emotional. Where this handling and holding is not adequate for the child's needs, then the child is faced with the necessity to survive without a critically important support. It is known that if the deprivation is too great, then children will not in fact survive, even if their basic physical needs are met (e.g. Spitz, 1945). However, human beings are endlessly inventive; the child who is deprived will attempt to redress that deprivation from his or her own resources. Joan Symington (1986) has described how a baby will attempt to manage distress:

> If the mother is absent, or present but emotionally unable to con-tain the baby's distress, the baby has to resort to ways of holding himself together. He is driven to this by the precariousness of the situation in which he finds himself. In other words he is driven to act in order to survive. His catastrophic fear is of a state of un-integration and spilling out into space and of never being found

and held again . . . The baby holds himself together in a variety of ways. He may focus his attention on a sensory stimulus . . . When his attention is held by this stimulus he feels held together. He may engage in constant bodily movement which then feels like a continuous holding skin . . . An adult's pacing up and down to help contain anxiety is a remnant of this continuous movement. A third method consists of muscular tightening, a clenching together of particular muscle groups and maintaining them in this rigid position.   (Symington, 1986: 481)

Symington goes on to say that such methods of dealing with anxiety become habitual in the baby as it grows up into a child and an adult:

We can see that their ways of coping are the same as the infantile ways of holding the self together and that these are trusted as the first line of defence. They are readily resorted to or fallen back on because they are at least relatively effective; they are familiar and are felt to be safe and trustworthy. They can then become part of the character structure.   (Ibid.: 482–3)

She then points out that these ways of coping may turn into useful ways of behaving or may not:

Some will lead on to socially adaptive behaviour and special skills; others will remain as the basis on which other omnipotent defence mechanisms are superimposed, which further block emotional development.   (Ibid.: 486)

Dance is undoubtedly one of those special skills that can be used to aid development or conversely to block it. Turp (1997) comes to identical conclusions about the possibility of negative or positive use of the exercising body.

So now let us try and examine what our unsuccessful student is doing with dance. In the first place she is using dance as a substitute for relating to people. She uses movement for comfort and as some kind of companionship. If you find her on her own in the studio or the body conditioning room working at an exercise or see her on her own early in the morning when she has come in to warm up, long before other students, you will not get the impression at that moment that she is unhappy; rather the reverse. The movement soothes her and makes her feel safe and maybe even good. The movement is the safe place into which she can escape from a world that seems too frightening (Wilson, 1995).

Now, as Symington points out, these moments come to all of us; we are all capable of retreating into a little mindless physical activity. Many people are consciously aware that if they feel upset it helps if they undertake some familiar task, even if it is only cleaning the car or sweeping the kitchen floor. The difference lies in the extent to which these solutions are applied to the exclusion of communicating feelings to other people. It is the difference between cleaning the car in a state of upset as a preliminary to sounding off when your partner comes home, or cleaning the car and not saying a word to anyone. It is the difference between going into a studio on your own to master an exercise that defeats you and then coming out to express your frustration to your friends, and going into the studio on your own and never saying anything to anyone. The problem about this, so far as professional dance training is concerned, is that dance is a communicative art. That is why our problem student does not project herself in class; that is why she does not make the movement her own. She is not using dance as a mode of communication – she is using it as a substitute for communication. For whatever reason, she has learned that people are not to be trusted and she has no intention of having any more to do with them than she absolutely has to. On the other hand, our successful student wants to communicate and uses dance as a means of doing so.

Secondly, our problem student uses dance technique as a ritual movement. It is the repeated and ritualised movement that she values for its capacity to protect her from feelings, or even to give her some relief from feelings. That is why she does not make the movement her own; that would require her to be in touch with her body and thus with her feelings. The whole point about her use of dance is that it is a defence against feelings that are probably unnamed and unknown but that are felt as a threat against which she must protect herself. Again, we are all capable of using ritual as a defence against feeling, or indeed as a way of escaping into a place where there is no feeling. Many everyday activities, such as washing up, can be used in this way to give us a temporary rest from feelings. Often people use the radio or television for this purpose (Tustin, 1986). Used occasionally, it is of little account. For our problem student, however, it is a way of life and a way of life that is incompatible with an expressive art such as dance. She does not want to perform or to improvise or to watch other people perform because these activities require her feeling participation. Feelings are what she is trying to avoid. By contrast, our successful student is constantly trying to find new ways to embody her feelings in dance.

Thirdly, our problem student is using dance technique as a way of defending against memory and desire. It is pretty obvious from the way she behaves that all is not well with her. Probably she has a painful and difficult story to tell about her past. If she could tell it, if she could put it into words, if she could begin to think about her pain (Bion, 1967) then she would not need to use dance in the way she does. Sadly, she hasn't reached that stage yet and consequently she uses dance to block her past and her future, to obliterate memory and desire. That is why she cannot improvise or choreograph, because the dancer's own experience is the major resource for such activities and our problem student cannot bear to come anywhere near expressing her own experience. Again, this is precisely what our successful student does; she is using her own history and desires as a resource for dance.

Fourthly, by ignoring her own pain or tiredness or hunger, as such a student is very apt to do, and continuing to dance anyway, our problem student both demonstrates how little she has internalised the capacity to take care of herself, but also uses her body as a way of expressing her emotional pain that as yet has no words or thoughts (McDougall, 1989). Like a baby, she uses her body to tell her story. She cannot soothe herself by talking to herself or seeking comfort from others, so she copes with her emotional pain by causing herself more pain (Turp, 1999; Wilson, 1991). I remember one such student showing me her feet which were a mass of raw sores created by blisters which she had left untreated. To her, the pain was not important; her feet were the voice of her unverbalised enormous distress.

So, then, by using dance in these ways our problem student has obliterated the need for other people and conscious awareness of memory, feelings or desire. Unfortunately she has thereby deprived herself of the vital ingredients for emotional growth. Without people, relationship, friends and human interaction, we can none of us develop. Without memory, feeling or desire, she deprives herself of the raw material for becoming a person. Her use of dance is almost certainly very important to her as a survival mechanism. Perhaps in time and with appropriate help she will be able to change her relationship to it, but as she is, her use of it is not compatible with training to become a professional dancer.

So let us turn now to our successful student who by contrast probably sounds too good to be true. What can we learn from her about the meaning of her use of the training? It may seem as if there is nothing to be learned; she is successful, a natural, there is no problem. This is true; however, we are trying to understand how dance training can promote the creative use of the training and discourage its destructive use. It will be helpful if we can garner some principles from our successful student.

The first point is that she may also have difficult experiences in her history. Our problem student by no means has the monopoly on emotional distress. However, our successful student has been able to use dance as a way of *dealing with* these difficulties, rather than using it to defend against them. Why she can do this while her fellow student cannot is probably a long story and not part of the focus of this book. We can suppose that she may have a more resilient temperament and that even in difficult circumstances there were people in her life to whom she could turn and who took notice of her pain. Whatever the truth, it all happened before she got to the dance school and cannot be much affected by the training. What we can notice are the coping mechanisms she uses in the present so that we can make use of them within the dance school with the vast majority of students. They may have temptations to occasional destructive use of the training and can be encouraged to seek more creative solutions to difficulties and bad patches during it.

The first thing to notice is that our successful student makes the most of the people in the dance school, both staff and students. She allows herself to get as much as she can from those who teach her; she uses them for information, for feedback, for support, for inspiration, for encouragement, for advice and for their experience. Similarly, she allows herself to get what she can from her fellow students; she uses them for friendship, for feedback, for support, for collaboration, for a sounding board and for comfort. In this way she provides herself with a network within the school that means that when she feels bored or discouraged or depressed or frustrated she does not go off by herself and sulk for days, or turn away from other human beings (Symington, 1993), but gives those she knows the chance to help her. In return of course she allows herself to be used in the same way.

What can the institution learn from this? It can learn first of all to ensure that in formal and informal ways the staff are available to the students as much as possible. This can be done formally by the establishment of a tutorial system. I will describe how this can be set up in the chapter called 'Dealing with Crisis in the Life of a Dance Student', but briefly it involves allocating a small group of students to a member of staff who is responsible for monitoring their welfare and progress within the school. In that way no student should become totally isolated and unremarked. Informally, staff can establish a tradition of being available for a few minutes before or after class, or perhaps of making themselves available in a public place (such as the canteen) at a regular time. Staff can also be invited to accompany students to art galleries, concerts, performances, and so on, perhaps with the modest inducement of their ticket being paid for by the school. Within some dance schools a rigid boundary is maintained between staff and students but I think it preferable that staff become known to the students to the extent that they can be approached easily. After all, staff teaching at the elite level that we are discussing have a huge fund of knowledge and experience of dance and the dance world which they might enjoy sharing, and from which students could certainly benefit. I also think staff contact on a frequent and informal level improves the development of the students in that it encourages adult behaviour. I am not of course suggesting that staff conduct their social life with students, but rather that they are sufficiently available to make the institution a more cohesive and integrated place where students are contained within a network of connections and contacts.

Secondly, I think the institution can learn from our successful student the huge importance of the peer group to the emotional welfare of the individual student, and take steps to foster connections between students. Again, this can be done in formal and informal ways. I think it desirable that there should be something along the lines of a student union, with elected officers and a budget for activities. Participation in such a body helps students to take responsibility and to mature but it also provides networks which act as supports for fellow students.

Collaborative learning is another huge aid to establishing peer relations. Despite the fact that dance is virtually always taught in a group, very little of the work is conducted in peer groups. Often it is as though the class is a group of individuals relating to the teacher as if no one else were present. This seems to me a wasted opportunity and a prodigal use of the teacher's energies. I will return to this subject in the chapter called 'Learning in Groups', but for the moment I want to emphasise that contact with other students in the learning situation establishes connections which again develop cohesion and integration within the institution.

Class Representatives

Shortly after you arrive in the school you will vote for a **class representative** who will then join the Student Union. They will meet with the Director of Student Support to co-ordinate information from students to staff and vice versa. They will bring a variety of matters to your attention e.g. teacher changes, special events, student union issues, feedback from faculty and technical meetings or news that needs to be imparted quickly. They will also inform you of **year meetings**, when each class will have the opportunity to meet with the Principal and the Director of Student Support. The class representatives should raise relevant issues at class and year meetings, so that the agenda for discussion is clear. This is your opportunity to discuss issues and exchange information collectively as a year.

Student Union

Our main role is as a medium between the student body and the faculty. We also keep you informed about national and regional issues and events that are particularly relevant to students. We are here to represent your rights and needs, so please feel free to come along to a meeting or talk to a rep. If you have anything that you want to say, or even if you just want to see what the Student Union is all about.

Our main aims are:

(a) To advise on the education of our members

(b) To promote the general welfare of our members

(c) To act as a representative of students' opinion in communications between its members, and the staff and administration of the School

(d) To act as a channel of communication between its members and other institutions.

London Contemporary Dance School, Induction and Advice Notebook

---

Informal contacts between students are probably the most important element of all in enabling them to support, stimulate and help each other. For that to happen easily there needs to be both time and a place. The canteen is often the meeting place, but a common room is also desirable. Attention needs to be paid to timetabling so that there is enough time for informal contact during the school day.

All the opportunity in the world probably would not persuade our problem student to turn to staff and students for support, but she is in a very small minority. The vast majority of students will use both staff and their peers to help them in difficult moments if the institution makes it plain that such interdependence is welcomed and encouraged. Dance training is arduous; it will be less so if individuals feel held and supported in their struggles rather than isolated and abandoned.

What else can we learn from our successful student? She is in touch with her body and her feelings in the present. This both enables her to be expressive in her use of her body and protects her against injury or self-harm because she is aware of and attends to the messages her body gives her. She has learned how to use dance creatively as a way of expressing and coping with day-to-day life (Turp, 1997). Again, there are things the institution can learn from this. Students can be taught to be more aware of their feelings simply by being asked to identify them and asked to use them to inform that day's class. In some institutions even such a simple initiative may require a change of perspective since there is an old convention that dancers ignore and repress their feelings so that they can dance despite fatigue, pain, and so on. In some cases this amounts to a systematic education in not knowing what you feel.

However, in the last few years it has become much more generally understood both that an expressive art requires dancers to be in touch with their feelings and that awareness of feelings protects against injury. What is implicitly demanded of teachers, then, is that they refuse to condone behaviour from dancers which is destructive and self-harming. For this reason I would not allow a dancer who is anorexic to take class because to allow her to do so would be to condone self-damaging and destructive behaviour. If dance is indeed 'a celebration of life' then behaviour that is damaging and destructive cannot be part of dance.

When dancers have been trained in an environment which condones, and may even reward, self-destructive behaviour, the dancers who emerge from it are ill-prepared to defend themselves in the professional world against demands on them, for example from choreographers, who take risks with their welfare. If we care about the welfare of professional dancers we must train our students to be able to take intelligent care of themselves through a developed awareness of their feelings. This may not come easily to teachers who are unlikely to have had a similar carefulness exercised on their behalf. The care and welfare of teachers is therefore a subject that I will address later.

So what else can we learn from our successful dancer? She is in touch with memory and desire, that is to say with the past and with the future, and uses dance to integrate her experience. Personal experience is the raw material of creativity. Student dancers need to be given opportunities to dance their own lives. This can of course be done by improvisation, but it can also be done in technique classes. I am told (Joysanne Sidimus, personal communication) that Balanchine was full of imagery for dance movement. It is well known that Martha Graham's floor exercises were given rhythm and energy by imagery she proposed (de Mille, 1991). My wish would be that the students provided their own imagery, actively derived from their own experience, perhaps with some prompt from the teacher, a word or a time (for example, think of something that happened to you in junior school). In this way they will learn to use dance to integrate their experience, to make it more fully their own, and thereby enrich their dancing. To ask that a teacher provide these opportunities is to endeavour to broaden and deepen the emotional use that the student makes of the training and thereby to guard against its use as a sterile and defensive ritual.

What I am suggesting, then, is that at either extreme the dance school can do relatively little to affect how the student uses the training. However, it can be very effective in encouraging positive and creative use of it for those very many students who are willing to grow and develop as young people. What is more, it can help them to grow by the provision of a nurturing environment. If a cohesive network of relationships can be established, accompanied by a consistent facilitation of the integration of the students' inner world of feeling and imagination into dance, then tendencies to withdrawal and self-harm should be very much reduced.

4

Adolescence and Professional Dance Training

As I have already indicated in the introduction, the issue of how adolescence is to be negotiated within professional dance training is one of crucial importance in considering how training can facilitate and enable emotional growth in students. In this chapter I will focus on various aspects of adolescent development and explore how they impact on dance training. My intention is to consider how dance training may contribute towards the development of autonomy and maturity in young people, and where it may limit that development. Wheeler and Birtle (1993) and Coren (1997) both give accounts of the impact of adolescence on the student's learning in a more general setting, which are a useful addition to the more particular problems of adolescence for the dance trainee.

The Mature Child

By the time an ordinary healthy child, especially a girl, is eleven years old, she is very likely to have achieved an age-appropriate maturity that allows her to feel rather competent and capable (Orford,1993). She will have mastered the basic functions of reading, writing and arithmetic; she will be physically co-ordinated and reasonably strong; she will have been given some responsibility and will be capable of helping and collaborating in both a home and school setting. Although her emotional base will still be at home, she will have made friendships, and interaction with her peer group will be increasingly important. Her position at the top of her junior school will give her considerable status. As a number of adolescents told me with some regret, 'It was very nice to be eleven'. She will have achieved some kind of equilibrium and a certain degree of confidence. We could say that in the light of the processes described in the previous chapters, the emotionally and physically healthy child of eleven will have a strong sense of being in her body; will have a good idea of what she feels and be able to express it reasonably well through a combination of words and appropriate body language; will have a sense of competence and confidence appropriate to her age; in short, will have a good sense of self. She has successfully negotiated childhood (Orford, 1993).

For the appropriately mature child who has begun dancing classes (probably a large majority of those who go on to professional dance training) there will very likely also be an equivalent sense of confidence and competence in herself as a dancer. She will have become accustomed to her physical self and may very well have developed excellent co-ordination and movement skills. Her dreams and fantasies of being a dancer do not seem impossible.

The Child in Transition

This plateau in development does not last very long. Soon virtually every aspect of a youngster's life will be changing as part of the transition from child to adult. In this process there will be very little rest until the young person has got to seventeen or so; then life may be a little easier and the remaining tasks of adolescence may cause less anguish. However, for the child of twelve, just embarking on secondary education, it may well feel like starting again at the very bottom. (Middle schools, for children of eight to thirteen, have been one of the ways that some education authorities in England have sought to modify this problem.) It is difficult both for youngsters and for the adults involved with them to deal with the constantly changing nature of adolescence. Paradox, contradiction, uncertainty, ambivalence, ambiguity and indecision are the hallmarks of this stage of life (Wilson, 1991). Parents and teachers as far as possible need to tolerate the constant flux and change and recognise it as part of the journey towards a more definitive version of the self. For these reasons the commitment required of the dance trainee in adolescence presents a problem. No teenager is capable in any real sense of saying at the age of, let us say, thirteen, 'I am going to be a dancer' (although many thirteen-year-olds say exactly that). There are too many unknowns in the life of an adolescent for such an assertion to have much weight. However, the adolescent cannot know this; it is the responsibility of the adults around to recognise the provisional nature of the youngster's commitment. It might be most useful if the adults had in mind the sort of commitment that Alcoholics Anonymous recognise – 'one day at a time'. No one knows when a youngster is thirteen whether in three or four years time she will have the talent, the physique or the desire to be a dancer. It is important that the desire to be a dancer is 'demand led', that is to say that we, the adults, support the student's desire, rather than that we fuel it with our own sense of her possibilities (Buckroyd, 1986). Conversely we need to listen with a certain amount of detachment to her declarations that she wants to stop dancing immediately. It is best if we, the adults, can maintain a position of detached goodwill so that our needs and opinions do not become confused with that of the adolescent. She will find it quite difficult enough to identify her own desires and motivations without having to detach them from ours.

Physical Changes

The physical plateau reached by the eleven-year-old, with its accomplishment of control and competence, is disrupted, in the course of nature, within one to two years by the changes of puberty (Wilson, 1991). In what follows I propose to focus on the changes to the female body because it is these that can be seen as more problematic for professional dance training. The changes in the boy's body, although they may cause him a good deal of anguish, are needed and fostered for his functioning as a dancer. A male dancer is used for his power and strength so his pubertal development is welcomed. These changes also take effect later, often not until he is fourteen (Orford, 1993), and are less radical in their effects in terms of dance training. These themes will be taken up later in the chapter on male dancers.

In contrast, a girl's physical changes will begin with the development of breasts when she may be as young as eleven. Menstruation will follow, often in the next two years or so, accompanied by growth in height, increase in muscle mass and the proportion of fat, and a tilting of the pelvis. These changes collectively constitute a major change in a girl's physique which will alter her centre of gravity and alignment (Schnitt and Schnitt in Ryan and Stephens, 1987). It is difficult for any girl to manage these changes; they arouse so many conflicting feelings (Orford, 1993). On the one hand, they constitute the evidence that she is a female, a woman, with the potential for fertility and childbirth; for the vast majority of girls this thought will be confirming of identity. On the other hand, the changes provide the incontrovertible evidence that childhood is over; for many girls this is the occasion of some sadness and regret (Wilson, 1991). For the child whose beginnings have been good, life is never likely to be so simple and so safe again. This conflict produces uncertainty and a challenge to the sense of self that has been built up during childhood and has been invested so strongly in body-indwelling. 'The body is changing in size, shape and hormonal structure. Just as pregnant women focus on their bodies, so adolescent girls focus on their changing bodies. They feel, look and move differently. These changes must be absorbed, the new body must become part of the self' (Pipher, 1994: 54–5). All of a sudden the pubertal girl feels a stranger in her own body. The child who has played and tumbled, climbed trees and done cartwheels, may well find herself reluctant to continue these activities. Physical education for girls in secondary education is often experienced as humiliating rather than positive and confirming (Pipher, 1994). A recent report by the Girls in Sport Partnership found widespread disaffection with physical exercise. 'Competitive sport is seen as masculine and the onset of puberty makes girls hypersensitive to anything that seems to detract from their burgeoning femininity' (*Guardian Education*, 23 March 1999). These feelings may well be compounded by the strangeness and discomfort of menstruation. Having been relatively unselfconscious about her child body, the pubertal girl becomes acutely conscious of her developing body. She may well stoop, round her shoulders and blush easily. The same report quoted above found that 'forty percent of girls drop out of sport by the time they are fourteen partly because they are self-conscious about their bodies' (*Independent*, 18 March 1999).

For the girl who is strongly invested in her identity as a dancer the conflict is likely to be that much more acute. It is the moment when many drop out (Schnitt and Schnitt in Ryan and Stephens, 1987; Pruett, 1991). Her genetic inheritance in terms of physique will start to become apparent which may make it clear that she does not have the body shape which is thought suitable for a professional dancer (for example, the ballet culture demands small breasts). This can be extremely painful for the girl who wants to dance but finds herself with a body that is thought unacceptable. Her body, her very self, is being rejected and, as Simone de Beauvoir says, 'to lose confidence in one's body is to lose confidence in oneself' (quoted Pipher, 1994: 57). Needless to say, decisions made by dance schools about physical suitability, especially when a student is strongly invested in her identity as a dancer, need to be conveyed with the utmost tact and sensitivity. (This applies equally to candidates for dance schools who are informed at audition that there is some physical characteristic, which may have gone previously unnoticed, that renders them unsuitable for intensive training.) It should be emphasised as far as possible that the girl is not wrong for ballet (for example) but that ballet is wrong for her. This is the difference between 'you are too big for this dress' (there is something wrong with you) and 'this dress is too small for you' (there is something wrong with the dress). Opportunities for the student to discuss the decision that has been made should be provided. ('You will want to think about what I've said and discuss it some more. Please come back and see me on Wednesday at 3 p.m. if you would like to. I am willing to talk to you as much as you like about it. I know this is very bad news for you and I'm sure you will feel angry and upset when you start to think about it. I want to help you get used to the idea and think about what the next move might be for you.') It is very hard to be forced to leave professional dance training because of perceived lack of talent or injury – situations that will be discussed in due course – but for the young person to be rejected on the grounds that her body is not right can easily be traumatic. Her identification as a dancer is likely to have been very important to her since adolescents are urgently seeking an identity; to have that identity taken from her (rather than to have given it up herself) is likely to feel annihilating – literally that she has been made nothing. The responsible adults need both to permit grieving for the loss and to help the youngster to begin the search for an alternative, perhaps in another dance form, perhaps in another expressive art. Even if these suggestions are not pursued they may sustain the hope that another identity can be found.

Even if the effects of pubertal physical development are not as serious as those described above, the young dancer will have to cope with changes in her appearance and sense of her physical self. 'Ironically, it is at this most physically awkward stage of life that the dance student is faced with the inner demand (and the teacher's requirements) to remain the same: co-ordinated, slim, graceful' (Schnitt and Schnitt in Ryan and Stephens, 1987). To remain the same is impossible, even though heroic attempts may be made in that direction. The task for student and teacher, together with other concerned adults, is rather to acknowledge, accept and manage the changes that are occurring. Youngsters are frequently not as well informed as adults think they are. Consequently, it might well be helpful to provide information about the physical changes that they are undergoing and to initiate discussion on the likely effects of those changes on the student's dancing (Geeves, 1997). Students could be invited to identify the problems they have experienced and to share the feelings that these problems create in them. ('Those of you who have grown a lot in the past year, can you say how that has affected your dancing?') In that way the changes would be signalled as ordinary, to be expected, perhaps difficult, but manageable. So the empathy of the concerned adults, together with the peer group, could enable the containment of what is potentially very distressing.

An alternative mode of dealing with the physical changes of puberty is to prevent or reverse them. This is extremely simple to effect by starvation. It has recently been well documented that young gymnasts have been deliberately required to remain at a weight below which the changes of puberty would take place, so that they would retain their childlike bodies and consequently the competitive edge that was thus obtained (Ryan, 1996). Something very similar, although one hopes not as deliberate, happens within the ballet world, when the demand for thinness becomes incompatible with the establishment or maintenance of menstruation. Some recent research demonstrated, not surprisingly, that those dance trainees most vulnerable to eating disorders were those whose natural shape did not conform to the requirement to be very thin (Hamilton et al., 1988). Girls who retain a child's body do not have to struggle with the changes that have been described above and in some quarters of the ballet world will receive favourable attention because of it. The price to be paid, however, is exceedingly high. It is now well understood that failure to menstruate results in a thinning of bone density and consequent risk of fractures and later osteoporosis. What is more, it seems likely that the bone mass thus lost cannot ever be completely regained, even when menstruation is later established or resumed (Wolman in Brinson, 1991). There are further anxieties about the effect on later fertility of delayed or interrupted menstruation. It is also un-

certain whether skeletal changes to the pelvis which have been prevented by low weight will ever take place once the age at which they
should have occurred has passed, with consequent implications for childbirth. Now that these things are well understood, the dance community
is in a position to consider whether the aesthetic of extreme thinness is
ethically tolerable and to refuse to comply with choreographers whose
vision of the female dancer is actively harmful to her physical welfare.
Dance schools can similarly alter the drive to extreme thinness by refus-
ing to allow girls who are underweight to continue with classes, by
developing a culture within which not menstruating is regarded as an
unacceptable failure to take care of oneself, and by providing continuing
nutritional education and support which will constantly reinforce the
message of the necessity for a proper diet (Geeves, 1997; Piran, 1999). In
this way the reality and necessity of girls' pubertal development will be
recognised and accepted by the training institution so that the temptation for the student to run risks with her health and welfare will no
longer be tacitly condoned.

Being Seen

The usual emotional effect on an ordinary teenager of the changes
described above is the development of an acute self-consciousness. The
young person has a terrible anxiety about being seen and about the
presumed reactions of those who might see her. Bearing in mind the
discussion in chapter two, this way of being may be understood as a
great anxiety as to whether her changing self is acceptable to herself and
others. The child whose security and self-confidence has not been well
established during her pre-pubertal development is likely to suffer more
than ordinarily from these worries. It is typical, however, that the attack
on self-esteem that is the result of pubertal changes is displaced on to
clothing, hairstyles, and so on. The adolescent thus retains some power
by convincing herself that if she presents herself in a certain way she will
be seen to be acceptable. As she becomes more used to her changed
body and can identify it as herself, this self-consciousness will fade, but
at its most acute, can make her feel unable to mix socially or even to go
to school. Careless or cruel comments on her appearance from adults or
her peer group ('You're putting on weight'; 'Look at your tummy'; 'You're
going to be really tall, aren't you?'; 'Why don't you get your hair cut

properly?'; 'You should do something about those spots') can cause terrible distress and a deep sense of worthlessness.

The dance student is not exempt from these anxieties but they are
made very much more complex by the very fact of wishing to be a
professional dancer. To wish to be a professional dancer is to wish to be
seen dancing. The person for whom this way of life is attractive may very
well have been the sort of child who loved performing and found the
attention exciting and satisfying. All of a sudden that wish, which may be
a strong part of her sense of self, is in conflict with anxieties about
changes to her body and a wish not to be seen (Pruett, 1991). As a
trainee, she will be in an environment where she *will* be seen, in mirrors,
by teachers, by her peer group, dressed in a minimum of clothing so that
her body is revealed without possibility of disguise. The level of stress
created by this conflict can be very great indeed and has as one of its
more ordinary manifestations an extreme sensitivity to comments about
her body. The student puts herself in a position to be seen, she wants to
be seen and yet it is torture to be seen. In this situation, the teacher and
concerned adults have a very great responsibility to be careful in what
they say about a student's body.

In the first place, insulting name-calling should be seen as absolutely
unacceptable in any circumstances. It is at best offensive to call a student
an 'elephant', 'hippopotamus', 'whale'; to use words such as 'waddling',
'clumsy'; to mimic students' mistakes. To behave in such a way with
adolescents, who have no opportunity to protest or respond and whose
sense of self is immature and fragile, cannot be helpful, even if that is the
conscious intention of the teacher. The teacher may feel she is merely
'joking' but such comments can be grossly wounding to students. It can
be said in explanation of such teaching that it has a long history within
dance and that teachers are often merely reproducing the mode in which
they were themselves taught. That is probably true, and the paucity of
available teacher training for dance teachers in professional dance schools
has allowed such methods to be perpetuated. However, in the light of
what is known about teaching methods and the needs of teenagers, such
ways of behaving can and should no longer be condoned.

Secondly, teachers and other responsible adults need to keep at the
forefront of their minds the central premise on which this chapter is
based: that adolescence is a time of change. Trainees need supporting
through the changes they experience. It may well be that for a time their
co-ordination is not as good as it was, that their alignment needs correc-

tion, and so on. The student is undoubtedly aware of these difficulties and doing her best to deal with them, even if she cannot explain them. What she needs from her teacher is recognition of her struggle, rather than attention to what she cannot for the moment correct ('I can see you're working on that'). She needs recognition of the difficulties she is facing ('When your body is changing quickly it can feel as though you have to start at the beginning again'). She needs support to go on trying ('This is difficult for the moment, but it won't be too long before you become accustomed to the changes in your body'). The teacher has the advantage, unlike the student, that she can imagine when this particular stage of development will be over. Her task is to support the student through it (Wilson, 1991; Rachel Rist, interview, 1 February 1999).

Thirdly, teachers should think about the implications of touching students in class without expressly asking permission. The teenager is striving to develop and maintain a sense of self which is highly invested in her sense of her body. The body confidence which she reached as a mature child will have been shaken by the changes of puberty. For the teacher to respect the physical being of the student by asking permission to touch or move her body, when she sees something that can be corrected, is to strengthen the sense of body-self. Not to do so implies that the student has no separate existence, no discrete being, and is therefore to undermine her sense of herself as an autonomous person. Such asking for permission, perhaps by saying quietly, 'May I?', as I have sometimes seen done, may seem ritualistic and meaningless, but has enormous symbolic value. It allows the possibility to be imagined that the student will say, 'no', and thus underlines the dignity of the student and the collaborative, rather than coercive, nature of the relationship between student and teacher.

Teachers might reflect upon the use of the mirror for adolescent students in the light of what has been said so far. The problem with mirrors is that the image the adolescent student sees is not so much the one in the mirror as the one in her head. The changes she is going through make it very unlikely that she is capable either of receiving an accurate image from the mirror, or of detaching 'herself' from what she sees in the mirror. It is the work of maturity to be able to look at an image of oneself and use it creatively. What is more, immature and insecure students can use the mirror as some kind of demonstration of their existence (Blackmer Dexter, 1989). The student who looks as if she is drowning in the mirror is a well-known member of the dance class. What she and all the other class members need is for their sense of themselves from the *inside* to get stronger. There may well be a case therefore for covering the mirrors or working facing away from them except perhaps when they are being used to develop a limited and specific awareness. In due course, when the worst of the trials of adolescence are over, it may be possible to learn to use the mirror in a way that is less damaging.

Lastly, it may be worth considering how the student group can be used to provide mirroring for each other. In the struggles of adolescence the peer group has a lot to offer. It may well be that to be seen by one's peers is the least frightening and most supportive way of being seen that is available to the dance student. Virginia Gallagher describes how she evolved a system for doing exactly this with younger children, while teaching some of the principles of sports psychology, and was positive about its benefits. She urged those teaching older children to try her methods (Gallagher in Brinson, 1993). My feeling is that if students were trained in giving and receiving feedback, which will be described later in the chapter called 'Learning in Groups', the group might be used much more extensively than it is now, and to good effect.

Becoming Separate

The physical changes of puberty may be difficult enough, but during that same period the adolescent must accomplish a number of psychological tasks. The most important of these is the establishment of a degree of psychic separation from significant adults, especially parents. The purpose of this development in Western culture, to which most young people have a very strong urge, is the eventual capacity to leave home, in an emotional as well as a physical sense, and to establish oneself as an autonomous person (Wilson, 1991). Separation is also the essential prerequisite to the establishment of adult sexual relationships and therefore to the creation of a new unit. In the old literature, separation was described as if it meant a complete cutting off from parents, a denial of their continuing emotional importance. Since women are not particularly good at this, men's apparently greater detachment was admired, and women's continuing attachment deplored. However, in more modern writing on the subject, separation has been seen more in terms of being able to identify and act on one's own feelings and needs, whether or not they coincide with those of one's parents, but without feeling the need to cut off from one's family in order to do so (Eichenbaum and Orbach, 1983).

The commonest way for adolescents to begin on this process of separation is via what is called 'adolescent rebellion'. In order to establish themselves as different, adolescents will find ways of not agreeing with the opinions of their parents and not conforming to what is expected of them. Where parents can tolerate this pulling away from them by their youngsters, rebellion can take relatively benign forms (Wilson, 1991): maintaining a style of dress, for example, which is known to be less than pleasing (I knew a boy who wore a hat in all circumstances, all his waking hours, for several years); adopting an appearance that is slightly unconventional (via hairstyles, make-up, body piercing, and so on); flouting parental injunctions (failing to tidy bedrooms, coming in at later than the permitted time, failing to telephone to indicate whereabouts); using forms of language that offend parents (swearing, muttering, failing to reply to questions, or replying in monosyllables, using street language). All of these may be irritating, but are not threatening to the welfare of the young person. At the same time parents can give youngsters the opportunity to choose and to assert their preferences in age-appropriate ways; common examples are giving a teenager a clothes allowance and allowing her to choose her own subjects for examination courses.

Where parental control is tighter, youngsters may have to adopt more dramatic ways of asserting difference (Wilson, 1991). For boys, this may take the form of failing at school or of delinquency; for girls it can take the form of eating disorders, risk-taking sexual behaviour or misuse of drugs and alcohol. However, if the emotional risk of defying parents is felt to be too great – that their love is likely to be forfeit – then the youngster will have no option but to comply. That is to say that some adolescents fail to make the move towards emotional autonomy and remain psychologically under the control of their parents, as if they were children. In neither case do they learn to make age-appropriate choices or to exercise an appropriate independence. (There is a further group of youngsters whose family environment and/or emotional health is so poor that their behaviour is disturbed and delinquent. Such a youngster is most unlikely to be able to sustain dance training and so will not be discussed here.)

How can professional dance training deal with the necessity for 'rebellion', for self-assertion, among dance students? Or, to express the same question slightly differently, how can dance schools give their trainees an appropriate independence and responsibility? The trainee of course has her own responsibility which will be discussed in due course; for the moment I want to focus on the responsibility of the institution to the development of the student. With rare exceptions, institutions involved in professional dance training enact the parental functions that are appropriate to the care of children rather than adolescents. There are many rules about appearance, behaviour, punctuality, and so on, which collectively recreate a highly controlling environment more appropriate for young children. In this situation, to rebel is to risk being excluded from the training, whereas to conform is to fail to perform one of the most important tasks of adolescence.

When I have talked to dance teachers about these issues I have often been thought to be attacking the old-fashioned courtesies that are common in the dance world between teacher and student, for example formal modes of address to teachers, ritual expressions of thanks for a class by clapping, students rising to their feet if a teacher enters a room, and so on. My view of these rather charming behaviours is that in themselves they are not objectionable, but that they can have a symbolic importance in underlining a relationship between student and teacher that is often experienced as hierarchical and that consequently implies a power imbalance. I am not suggesting that teacher and student are or should be *the same*. Clearly the teacher's knowledge and experience mean that she is not the same as the student. However, what the student needs to feel is that the relationship is collaborative and not coercive. The student needs to be able to express her individuality in ways that are not harmful and needs to be given opportunities to make choices and to take responsibility for herself in age-appropriate ways.

The dance class, like any other teaching and learning environment, needs to be interactive in order to liberate the energies and intelligence of the adolescent. The dance class needs to promote her development as a young person in touch with her own feelings and capable of expressing them, knowing how to make choices based upon them as part of her growth towards independence. The stereotypical dance class and dance training institution, however, require very little input from students in terms of their feelings, ideas and opinions about their training. There are very few institutions that have a system of asking for student evaluation of the training. It seems to be assumed that the student has nothing to offer in that way and that on the contrary she is there to be told and to be trained.

> **Teachers should** develop better liaison between students and teachers and among teachers themselves, including the practice of reports by student groups on their teachers.
>
> **A Dancers' Charter** Appendix Three

It would be ridiculous to deny that the teacher has a fund of knowledge and experience, hugely valuable to the student, indeed essential to her development as a dancer. However, the function of the training institution is not only the development of the student as a technical dancer, but also as a creative and expressive person. For that reason students need to participate and engage in their training as much as possible. It is the responsibility of the institution to facilitate and develop that aspect of its work. I will return to these issues in the next chapter; here I want only to propose that time is used inside and outside class for discussion between the teacher and the group, for peer interaction, for the soliciting of student opinion, for sharing current debates within dance training, for personal goal setting, for self- and peer-evaluation. These are some of the methods whereby students can be systematically educated into a mature responsibility for themselves and their training.

The failure to develop this aspect of dance training leads to exactly the kind of acting out from students that is so damaging to them and to their training. Discontent and misunderstandings in class, that could be resolved by open discussion between teacher and student, turn into destructive gossip and covert aggression. Interactions between teacher and student that arouse angry or hurt feelings in the student, which she is not allowed to express, easily become converted into self-destructive behaviour. Impulses to creativity and expressiveness from students in relation to the dance class that cannot be accommodated, are lost and replaced by passivity and conformity. Opportunities for interaction between peers, which would develop skills and relationships, are not seized so that vulnerable students become isolated. It is possible to make youngsters passive and conformist in relation to their training, but the dangers that are thereby courted and the opportunities for the development of the adolescent that are thereby lost (Schnitt, 1990) suggest that this is an area where reflection on current practice might be useful (Geeves in Brinson, 1993). Butler (1987) makes the same point in relation to elite music students.

LONDON CONTEMPORARY DANCE SCHOOL Student Evaluation for Technique Classes

Please circle BALLET or CONTEMPORARY. Please explain your answers where possible. The more detailed your comments, the more helpful this questionnaire will be to your teachers.

1. Did the course challenge former ideas and assumptions about dance training?
2. Did the course add new information and/or give a new perspective to your existing knowledge and understanding of the subject?
3. Was the material, as presented by the teacher, well organised?
4. Did the class follow a logical sequence throughout the week and the term as a whole?
5. Were the specific demands of the technique clearly presented?
6. Were you able to integrate knowledge gained from other practical courses in this school with the information presented in this course?
7. Did the course follow on logically from previous techniques studied in the school?
8. Did this course add a new dimension to your understanding of those techniques?
9. Did you discover contradictions between information given in other practical courses and this course?
10. Were these contradictions resolved?
11. Were the physical demands made by the teacher appropriate?
12. Was the expectation of good performance realistic in relation to the class material?
13. Did the teacher provide fair, constructive, individual attention during the classes?
14. Did the teacher provide time for discussion outside class time and were these discussions constructive?
15. Was the duration of the course sufficient for you to investigate and assimilate the work conceptually and physically?
16. Did you find your record of attendance acceptable?
17. If you missed class, how many classes did you miss?
18. Did you participate in the course as fully as you could have?
19. Did the course encourage independent work and thought?
20. Did you give time to course work outside the class?
21. How would you assess your capacity for independent thought?
22. How would you assess your capacity for perceptive self-evaluation?
23. Was the method of course assessment made clear and was it appropriate to the subject?
24. Was the method of course assessment closely related to course content?
25. What did you gain from this course?
26. In what ways was this course exceptional, that is inspiring, exciting, etc.?
27. Please add any comments that you think are important to this evaluation.

Social Development

From about the age of twelve, the adolescent starts to turn away from her family of origin and towards her peer group for her emotional satisfactions. Over a period of about a decade she will come to the point where the single most important person in her life will no longer be one of her parents, but one of her peer group. In order to make this development she will spend very long periods of time with her peers, learning the many skills required in forming friendships and eventually sexual relationships. The youngster who does not undergo this process is likely to be seriously disadvantaged in acquiring the skills of social interaction and will therefore become isolated.

The average youngster attending a mainstream school has a great deal of time and opportunity for interaction with her peer group. The school day includes many classes where pair and group work will be part of the teaching methodology. There are frequent breaks and often long lunch hours. The school day finishes early and there is no school at the weekend. All of this time, together with long holidays, allows for virtually constant peer group association and interaction. For the vast majority of youngsters, these times are energetically used for developing friendships and relationships.

By contrast, the student at a vocational school has an extraordinarily busy life. As well as continuing formal academic education until at least the age of sixteen, she is undergoing an intensive training as an elite athlete. There will certainly be far less unstructured time available to her even in terms of breaks during the day. The physical demands of doing so much are likely to make her too tired to have a very ambitious social life, so that the dance student may very well meet only other dance students and have a much more restricted and limited social life than the average youngster of her age. Even during her training, the traditional mode of dance teaching, where a teacher does whole class teaching or addresses individuals within the class, means that there is very little interaction between students in the course of the learning. Collectively these limitations often mean that the dance trainee does not mature as a social being in the way that is usual for her age group. Agnes de Mille was one of those who failed to achieve the ordinary social development of the adolescent, as she describes in her autobiography. At the time she appeared to manage, but paid a price later: 'I got through adolescence without a pang. I postponed it' (de Mille, 1952). Immaturity contributes to the dancer's vulnerability once she leaves training and has to function in the adult world.

Clearly, dance training organisations need to think about these issues and how they can be addressed. I can see a number of ways in which the problem might be approached. The opportunity might be taken in the academic work to include as much peer interaction as possible and to introduce contact with non-dance students. A number of training institutions are embedded in larger organisations where such contacts are relatively easy. Dance classes themselves might involve a great deal more interaction between students; later in this book I will discuss this possibility at greater length. Collaborative ventures, such as working with other performing artists, might be tried. Appendix Four describes two such collaborations: one, organised by London Contemporary Dance School, involves collaboration with music students; the Central School of Ballet participates in another similar scheme with design students.

There are dance students, as described in the last chapter, whose devotion to dance seems to be fuelled in part by the very fact of the social isolation and restriction of a trainee's life. Youngsters whose social adjustment is poor or who are afraid of engaging in social interaction with their peers may be attracted to dance training as a way of hiding from the tasks of adolescence (Buckroyd, 1986e). Clearly, structured opportunities for interaction with their peers are particularly desirable for such students.

In a more radical way the implications for student development of ever-increasing intensity of training might be reassessed. Over the past twenty-five years the amount of training that students undertake has increased hugely. On the physical side this leads to stress fractures and amenorrhoea with their attendant problems (Wolmar in Brinson, 1991); on the psychological side, students are deprived of appropriate opportunities for the emotional work of growing up. A number of authorities are starting to suggest that the constant repetitions of conventional dance training may not be the most effective way of training, and that less, with a more focused approach, might well do more (Koutedakis in Brinson, 1991; Geeves in Brinson, 1993). Perhaps training organisations might explore equally whether the work needs to take up quite as much time as it currently does, and whether there may be more time for peer interaction.

If, by whatever means, the opportunities for interaction were significantly increased, the benefit to the development of trainees would be considerable. However, it is likely that the training would also benefit from the increasing maturity and confidence of trainees whose development towards adult life had been facilitated in this way.

Sexuality

Adolescence is a time when hormonal changes bring about a powerful upsurge in sexual feelings. In an ordinary environment youngsters gradually experiment with intimacy through fantasy and through a great deal of ritualised interaction which eventually leads to pairing off. To miss out on this stage of development is to find oneself ill-prepared for the world of adult sexual relationships and therefore vulnerable to harm.

Dance training institutions have a number of difficulties in facilitating this aspect of adolescent development. The first is, again, time. Many dance schools have a large majority of female students; whereas in mainstream education the pupil at a girls' school will have plenty of time and energy to seek out the company of males, the dance student will have much less opportunity to do so. Secondly, the delay in menstruation and the maintenance of low weight greatly diminish sexual feelings. In effect this keeps some youngsters in an emotional pre-pubertal state; they are children so far as sexual feelings are concerned. Thirdly, dance training takes place when numbers of young people are gathered together dressed in garments that are designed to be very revealing of the body. In order to manage this situation, students must operate a denial of the sexual feelings likely to be aroused in these circumstances. Whereas physical education in secondary schools is segregated for precisely this reason (among others) in dance schools students are required to deny the significance of the physical closeness the dance class creates.

None of these circumstances is likely to facilitate the development of an ordinary progress to sexual maturity. That process is difficult for most of us, even in ordinary circumstances – how much more difficult for a dance trainee. Yet this is an area that deserves some thought since there is anecdotal evidence at least (Kirkland, 1986) that dance trainees are vulnerable to engaging in risk-taking sexual activity, or alternatively to failing to engage in relationships at all (Schnitt, 1990). Training institutions can promote interaction with students from other institutions, as has already been suggested. They can also promote a policy of using the establishment and maintenance of menstruation as a benchmark of appropriate self care, as I have already suggested, but also with the aim of protecting psychosexual development. But perhaps most importantly, dance schools can ensure that discussion of these issues is facilitated and encouraged among both staff and students.

It is a commonplace to observe that it is unfortunate that so much has to be learned at school at a time when the turmoil of adolescent change and development is under way. If this is true of mainstream education, how much more true it is of professional dance training. Certainly, many dancers (and other elite athletes and performers) *do not* have an adolescence (Schnitt, 1990). Nevertheless, whatever the difficulties, it is vital to ensure as far as possible that adolescent development is facilitated. The alternative is either the dancer who never grows up emotionally and whose expressive and artistic capacity is thereby limited, along with her whole personal potential, or the dancer who remains a little girl throughout her training but then spends her twenties having the adolescence of which she was cheated. This timing is likely to threaten her career as a dancer. There is also a third possibility: the dance trainee who fears that adolescence and dance training are incompatible and who drops out to safeguard her development as a person (Schnitt and Schnitt in Clarkson and Skrinar, 1988; Pruett, 1991). If training institutions can wholeheartedly incorporate the value and necessity of adolescent psycho-social development in their goals for their trainees, then the waste of human potential that is implied in any of these scenarios may be avoided.

5

The Dance Teacher

If education is essentially about the eventual acquisition of qualifications or skills, and [also] the involvement in and the engagement
with a culture which nurtures, protects, and facilitates personal
development, then these two aims need to be complementary. The
danger is in assuming that the former will inevitably lead to the
latter, rather than recognizing that the latter enables the former to
occur and flourish.   (Coren, 1997: 139)

Truly effective teachers are realistically positive, supportive and
enthusiastic. They provide specific feedback to their students that
is primarily couched in positive language, They focus on the future
rather than the past. They exercise control through consensus
rather than coercion and deal with behavioural difficulties early in
their generation before they become real problems. They intui-
tively understand and manage social dynamics.
                                                    (Thomas, 1993: n.p.)

In this chapter I would like to attempt to delineate the role of the teacher
in professional dance training, in the light of the concepts and ideas that
have been explored so far. Many teachers of dance at this level have a
passionate commitment to their students; however, because they have
almost always had a career as dancers themselves, they will often not
have had the opportunity to consider in any detail the concepts I have

> **Teachers should** recognise that changes in the profession need to start with teacher training to encourage a rounder approach involving personal growth and care for the whole person.
>
> **A Dancers' Charter** Appendix Three

been presenting, or their relevance to dance teaching. It is still rare for teachers at this level to have had the benefit of teacher training. Indeed that is one way in which the dance community could vastly improve its awareness of the psychological and emotional implications of dance training very rapidly (Brinson in Brinson, 1993; Bannerman in Brinson and Dick, 1996).

Yet teachers, trained or not, 'play a very important part in the lives of young people; they provide a framework which either assists or hinders emotional and mental growth' (Salzberger-Wittenberg, 1983: xi). As Skrinar and Moses observe, 'Teachers, as vehicles for . . . training, are key figures in a dancer's accomplishments. Their methods of guiding and selecting students can facilitate or thwart the physical, psychological, sociological, and spiritual development of students, irrespective of class purpose or level' (in Clarkson and Skrinar, 1988: 289).

To the former dancer, however, trained in less psychologically aware times, and doubtless a survivor of considerable emotional trauma during her own training, these concerns may seem trivial or self-indulgent. On the other hand, such a person will undoubtedly be able to bring to mind a long list of fellow dancers who, one way or another, went to the wall because of emotional difficulties. There have been too many tragedies through injury, drug addiction, eating disorders, failure to take appropriate care, and emotional breakdown. We in the dance community really owe it to our students to help them to greater security, maturity and sense of self than many dancers of earlier generations were able to achieve. Nowhere in these pages do I wish to suggest or imply that the great gifts of knowledge and experience that teachers bring to dance students are not hugely valuable. However, I would like to encourage teachers to use those gifts hand in hand with an informed concern for the student's development as a person. It is my conviction that thereby the standards achieved would be higher and at less cost to the teacher: 'The imparting of knowledge . . . is highly dependent on the nature of the relationship between student and teacher' (Salzberger-Wittenberg, 1983: xi).

> I believe that we should honour the past and the past achievements of those who have done so much for dance. We would betray that great tradition if we did not consider and reconsider the appropriateness of the present teaching and learning of dance. That is what those who created this tradition did in their own day and it is what we need to do now. Our world has changed, our society has changed, dance has changed and we must change.
>
> (Bannerman in Brinson, 1993: 34)

Class

The central experience of learning to dance is the dance class, and it is on what goes on in the dance class that I will focus during this chapter. Class is the vehicle for the vast majority of the learning that will take place and is the mode in which that learning will take place. Or, to say the same thing the other way round: nobody learns to dance from a book; nobody learns to dance just on her own; nobody learns to dance without a teacher. Class is the most important element in the training of a dancer, the repeated experience in her daily learning, the most continuous of the methods through which she will be formed and developed, not only during her training, but also throughout her life as a dancer.

Class is seen first of all, at an elite level, as a preparation for performance and the means by which the capacity to perform is sustained. It is also, and needs to be, more than that. Since so few of those who have trained as dancers find work as professionals after their training is over (in our times of serious underfunding of the arts in Britain) class may well be not only the experience of *learning* to dance, but also the principal experience of dancing. Certainly most students will be involved in performance during their training, but the proportion of time that this takes compared to the time spent in class will be very small. For a large proportion of dance trainees, there will be no progression to a career in dance; the training will be all there is. There is also a very significant further group of those for whom the experience of learning to dance will be the experience of dancing, and that is that majority (in some schools, a large majority) who, for one reason or another, do not complete the course. The reasons for not completing are very many, including accident, injury, lack of talent, financial circumstances, and so on, but whatever the reason, for these students, the experience of class will have been absolutely dominant in their experience of dancing.

Clearly, then, it is utterly vital that the experience of taking class is as good as it possibly can be. When the numbers of those who continue to a dancing career are so very small it is essential that the training can stand alone as a positive and creative experience that contributes to the development of the student as a person in every way, whether or not she goes on to be a professional dancer. There is an analogy to be made with a liberal education, which does not necessarily prepare a student in terms of content for future employment, but teaches her *how* to learn and develops self-discipline and intellectual training. These skills are then available for use in any context. The self-discipline, perseverance and application that are required to undertake professional dance training, whether or not they are eventually used for a career in dance, can perfectly well constitute the basis of further learning in any direction. However, an aspect of such a liberal education is the development of the mature person. Dance training must seize the opportunity to develop that aspect of its responsibilities.

The Teacher's Aesthetic and Physical Expertise

The most obvious function of the dance teacher is to teach her students how to dance. By virtue of her own training, her experience of dancing and her training and career as a teacher, she brings to the dance class a wealth of knowledge to convey to her students. Traditionally this knowledge and experience have been encapsulated first in the teacher's ability to demonstrate in her own body, or that of a suitably instructed demonstrator, the movements and positions that she wants to teach, and secondly in her eye which could identify when and how students failed to reproduce what she demonstrated. These skills are the fruit of many years of hard work on the teacher's own body, and of a prolonged education in looking at her own body and at other dancers. By a kind of apprenticeship, therefore, the student dancer learns to use her body, rather as an apprentice craftsman or musician learns to use his tools or instrument to produce a result that is then evaluated by his teacher.

At its best, such teaching can be extraordinarily inspirational. The student sees the movement enacted by the teacher and is filled with pleasure and admiration and the wish to be able to do the same. This is the kind of experience that inspires a dancer in the first place. As a system it has also had the virtue of carrying down and developing through generations of dancers the accomplishments and discoveries of previous masters of their art: Russian ballet, for example, or the work of Martha Graham.

The Widening Scope of the Teacher's Knowledge

Although the capacities described above are central and crucial to the dance teacher, increasingly the remit of the dance teacher has been widened to include a knowledge of other subjects. As the field of dance medicine and science has expanded, so it has become increasingly necessary for teachers to know more about anatomy and physiology and to have an understanding of nutrition and fitness. As it becomes ever clearer that injuries are very often caused by faulty technique, so the responsibility on the dance teacher to be able to convey how a movement is made becomes greater (Bannerman in Brinson and Dick, 1996). In other words, the traditional model of the teacher as former dancer whose sole concern is with transmitting the aesthetic heritage that she embodies, has begun to modify. Dance training organisations are beginning to provide their teachers with in-service training in all these fields; recent conferences have provided experts from a number of related fields to share information on the health and fitness of dancers in the broadest of terms (for example, the conferences of the International Association for Dance Medicine and Science). The BA at the Royal Academy of Dancing, which is a dance teaching degree, incorporates significant elements of anatomy and physiology. The same is true of the teaching course at the Royal Ballet School.

This development of the scope of the dance teacher's role has also begun to include a growing psychological awareness. I have, for example, been invited to a considerable number of dance training organisations to talk to staff about eating disorders in dance students. Both of the teacher trainings mentioned above included psychology courses. In what follows, then, in this chapter I am attempting to build on these changing percep-

---

Teachers should provide more and earlier information about how the body works, about anatomy, physiology, the reasons for important aspects of dance such as warm-up, warm-down, the sequence of exercises and the causes and treatment of injury.

A Dancers' Charter Appendix Three

tions of the dance teacher's role in professional training, and to widen it further in terms of the teacher's awareness of psychological issues relevant to teaching class.

The Underlying Objectives

What is implicit in the concept of the enlarged role of the dance teacher is that the goal of elite dance training can no longer be simply that of technical dance training. That single goal is no longer justifiable in terms of what any educational experience must nowadays provide. The implication of the growth in our understanding of young people and their needs, as described above, is that a more complex description of the goals of the training is required.

I would like to propose the following list of fundamental purposes of a psychological nature for professional dance training. They derive from the discussions of the previous four chapters:

- The provision of the optimum emotional environment for the facilitation of learning.
- The maximum development of the creative and expressive potential of the student.
- The facilitation of the student's autonomy and responsibility for the training.
- Continuing attention to the enabling of the student's development through adolescence to maturity.

The Facilitating Environment

In this section I would like to describe the characteristics of the emotional environment of the dance class where the facilitation of learning is being addressed.

In a very interesting article on dance teaching, Brian Thomas concludes, 'The challenge in teaching is to manage the balance between stretching and supporting our students' (1993). 'Stretching' is what the vast majority of teachers of professional dance are good at. They know how to identify further goals to be pursued, to introduce new material, to raise their expectations of the standard of work, and so on. What most are not so good at is providing a supportive atmosphere in which students can strive to achieve what their teachers ask. Yet it is increasingly understood that without an environment of safety and trust it is very difficult for the student to learn (Coren, 1997). What are the elements of 'support'? First is the use of positive forms of speech.

> Every negative statement can be converted into a positive one: 'Don't slouch' becomes 'Stand erect' . . . 'You're not lifting your leg high enough' becomes 'Lift your leg a little higher on the turn.'
>
> (Thomas, 1993)

Second is the recognition of achievement and effort, even where the results do not reach what is eventually wanted: 'Good attempt', 'Much better', 'Almost did it', are phrases that might be generously employed. Pleasure and satisfaction in the students and their work are also strengthening to class morale and to the individual's efforts. So, for example, the teacher might take care to say in appropriate circumstances, 'That was a good class today, you worked well' or 'I enjoyed teaching you today, that was fun.' I have been told that praise is handed out so seldom by some teachers that when a student finally is commended for her work, it produces terrible envy among other students. Generous praise never did any harm; teachers who find nothing to praise might wonder what that says about them, and make it their task to find as much as possible. Dickinson, who works on developing effective teaching in mainstream education, notes, 'It is challenge with success that builds self-esteem . . . This connection between self-esteem and achievement is quite crucial' (Dickinson, 1996). He goes on to quote White, who has done work on self-esteem: 'Self-esteem is the pivotal point between success and failure; it has a marked effect on learning' (White, 1991, quoted in Dickinson, 1996). McFee, who writes on dance education, quotes from an HMI report with approval, 'Active learning, and a sense of purpose and success, enhance pupils' enjoyment, interest, confidence and sense of personal worth' (1994: 158–9).

A third element of 'support' is specific, focused and particular feedback which identifies the precise movement or position that is being commented upon. Thus 'Left leg a little more extended' is infinitely preferable to 'What on earth do you think you're doing with your left leg?' or, worse, 'A dog could raise its leg higher than you do.' Such comments may raise a laugh, but are wounding to the student who is doing her best. More important, they are likely to scare other students who will fear that their inadequacies will receive equally harsh judgement. Being publicly humiliated does not promote learning. Similarly, commendation needs to be specific: a general 'Good' does not use the opportunity to help the student realise exactly *what* was good, whereas 'Good, you really stretched your foot that time' gives clear and particular indications of what has improved (Rachel Rist, interview, 1 February 1999).

Alongside support goes the necessity for the teacher to provide a calm, good-tempered, friendly, tolerant and compassionate presence. It takes great courage for an adolescent to risk her self in learning to dance. In order to do so with the minimum of distress she needs an environment of safety in which she can be sure that her mistakes and difficulties will be tolerated and in which she does not feel at risk from temperamental outbursts from the teacher. The student will almost certainly be struggling with her own perfectionism and sense of inadequacy; she certainly does not need those feelings to be reinforced (Thomas, 1993; 1997). Moreover, the teacher is likely to be a very important person to the student. She has the opportunity to model to the student a self that is accepting and compassionate, which the student may then be able to internalise. Such a presence in the teacher will affect profoundly the emotional atmosphere of the class and is likely to promote learning. As Linda Hamilton expresses it, 'Is the classroom "safe" from public humiliation? Are the teacher's criticisms geared toward a problem-solving approach? If the answer to these questions is "no" then the student would be better off with someone else, regardless of the teacher's reputation in the profession . . . Even if this teaching approach could be justified on technical grounds (which it cannot, given the negative repercussions . . .) there is no excuse for the destruction that these instructors inflict on young performers' self-esteem without regard for the long-term consequences or emotional costs' (Hamilton, 1997: 8–9). We cannot comfort ourselves either with the idea, put to me by a good number of dance professionals, that destructive teaching is a thing of the past. I have only to raise the subject with dancers and trainees to be given examples of teacher interventions that are alarmingly insensitive. Brinson and Dick (1996) found that two thirds of the ballet dancers interviewed felt that their teachers' criticism had affected them negatively and provided examples of comments that were critical and unhelpful.

When I have discussed these issues of positive feedback, support for students, recognition of achievement, and so on, with dance teachers, they have sometimes said to me that my ideas are totally unrealistic for dance training. First they say that the real world of professional dance is not benign and careful of the welfare of dancers, so to treat students carefully is to fail to prepare them for the reality of professional life. My answer is that I can well believe that the world of professional dance is often careless of both the physical and emotional welfare of dancers. Brinson and Dick (1996) demonstrated as much in their book. The issue is how we prepare students for that world. My view is that they are best prepared by the experience of being treated well and being encouraged to take responsibility for themselves. In this way they have the chance to mature in such a way that they are less vulnerable to being treated badly in the professional world. My analogy would be with the care and nurture of children within a family; we all know that children will have to deal with difficulties and take responsibility for themselves when they leave home. We prepare them by providing a supportive and encouraging environment within which they are given increasing responsibility for themselves. We certainly do not prepare them for the rigours of adult life by treating them badly and carelessly. Where dance trainees are enabled to mature and develop in an appropriately nurturing environment, I am convinced that they will do better professionally and be less at risk personally.

A second objection teachers have made to the idea of the facilitating environment is that being pleasant to students will simply never get them to the standards demanded by the professional dance world. Here, it seems to me, there is a confusion between respect and good behaviour between teacher and student, and being soft and easy-going about training. I am sure that standards of professional dance these days are extremely demanding, but my argument is that those standards will be more easily reached in an environment where the student is not distracted from the task by the fright produced by a hostile teaching environment. It is perfectly possible to demand high standards without being unpleasant. Indeed if the student's energies are enlisted in a collaborative venture with the teacher, those standards are more likely to be achieved. Rogers did a good deal of research to demonstrate this truth (1994) for academic subjects. Research is needed to test the hypothesis for elite arts students.

However, it is not difficult to understand that teachers trained in a very different environment might find it strange to provide for their students a setting that nurtures and supports. We all tend to repeat what we know. What is more, it is easy to feel envious of students to whom we may well be giving a better experience of training than we had ourselves. I have several times heard teachers say 'I had it hard and it never did me any harm'. I think hard treatment does do harm to students and there is ample evidence of that around us. Linda Hamilton, a psychologist who has done more research than anyone else on the welfare of dancers, reports that 'Dancers with critical teachers were unable to achieve their goals as professionals because of problems with self-sabotage in their careers' (1977: 73). Rather, teachers need to find within themselves, as so many do, the courage and the generosity to be more humane teachers than those who taught them.

A further constituent of the facilitating environment in the dance class is the provision of structure. Dance classes frequently have a traditional structure which is the order in which elements of the training take place. However, I refer to a structure, devised by the teacher and shared with the students, that is designed to focus the work of the class and provide goals. At an earlier stage of dance training one might perhaps use a syllabus for this purpose, but once a student is in elite training it is unlikely that there is new material to be covered in the way that a syllabus describes. Rather, the task is the unending refinement of what is already known, and revisiting it in ever new combinations. In these circumstances for the teacher to devise a series of different focuses and goals for the learning over time is likely to energise students while providing a framework within which to direct their efforts. Students can be invited to contribute to the formulation of this framework (Thomas, 1997). Dickinson comments on the value of this kind of structuring for mainstream education: 'For at least two generations teachers have been setting out aims and objectives for their schemes of work. What may be new is the importance that is now attached to learners being clearly aware of the aims and objectives of the work they are undertaking' (1996: 13). Beginning professional training may well de-skill students: they will have come from smaller organisations within which they will have been the senior and best students. Now all of a sudden they are in an environment in which they are the least skilful and the least capable (Wittenberg, 1983). Structure provides a framework within which the frightening task of beginning from the beginning all over again can be broken down into manageable sections. It is a safety measure.

A further constituent of this list of elements of the facilitating environment is an interactive style between teacher and students and between

Teachers should seek to develop thinking dancers able to respond intelligently to all aspects of their training, including new ideas, rather than dancers who 'react as puppets' with good technique.

A Dancers' Charter Appendix Three

student and student. In the chapter on adolescence I stressed how important it is that a collaborative rather than a coercive style is adopted for adolescents in the dance class. In an environment where students are invited to contribute their ideas and opinions to the class group and are encouraged to formulate their thoughts and ideas in pair and group work within the class, trainees can be involved in planning work, agree together rules for classroom conduct, assume responsibility for identifying individual goals and generally be involved in decision-making. Two distinguished teachers with whom I discussed this issue told me that they thought it was very important that the students spoke and articulated their thoughts in the class (Charlotte Kirkpatrick, personal communication; Rachel Rist, interview, 1 February 1999). The teacher, then, instead of taking the entire (and exhausting) responsibility for everything that goes on in the dance class, works collaboratively with students, giving them appropriate freedom and responsibility within their training.

Although there is a strong argument for devolving as much power as possible to students within the dance class, there are a good number of situations where the teacher needs to be active in her concern for the emotional welfare of trainees and thus maintain the facilitating environment. In this section I would like to describe those situations and how the teacher can respond to them.

In my view the most difficult and damaging dynamic within the dance class can be that created by the inevitable competition between classmates (Wittenberg, 1983; Greben, 1990; Schnitt, 1990; Orbach and Eichenbaum, 1994; Coren, 1997) and the envy created in less gifted students by the talents of the most accomplished. In the chapter called 'Learning in Groups' I will explore how management of these difficult feelings can be discussed with the group. In this chapter I am concerned principally with the teacher and her response. It is first of all necessary for the teacher to allow herself to be aware of competition and envy between students. Some teachers with whom I have discussed these matters deny that they exist. Students on the other hand have talked to me at length about the inhibiting effects of a 'pecking order' within the dance class.

They often perceive the teacher as consolidating a 'rank ordering' which makes improvement and development out of one's 'place' very difficult. A teacher who is aware of the dynamics of competition and the anxieties of students in relation to achievement can be careful not to have 'favourites' or to excite envy by too lavish praise and attention to the best students. Conversely, she can avoid expressions of contempt and irritation towards the least able. The teacher's responsibility is to the whole class. Obviously the abilities of individuals will differ, but the teacher's task is to create a positive learning environment for all students, irrespective of talent. Within such an even-handed environment it should be possible for each student to reach towards her own potential.

A related issue is the teacher's responsibility to be aware of and manage her *own* envy (Wittenberg, 1983). It is common to acknowledge that parents, adults and teachers see the young people for whom they are concerned enjoying opportunities and privileges that the older generation did not have. That old saying, 'Youth is wasted on the young', conveys exactly this sense of 'If only I had your opportunities, how well I would use them.' The dance teacher finds herself among young people, at least some of whom will be as talented as she herself was at that age. It is difficult for her not to feel a pang of envy for the fact that those youngsters have in front of them the prospect of a performance career, whereas for the teacher the performing days are probably over. All of this is perfectly ordinary and understandable. However, where these feelings are not acknowledged they can take the form of carping and criticising rather than generously encouraging. I have sometimes listened to dance teachers tell me that students today are lazy and undisciplined and have nothing like the devotion to dance that they had themselves; that seems to me the voice of envy of those for whom everything is yet to win. When teachers have had their fill of performing and have achieved their potential as dancers then these feelings are less troublesome, but of course very many dancers do not get their fill of dancing, for a whole variety of reasons, and still long to dance when that opportunity is gone. What I would like to stress is that envy as a feeling is ordinary and need not necessarily do harm where it is owned and acknowledged. It is only harmful when it is acted out and undermines the efforts of trainees.

Conversely, teachers can be the object of students' envy. When the accomplishments of the teacher seem too difficult for the student to achieve then one way of dealing with the difficult feelings aroused is to rubbish the teacher. An envious attack of this kind seeks to destroy the greater competence of the teacher and thus get rid of the feelings of incompetence and vulnerability in the student. Teachers will do best if they try and understand the source of such attacks and refrain from retaliation.

A second damaging dynamic is bullying within the dance class. This can be related to the competition and envy described above and takes a number of different forms. The one that I have observed and been told about most frequently happens when a weak student is (literally) elbowed out. She is relegated to the worst position at the barre, hidden at the back during centre work and made to go last (or to miss her turn completely) coming across the floor. Where this meets the student's own anxiety and poor sense of self, the stage is set for bullying. In mainstream education these dynamics receive a lot of attention and are repeatedly discussed in class groups and raised by teachers. So far as I am aware this is very rarely the situation in dance schools. The group needs to be faced with this issue, which will be discussed in the chapter on groups, but the teacher also has a responsibility not to allow the student to be made a scapegoat for the group's fear of its own weakness, inadequacy and lack of talent. Simple devices, such as teaching the class from the opposite end or the side of the studio, or reversing the order in which students come across the floor, together with even-handed attention to all students, will go some way to avoiding collusion with these destructive dynamics.

The teacher, however, is the one who is most commonly the bully in dance classes. I have been a witness to and have heard many accounts of examples of the insulting and humiliating of students and of temper tantrums that included shouting insults, swearing and name-calling. I have also seen teachers coerce students on to yet greater efforts when they were long past useful exertion. Yet it is clear that many dance teachers deplore such bullying (Independent, 14 July 1997). Where it does arise, I have come to understand that usually the teacher who uses methods of interacting that are experienced by the students as abusive is repeating ways of teaching that she herself experienced, and, at a conscious level at least, thinks that she is helping students make maximum effort to use the class. That may be the reason for teachers' astonishment at the suggestion that they bully or coerce students. We thus return to the issue of the desirability of teacher training. Where teachers have not had that opportunity, I think it would be helpful for some in-service training to be made available. If teachers were asked to reflect on their own experience of training and to recall examples of good and bad teaching they would have a basis for considering their own teaching. We all often repeat what has been done to us, even if at a conscious level we disliked it, because we lack other models. We repeat what we know. If, however, we have the chance to think about that experience we begin to have some power to choose whether to repeat what we have experienced. In-service training would also offer teachers the opportunity to discuss strategies for managing difficult situations in class and to acknowledge some of the stresses that dance teachers endure.

It would also be useful for teachers to reflect on the power balance between students and teacher in a professional dance setting. It seems to me that dance teachers have far more power than teachers in mainstream education, and that students have much less. This imbalance needs correction, as I repeatedly indicate throughout this book, but given that it exists it demands of the dance teacher a very particular care in relating to students. Where students are forbidden to respond directly to teachers (which appears very often to be the case) then the teacher has more than usual responsibility for exercising power carefully and judiciously. Much of the acting out with food, cigarettes, and so on, that is so much of a feature of dance student behaviour seems to me to be an expression of rage with a system that treats students carelessly but does not allow them a voice with which to protest.

I have discovered very little describing or providing a critique of teaching that is not facilitating or is actively harmful, even though the autobiographies of dancers are full of such stories and they are the subject of endless conversation among dance students and dancers. However, Clyde Smith has done research on dance schools and professional dance teaching (Smith, 1997, 1998) which provides an analysis of the dance teacher's power. Smith's argument is that the student in what he calls the 'Conservatory' is isolated, by the nature of the dance training, from other peer group, social or educational settings and quickly becomes accustomed to a lifestyle as a dance trainee. This isolation, in which there is little or no relief from the institution and there is punishment for failure to conform, rapidly ensures that the student becomes submissive. He compares the 'Conservatory' to Erving Goffman's (1961) idea of the total institution, such as a prison or a psychiatric hospital, where the inmates have no basis on which the power of those holding authority can be challenged. Of course there is a crucial difference from those two situations which is that the dance student is not obliged to stay

"I felt very strongly, very strongly motivated to train in a way that I wasn't trained; to teach in a way that I wasn't taught. I felt that my training and my experience, especially with the Graham Company, was severe. It was very old school. It worked on the principle that you can never be good enough. It was always about what you *didn't* achieve. It was relatively negative. It was negative to create challenge, to see if you would make or break. It was 'No, no, no, no, no'; 'That's awful, that's awful, that's awful'; 'You'll never get anywhere.' You actually had to *fight* with that.

I think that may be part of the reason why I retired very early, because I felt that it was quite condemning as an experience, even though I achieved within it. Something about it didn't feel right by the time I was in my late twenties. I was victimised by it but also I'd allowed myself to participate. I don't blame the parties involved as much as I think that's how it functioned and I allowed myself to be a part of that functioning. When I really grew wiser, grew more aware, I did realise that it wasn't healthy, that it was relatively destructive.

As I moved into teaching I have for years now promised that I would never allow myself to participate in the same kind of teaching. So I approach teaching in a different way. I think you make a choice and some people continue to teach the way they were taught. I've been determined to break that cycle. I now approach training to provide a positive environment, a supportive environment, one that will encourage the student to identify for themselves what they want to achieve. They have to be self-motivated and I'm not going to achieve that motivation by beating somebody down. That's not to say there isn't discipline, there isn't work, there isn't a sense of what is being demanded and asked of you. That exists, but I think you can have all of those expectations and still encourage and support and try to draw somebody out of themselves and into a positive experience of what it is to live in and with and through such a physical experience."

from an interview with Lyndon Branaugh, LCDS, 16 September 1998

at the 'Conservatory', but, says Smith, the 'Conservatory' has made itself so powerful because of its influence within the dance world that students feel that they must endure what happens there if they want to get a job. The dance student therefore permits herself to be badly treated.

He argues further, following Foucault (1979), that the structure of the traditional dance class where students are separated from each other, wear revealing clothing and are easily observed, makes the teacher able to command and observe 'docile bodies' in order to improve them. The potential for abuse in that situation is very great. Using Deikman (1990), he compares the dance school and its classes to a cult. In any cult there is compliance with the group, dependence on a leader, devaluing of the outsider and avoidance of dissent. Those who join the cult claim that the leader and the cult members are special; the sense of specialness, the sense of being an elite, makes cult members willing to accept any behaviour from the leader in the service of the ultimate goal, which is usually some form of enlightenment, and in the case of the dance school, getting a job as a dancer.

These comparisons are very stark and (one hopes) not directly applicable to the average dance school. However, Smith does provide a way of understanding why, in some situations, teachers place themselves and are placed in such a position of power, how that power can easily be abused and why dance trainees can tolerate abusive treatment. He concludes, 'Ultimately we must find new ways of being in the classroom. These ways would recognize the ultimate autonomy of each participant as well as the relative wisdom of teacher and student. Perhaps extreme situations like that at the Conservatory are not aberrations but are instead indicators of the worn out and destructive paradigms in which we all participate' (Smith, 1998).

The Development of Creative and Expressive Potential

Not very long ago I had a conversation with a dance teacher who was telling me about the extraordinary difficulty of mastering ballet technique. He went on to say that when, after continuous and repeated effort, the trainee has mastered the technique, then emotional expression can be added. This concept is about as far from Isadora Duncan's description of dance as 'an expression of life' as it is possible to get. It implies just that separation of technique and feeling that is so dangerous within dance training because it allows students to be misused and to misuse themselves. Feeling, emotion and expression cannot be turned off and on like a tap, to be used for performance but put away at other times. Too often, dancers seem to learn to turn off their expressive and imaginative powers and then are unable to access them for everyday use.

I have already made a number of suggestions about how the student's imaginative and emotional capacities might be brought into the dance class rather than left at the studio door. In this section I am concerned rather to explore the purposes and concept of dance training in the mind of the teacher. The conversation reported above reveals how the high standards of technical competence demanded in professional dance, contemporary as well as ballet, can have an overpowering effect on the

The School's curriculum is designed to provide a professional theatre training and to make students critically aware of art forms other than dance. Students are under the personal tuition of staff members who encourage them to study dance within a broad cultural and social context. Although there is a strong emphasis on technical excellence, the School has always encouraged individuality, experimentation and creativity. For this reason the School's work has been conspicuously important and influential and has substantially contributed to the development of dance in Britain.

As well as these practical dance subjects, all degree students undertake a programme of supporting study in subjects designed to underpin their training and equip them as articulate dance artists of the 1990s. In the first year of the course, compulsory subjects include music, anatomy and stagecraft, and in the second year students undertake a studio-based course in the structure of movement which helps them to make connections between different elements of the course and to find a language in which to discuss their experience as dancers and choreographers. Students are also encouraged to place their chosen art form in the wider context of contemporary culture, and first year students are given an introduction to other art forms such as film and theatre.

London Contemporary Dance School,
Induction and Advice Notebook Academic Year 1998/99

training, which becomes conceptualised as the acquisition of technique to which, at the stage of performance, feelings or expression can be added. Although this description may have elements of caricature about it, I would like to use it as a counterpoint to the idea of dance training as the nurturing of the artist in whom technical competence joins with developed imaginative and expressive qualities.

Implicit in the idea of expression as the final ingredient is the conviction that expressiveness can readily be produced. This seems to me unlikely. Rather, I think that the use of the self and the disciplining of the feelings and imagination that produce artistic expression are the result of years of development. Certainly in the fine arts, development of technique and imagination go hand in hand, as they do in performance arts such as acting or music (Butler, 1987). I would like to see a much more explicitly developed model of technical and artistic development proceeding hand in hand in dance training. In that way, professional dance might produce the flood of imaginative talent which would revivify dance as an art form. As Deborah Bull comments, 'It's as if it is considered enough to equip dancers with the technique necessary only to "do the steps" and no more, a sad diminution of what they may be capable of,

> In teaching dance at Tring Park, our aim is to develop thinking dancers with a high level of technical skill complemented by aesthetic awareness. We believe in training the whole dancer in body, mind and in artistic understanding. Dancers are encouraged to fulfil their own potential and each pupil's progress is monitored carefully.
>
> Arts Education School at Tring, publicity brochure

and a sad impoverishment of the art form itself. If ballet is to reaffirm its position as a creative art, then its artists must be educated as true creators rather than simple re-creators' (1999: 72).

The essence of art is its capacity to portray and give meaning to the human condition. Yet I think there is an argument for saying that professional dance training has erred so far on the side of technical expertise that it has lost too much of its capacity to convey meaning, and has often become a display of pyrotechnics. No professional dance school would like to think it was producing the equivalent of gymnasts, yet attention to technique at the expense of expression will do exactly that. The teacher's job is, then, at every point to elicit, identify, acknowledge and facilitate the expression of feeling, so that the body of the dancer is not only an instrument of technique, but also an instrument of developed human sensibility. Such a huge task cannot be left to repertoire or choreography classes but needs to be integrated at the heart of the training in the technique classes.

The Student's Autonomy and Responsibility for the Training

I have devoted a later chapter to this issue, but here I would like to say a little about the implication of the student taking responsibility for the dance training. One of the complicating features of dance training is that a commitment usually has to be made to it by a young person long before she can know enough about herself or the choice she is making to make that decision one that is properly informed. There is the same complication for young musicians and for some physical disciplines, such as gymnastics or tennis. In practice the youngster's desire to dance has to be translated into action by the concerned adults around. There are some mainstream institutions that have endeavoured to keep choices open for students by the provision of arts education within an ordinary school setting and some contemporary dance trainings allow for the training to begin at post-secondary school age. However, for most professional dance

> Teachers should accept the need to train dancers mentally and psychologically, as well as technically, for today's choreography so that the emphasis should be placed on versatile interpreters and artists rather than virtuoso gymnasts.
>
> A Dancers' Charter Appendix Three

students a clear choice has had to be made in favour of a way of life that as we have already seen is significantly different from that of most adolescents. The danger is that the student continues with training when her first motivation has died, because she is doing it to satisfy someone else. That someone can easily be the dance teacher. When a student is talented it is very tempting for the teacher to urge her to continue by saying things like, 'It would be such a waste for you to stop now.' Of course the student is often glad to hear such things, but one of the disciplines of giving responsibility to the student is to refrain from such statements, backed as they are by the teacher's power, and instead allow the student to sweat her way through her uncertainty to a decision that is her own. I believe that talented youngsters will have to deal with their own ambivalence many times during their adolescence and that the function of the teacher is to be a resource and a sounding board, but not the person who knows what is best for the student (Buckroyd, 1986d).

Similarly, in matters such as attendance at class, dress, weight, punctuality, focus and concentration, it is not the teacher's job to create an environment where delinquency is impossible. Students often do not consciously know what they want for themselves, and use the environment and their functioning within it to express their unconscious processes. So, for example, I worked with one student who steadily increased her weight to a point that her continuation as a student was threatened. That was the only means available to her to discover her own wish to leave training. Had that student been the subject of weekly weigh-ins, she would have been under enormous pressure to lose weight as soon as she started to put it on. She then would not have been able to recognise the message she was giving herself. Another student found herself unable to get out of bed in the morning to get to class. A very ferocious regime would have been so threatening that such behaviour would have been unthinkable. As it was, her lack of motivation became very obvious to her and its meaning could be discussed. In her case, family upset had made her depressed; when that could be attended to she reclaimed her interest in dance. If students are truly to be allowed

Discussion with Louise Donald, Director of Student Support, and Elizabeth Nabarro, Student Counsellor, on LCDS policy on attendance:

EN: Louise keeps a very careful eye on attendance which identifies people whose attendance is poor before that becomes a chuck-outable offence. It's a system which picks up a lot of problems.

LD: It's a good first alarm system.

EN: It picks up a lot: people who are becoming depressed, people where some crisis is happening which they haven't told anyone about.

LD: I interview students on a half-termly basis if they begin to approach the number of permitted absences, but those discussions, 99 per cent of the time, are about what is happening to get them to this stage.

EN: We're not just saying, 'You've got to get in to School tomorrow.'

LD: Students are obviously aware of the implications of going over a certain number of absences, but they also understand that absences are absolutely acceptable depending on the meaning of them. Discussing how we resolve the problem is part of the function of the monitoring system.

Interview, 16 September 1998

responsibility for the training then the teacher must relinquish the power to coerce conformity and rather be open to exploring the meaning of nonconformist behaviour.

The point that I am making is that urging the student to take responsibility for her own training implies a change in the self-concept of the teacher. She is not the one who must take responsibility for how the student uses the training and reprove or punish the student for failing to make the use of it that the teacher thinks best. Rather, the teacher becomes the one who observes the student and tries to engage her in a dialogue about what her behaviour means and what the student is trying to convey to herself or the institution. The very useful result of this way of thinking for the dance teacher is that she can let go of some of the anxiety involved in taking responsibility for other people, and use that energy more efficiently.

Adolescent Development

Last in this list of the emotional functions of the dance teacher is that of enabling adolescent development in students. It is unfortunately true, as has already been explored in an earlier chapter, that dance students are

> **Dancers should** be bolder in pointing out to choreographers the physical dangers of some newly-invented movements, excessive repetition and long rehearsals.
>
> **A Dancers' Charter** Appendix Three

often immature in terms of their psychosocial development (Greben, 1990). This immaturity is in my view quite often fostered within dance classes because it is convenient. Adolescence implies an attempt at self-assertion and self-definition which is very unlikely to be convenient for the institution. On the other hand, pre-adolescents, whether we speak chronologically or psychologically, are malleable and conformist; they are eager to please. To encourage adolescent development is, therefore, for the teacher to make a rod for her own back. The class will not be so easy to teach; on the other hand the experience of being in the class will be much more valuable for the student. On one occasion, reported to me by the student in question, the teacher made a sexist remark to one of the class. My informant then protested immediately and openly about what had been said. The teacher's response was to throw her out of the class and refuse to teach her again. Yet in my view the student's response was appropriate to a young person who wished to challenge what in her view was sexist behaviour. Teachers who genuinely wish to promote personal development in students cannot retain the absolute power traditional for the dance teacher. They must revise their concept of the teacher to describe someone who is involved in the very difficult and complex process of enabling the growth towards maturity of gifted young people. In my view it is the failure of dance training to permit this development which has allowed so much abusive behaviour towards dancers from choreographers and company directors and which has resulted in dancers very often having pay and conditions of work that are unacceptably poor (Brinson and Dick, 1996). The student who dare not protest in class is the dancer who dare not protest in rehearsal, and who dare not demand better conditions of work. Those who are, developmentally speaking, still children are easy to terrorise and manipulate.

Assessment

Assessment is a further complex area of the teacher's responsibility. In this section I would like to discuss how assessment can be thought

Assessment Procedures

Every term students will undergo assessment procedures in each technique. These will include continuous and class assessments. The continuous assessment is an indication of your ongoing individual progress. The class assessment reflects your progress on the day, compared to an accepted standard.

Teachers will also be available to discuss the assessment results with individual students. You should make every effort to make an appointment with your teacher to discuss your progress, whenever you feel the need. Towards the end of every term you will receive a class assessment and continuous assessment for each technique. They will look like this:

Contemporary Continuous Assessment

Name ....Class....................................Term...1....1998–99

1. *Understanding of Class Principles*
   The ability to adapt mentally and physically to the specific principles of a technique and the movement style of the class while showing a respect, understanding and responsibility for individual, physical structure at this present stage of its development.

2. *Physical Eloquence and Clarity*
   The ability to reveal the origin and detail of a movement and to move with simplicity and integrity in a co-ordinated way.

3. *Energy and Physicality*
   Commitment to, and pleasure in, working deeply in the muscles and in using space. Use of energy appropriate to the movement.

4. *Musicality*
   Having an accurate rhythmic understanding together with a sense of phrasing; that is, the ability to use music to shape the dynamic of movement.

5. *Stamina*
   The ability to sustain movement through concentration and efficient use of energy within the context of long movement phrases both fast and slow; to sustain that energy and concentration throughout the class and throughout the week and term as a whole.

6. *Elevation*

Having the technique and strength to jump with ease and to land with control.

7. *Quantifiable Commitment*

The ability to bring both a positive energy and curiosity to the class, fully and consistently participating in the work.

8. *Overall Progress*

Comments

Signature..Date.............................

Continuous Assessment Mark

Assessment Class Mark

Each category will be marked from A to E. The categories above are listed in order of importance.

London Contemporary Dance School Student Handbook

about in relation to the changing role of the dance teacher that has been explored so far in this chapter. Assessment of the supporting curriculum and of academic subjects is these days often conducted according to the requirements of external bodies, such as examination boards and universities. Assessment of technique classes, however, has historically been carried out in ways that could be further developed to the benefit of the student. A model of assessment that used to be very common in technique teaching, and may still survive, was that the teacher at stated intervals during the year made a judgement of the progress of her pupils according to criteria that were not shared with the students and may not have been explicitly stated by the teacher, even to herself. The result was a rank ordering of the students from 'best' to 'worst', as a result of which the best students might be promoted to other classes and the worst relegated or asked to leave. Students could find themselves on the receiving end of judgements that were not discussed and that ran the risk of being entirely subjective ('You'll never make a dancer'; 'We'll be seeing you in the company before much longer'). Many institutions, however, have developed beyond this model.

In what follows I want to describe the principles, derived from mainstream education, on which assessment can be based that will allow it to become a much more useful experience for students. The first is what is known as criterion-based marking. If students are aware of what in particular they are being marked on and how each of the criteria is graded, then they have the opportunity to see where their strengths and weaknesses lie and consequently to direct their efforts to improve much more precisely. Secondly, students can, according to this system, be graded with reference to criteria, rather than with reference to each other. The primary purpose of the assessment then becomes a monitoring of each student's progress rather than a listing in order from 'best' to 'worst'. Obviously the student who does well/badly on all criteria will be placed in some kind of ranking, but it changes the spirit of the grading from some kind of judgement to a form of monitoring in which the emphasis lies on identifying strengths and weaknesses. This system then enables the strengths of each student to be noted and valued, as well as indicating where improvement is needed. As we have already seen, achievement is essential to self-esteem and self-esteem is crucial to success; individual areas of strength therefore need to be identified even in weak students. Criterion-based marking is sophisticated enough to allow for much more than a blanket judgement.

A third principle that can be of value in the assessment of technique is that of continuous assessment. What this implies is that a student is graded on the basis of work over a period of time, rather than on a particular day; the distinction in written assessment is between course work and examinations. Many subjects use a combination of these measures, which would also be a possibility for the assessment of technique. Continuous assessment demands that the student again knows what is being assessed, which in turn leads to the establishment of goals and targets for a specified period of time ('This half term I want you all to work on your placement in this particular way . . .'). As I proposed earlier, structuring the work in this way is helpful for students in facing the task of learning, as well as in the mastery of particular skills.

These ideas on assessment are beginning to be more current in the dance world. With them goes the idea that students can be invited to self-assessment. This is not a particularly easy skill and one fraught with emotional problems, but its value is that it teaches students to become more conscious and self-aware and aids them in taking responsibility for their training. Rachel Rist discussed with me the process that she has evolved for self-assessment for ballet, and commented on the students' difficulties in owning their strengths; they found it easier to own weaknesses (interview, 1 February 1999). When this becomes clear it then becomes possible for the teacher to help students towards a more realistic self-assessment, with the increase in self-esteem that is its result.

Another way of talking about this same process of identifying precisely what is being taught and learned is via a system of aims and objectives. These state the content of what is being taught (beginning pointework) and defines what the student will have to be able to do in order to demonstrate that she has learned it ('By the end of the term, students will be able to . . .'). This way of talking, which is now very widely used throughout mainstream education has the additional value that it requires the teacher to be precise and focused about what she is trying to achieve and thus to use herself more economically and efficiently.

The development of a system of aims and objectives cannot usually be undertaken by one teacher in isolation from the rest of the technique staff, because what it implies is a map of the development of the student throughout the training. The working out of such a system is not particularly easy but it has huge benefits in providing a structure within which the training can be reviewed and discussed by technique staff. It is a system that is also capable of adaptation to take in new understanding of technique, and of revision to include more of some things and less of others. The process of generating the system enables staff to learn from each other and fosters collaboration so that systems of double-marking and/or moderation of marking become possible.

The underlying assumption behind all these methods is that students will be involved in the whole system of assessment and that the old practice of a judgement being delivered on a student's dancing without the opportunity for discussion will evolve into a more interactive way of doing things. Dickinson comments, 'Much is to be gained from engaging learners in a dialogue about their learning.' He summarises research about what students want to get from their assessments.

Able pupils . . .
- Care more about teachers' comments than about grades.
- Want comments to be truthful, realistic and challenging.
- Want work to be constructively criticised.
- Want time to talk to the teacher.

He then goes on to describe how teachers can respond.

Teachers can engage in a dialogue to . . .
- Negotiate tasks.
- Support, challenge and extend.
- Assess and record.
- Set personal targets.
- Monitor.
- Celebrate achievement.

(Dickinson, 1996: 28)

Support and Training for the Dance Teacher

Dance teachers and dance training institutions vary enormously and will find the arguments that I have been advancing above acceptable or not in varying degrees. I am not so much concerned to provide a prototype for the dance teacher as to provoke discussion of the issues that I raise which are urgently in need of greater currency within dance training. Yet for some teachers and institutions these ideas may be unfamiliar or downright ridiculous. How can teachers be supported towards reflecting on their practice as teachers in the light of psychological issues that I am exploring?

Dance teachers are very often employed on a part-time or hourly basis and are often expected to carry out their work without any formal means of support or training. As Brighouse remarks, 'Teaching can be a very lonely activity. The time-honoured practice of a single teacher working alone in the classroom is still the norm; yet to operate alone is, in the end, to become isolated and impoverished' (in Dickinson, 1996). Increasingly, however, institutions are providing at least the occasional day or half day of staff training.

If psychological issues could be included as part of the elements of such training then a start could be made on making these issues more

> **Teachers should** seek regular in-service/refresher courses to raise standards, update teaching, improve first-aid knowledge and remove old attitudes.
>
> **A Dancers' Charter** Appendix Three

familiar. One model for ongoing training is a monthly meeting for all staff for about two or two-and-a-half hours at which a particular subject can be raised for discussion. If such meetings were facilitated by someone with some training in groupwork they might be more effective than if the power structures within the institution were allowed to dominate the meeting. My experience of such training is that if lunch/coffee is provided, a solidarity among the staff gradually develops and a trust between members of the group, which will enable progressively more difficult issues to be raised.

An alternative or additional model could be the establishment of a staff peer support group which has as its agenda the discussion of psychological issues in relation to the training. One problem about such a group is that those most in need of this kind of discussion are the least likely to attend. However, given the urgent need of dance training to take these issues on board, attendance might well be required. Again, a facilitator might well be necessary to get such a group going and to develop ways of working together that enable trust to develop.

Another device for the development of teachers is a system of what is often called Teaching Observation. In mainstream education such systems are increasingly required by government bodies but in my experience have demonstrated their value for teacher development in very positive ways. The essence of such a system is that it uses peer review to facilitate the development of teaching skills. Teachers choose a partner (usually of roughly equal status and experience) and each observes and comments upon the other's teaching, according to a protocol. Good practice and strong points of the teaching are identified; areas where the individual is thought to be less strong are raised as matters for discussion, rather than for judgement. The point is that teachers are using each other's experience and skills as a way of creating a forum for discussion; this is not a system of monitoring or evaluation. In particular it is not a disciplinary system and there are no sanctions. The teacher to be observed chooses a particular class and explains beforehand to the observer how this class fits into the wider frame of the course or series of classes she is teaching ('This term I am introducing the first year to Graham

---

Teaching observation and review

The purpose of the exercise:

- To improve the students' learning experience.
- To aid the developmental improvement of teaching competence.

The process:

- Finding a partner.
- Choosing the session to be observed.
- Informing the observer of the teaching context within which the class takes place.
- Explaining the presence of the observer to students (so they know they are not the ones who are being observed).
- Feedback – this should be sensitive and constructive. It is a good idea for the reviewer to start by asking the teacher what they thought of their teaching in the session and what changes they might make, if any. The reviewer should then mention positive aspects they have noted before offering advice or comments on what could be improved.
- Action – all teachers will recognise that there are areas of their teaching that could be enhanced. Part of the task of the review is to identify realistic and achievable strategies for meeting these developmental needs.

Adapted from the University of Hertfordshire process of
Teaching Observation and Review, 1998

---

technique. Very few of the students have had any prior experience of this technique so I am concentrating on conveying the basic principles. This is the fifth week I have taught them; they have three classes per week. This week I am particularly interested in getting them to . . . In this particular class I will focus on . . .'). The process of identifying exactly what it is that one wants to accomplish in any particular class is a useful discipline in itself. After the class a time is set aside for discussion of the class by teacher and observer with reference to a list of desirable objectives (see the example above). Although it is useful if the observer has some knowledge of the content of the class it is not necessary, and certainly not necessary that she is an expert; the observation is to do with *how* the session is taught, rather than the content of what is taught. For that reason it is sometimes easier if the observer does not have expert knowledge because then she has a better chance of understanding (from a learner's point of view) whether what is being taught is described clearly. It is also easier for both partners to avoid getting involved in subsequent discussion of the content rather than the process if they do not share exactly the same expertise. It might, then, be worth trying to pair dance teachers across techniques, for example jazz/ballet, ballet/contemporary, and so on, to emphasise that it is teaching method that is being observed, rather than content.

From the discussion, strengths are identified in the teaching and an action plan is drawn by the pair working together to focus on areas of methodology that could be improved. If the whole exercise is carried out regularly, say once a term, then there will be repeated opportunities for discussing change and development. The report drawn up is the property of the teacher being observed; it goes to no one and is not in any sense a disciplinary document.

The boxed example above is drawn from material developed at the University of Hertfordshire for a Teaching Observation and Review programme in which all teachers were required to participate. Although it met with initial resistance (because it added to their workload) teachers have responded with some enthusiasm to the actual experience.

This basic outline can be elaborated for use in a dance school and filled out to provide more detail of what exactly is being observed. If this whole procedure can be undertaken in a spirit of willingness to engage in peer discussion of teaching in a structured and particular way it can become another means whereby the lack of teacher training for professional dance training can be redressed and which can improve teachers' confidence in their teaching.

6

Learning in Groups

The vast majority of dance classes are taught by one teacher facing a group of students. The teacher, in this traditional model, is the person in charge and the only one who speaks. Any interaction is between her and individual students and is initiated by the teacher. There is no formal interaction between students and any informal talking is usually forbidden.

The unspoken assumption in this model of dance teaching is that there can be any number of individual relationships between the teacher and students, and at the same time no relationships amongst the students themselves. Certainly, in traditional dance classes the teacher can wield enormous power and can forbid open communication between students so that it can seem as if all that goes on is controlled and orchestrated by the teacher. Students emerging from a class will very often comment on the teacher and her direction of the class, rather than on what they themselves have learned or done in the class ('She gave us a really good class,' as opposed to 'I worked really hard in that class').

However, my contact with students has demonstrated to me many times that even if the teacher is successful in forbidding open interaction between students, there is still an active and important dynamic going on among members of the class. The group interaction does not cease to exist because the teacher wishes it to do so. Moreover, the behaviour of the teacher influences and is part of the group dynamic.

Group Theory According to Bion

Group theory, according to one of its major theorists (Bion, 1961), proposes that any group is formed to carry out a task. It has work to do; in this case the task is to learn to dance. Bion thought that we would all prefer not to have to go through the process of learning, but instead magically know without having to go through the pain. For this reason the carrying out of the task is vulnerable to all sorts of evasions and diversions. These distractions are put in the way of the task so that the work for the moment takes second place to whatever else is going on. The quickest way to ensure the task is carried out is to be attentive to the group dynamic so that distractions can be noticed and attended to and the group can go back to work.

In what follows I would like to begin by thinking about the traditional dance class as a work group and to explore what gets in the way of the carrying out of the task. The teacher's best hope in the dance class is that each member of the class will use what she offers as a way of developing as a dancer. The teacher's ambition is that each student makes intelligent and discriminating use of the class. In other words, the group formed of teacher and students is, ideally, collaborating in the venture of the students' learning to dance, where each student takes responsibility for using the class to the fullest in the pursuit of that aim. The easiest way to sabotage that aim is for an unhelpful dependence to develop. The students (the group) give all the responsibility for the work to the teacher (leader) and disown their individual responsibility. Conversely, or additionally, the teacher (leader) may take all the responsibility from the students (group) for their learning and assume it herself. In either case the collaborative process of learning, where each person takes their own responsibility for the work of the group, is side-tracked and brought to a stop. The result is an exhausted teacher and passive, non-thinking students. From the outside it may not look like this. It may look as if the teacher is presiding over a class of hard-working students, but when students are focused on doing what they are told, rather than applying the teacher's instructions to themselves in an intelligent and responsible way, then the work of the group has been avoided and evaded.

There are other ways to undermine the work. The group can take flight from the task by engaging in some other activity altogether. For example, the teacher may become interested in the work of one particular student and suspend the work of the class to focus on one person while the rest of the group wait. Sometimes teachers try and use this device to continue the work of the group by asking the other students to watch and apply what is being said to themselves. However, more often students use the hiatus as an excuse to stop working. Sometimes members of the group will fight against the task by rebelling against the teacher. They do the exercises or otherwise behave in ways that will attract her negative attention (for example by talking), and in that way bring the work to a halt. They may also fight each other with the same result.

Sometimes the group hopes that the work can be done by a pair who will rescue the group from the task; so, for example, when one student is picked out by the teacher to demonstrate something being well done, the group can look on in admiration (or envy) while for the meantime the work of the group is carried out by the teacher and the selected star student. Sometimes the teacher herself will perform so that the attention of the class in focused on her and her superior capacities, rather than on the task.

An Alternative Model of the Group

Bion's ideas of group functioning are extremely useful for thinking about the way individuals behave within group settings. However, it may well also be relevant for teachers to be aware that individuals come to groups with a history of interrelationships in groups, especially the 'first' group, their family of origin (Foulkes, 1945; Yalom, 1985). It is not likely that the dance teacher will be well informed about the family history of many of her students (although she may be aware of some of the tensions in some of their families). However, even though she does not know and does not need to know these details, it will be useful to her to remember that students in class will bring with them ideas about how groups (families) function, and ways of behaving within them that may have little or nothing to do with the current situation. For example, the student who comes from a family where she has had to compete strongly with others for attention is likely to display that same competitive behaviour in class, perhaps positioning herself in such a way that she is constantly noticed by the teacher, perhaps asking questions or detaining the teacher after class, perhaps 'performing' within the class to attract maximum attention. In moderation, of course, all these behaviours would be acceptable and even desirable in a dance class, but used to excess they are likely to cause problems both for the teacher and for other students. If the teacher can bear in mind that what she is seeing is the acting out of an old dynamic from another situation she may be able to handle the situation without become irritated or retaliatory. Similarly, the student who has come from a family in which she has had very little autonomy or responsibility but instead has been told what to do and been obliged to conform may be very passive and compliant in class, to the point that the teacher feels that she hardly engages herself at all. Since such a student causes few ripples in a conventional dance class, her behaviour may pass unnoticed, but if some of the values of responsibility and ownership of the training that have been described in this book are applied to the dance class, then she may seem passive, disengaged and even disinterested. Again, the teacher who bears in mind that this behaviour has a long history and an emotional meaning may be able to encourage and support the student in a more robust engagement with the training, without feeling irritated or contemptuous.

Traditionally, dance teachers have persuaded themselves that it is possible for students to join a dance class leaving behind their history and their emotional lives. It will be plain to the reader from earlier chapters that I do not believe this to be either possible or desirable. It is no more possible in terms of the dynamics of the dance class as a group than it is for the individual. No trainee (or teacher) can leave her history of relating in groups at the studio door. The teacher, however, can help with the management of that history within the dance class if she is aware of some of these issues.

Problems with Whole Group Teaching

The fact is that it is extremely difficult for a large group of students to use the whole group teaching method as a way to learn effectively. Their history is ever present, and temptations to sabotage are too easy (even if they are completely unconscious) (Nitsun, 1996). This perception is by no means new in mainstream educational circles. There, whole class teaching in the way described above is known as 'chalk and talk', or the transmission model of teaching (Barnes, 1971, 1975). For many years it was almost completely discredited because of the problems in getting students to engage actively with what they learn in this mode and in commanding their sustained attention. Most recently it has been accepted that it can be useful in short periods for conveying information but that it needs to be accompanied by other interactive teaching methods.

Quite apart from the problems of group dynamics created by whole class teaching, it has other disadvantages as a method of instruction. The most obvious is that it presents the whole class with the same task, regardless of their varying needs and abilities (Skrinar and Moses, 1988). As a method it thus risks failing to stretch the most able and asking too much of the least able. Joan Blackmer Dexter describes the problem very clearly: 'If I told the class to stretch a certain muscle I could see that for at least some of my students it was the wrong command. For a person with a certain configuration of the knee, for instance, stretching was not what was needed but rather a special kind of contraction of the muscles which hold the kneecap taut. Yet with twenty students and a limited amount of time, I could not hope to tailor my commands to each unique body. I was forced to give a general instruction which would work more or less for most of the students, but not suit anyone exactly' (1989: 52) Secondly, it leaves the task of observing students to one pair of eyes, the teacher's. Clearly the group does not have to be very large before that task becomes very difficult. It has been demonstrated (Samaro and Skrinar, quoted by Skrinar and Moses in Clarkson and Skrinar, 1988: 292–3) that 'dancers to

Back of room

Teacher

The teacher's area of attention with the class (Samaro and Skrinar, quoted by Skrinar and Moses in Clarkson and Skrinar, 1998: 292).

the immediate right and left and back positions of the room received the least teacher input; front-center and right- and left-center received the most' (see diagram). In other words the teacher cannot attend to all students equally in this whole class teaching situation.

In earlier chapters in this book I have stressed the importance of peer interaction to the development of students; yet whole class teaching, in the traditional model, actively prevents peer interaction and thus denies students a powerful resource for their development. What is more, when the teacher is the dominating figure in the studio the energies and intelligence of students, which can contribute to the direction of the class, are wasted. Additionally, when the group is not engaged in discussion and collaboration with their peers and their teacher about their learning, then there is no mechanism for addressing problems in the group dynamic.

Only if the teacher has established a relationship with the students as a group, and they with each other as members of that group, can there be discussion of the group dynamic in relation to such issues as competition, bullying, attendance, lateness, group targets and goals, and so on. In mainstream education there are regular class meetings for addressing issues such as these via what is usually called Personal and Social Education (Adams, 1989; HES, 1998). In these classes, students are encouraged to develop a language in which to discuss such issues and the group identity is encouraged. To the best of my knowledge there is little of this kind of work done in dance training institutions in relation to what goes on in technique classes, and consequently the opportunities offered for growth and development are neglected. What is more, without the group as a developed unit, there is no opportunity to discuss trauma in the life of the group. In dance training some members of the group will leave in circumstances which will frighten other members of the group, for example when students are asked to leave the school because they are making inadequate progress, or when injury means that a student can no longer continue with the training. Groups find such changes very difficult and need to discuss them and share their feelings and reactions.

Later in this chapter I will discuss some of the alternatives to whole class teaching that could be adopted within dance training. However, it is only realistic to recognise that much dance training will continue to be in large groups. How can the less useful aspects of that mode of teaching be modified or reversed?

A Model for Brief Training Awareness of Group Dynamics

1. Participants are asked to consider first of all whether they think that the following statements about group functioning correspond to their own experience. They can be asked to work on their own first, bringing examples to mind of the situations described, and then share these with a partner or small group.

- Someone always takes the lead in a group, even if it is not the chair or the person who is named as leader. People are often very glad that someone else will do this.
- Some people get off the point in group meetings or discussions and talk about things that are not relevant. This prevents the group getting on with the business.
- Some people always want to argue with whatever is suggested, which takes a lot of time.
- Some people just sit there and say nothing, waiting for someone else to come up with answers. They don't really pull their weight.
- Some people are really focused and keep on dragging everybody back to the point. It's good if you have a chair/leader like that.
- Some chairs are good at getting other people to come up with ideas and discuss them without dominating the meeting themselves. This can result in a good discussion in which everyone participates.
- Some chairs just want to force their ideas through and don't give anybody much of a chance to discuss anything.

Participants can be asked not only to give examples of these things from their experience but also try and identify the role(s) they typically play in groups. This section of the training can be concluded with a whole group discussion and comparison of experience.

2. Once this awareness of group dynamics has been brought into full awareness, participants can be asked to apply it to dance classes. Although the correlation may not be quite exact between the situations described above and the dance class, it is close enough for participants to work with it. Participants can first be asked to think about what role they played in their own dance classes during their training and what role their teachers played. As before, this part of the training can begin with participants working on their own and then in pairs or small groups. When this section has been completed then participants can be asked to think about the dance classes they teach now and how these various situations apply.

3. Participants can then be asked to consider what role they typically play as teachers and whether that mode of behaviour needs to be modified in view of what they now understand. It is easier to recognise that one's mode of teaching needs to develop than to change it, so the last element of this part of the training can focus on how in practical

terms the teacher might enable her students to function as a work group more of the time. A whole group brainstorming exercise, where suggestions are put up on a board, could be used for this.

4. Finally each participant might be asked to spend a few minutes considering her functioning in the training group of which she has just been a part. If we can identify the ways in which we allow ourselves to be deflected from the task of the group and the roles we play in groups, we will be better equipped for facilitating groups in the future. As Barnes points out, 'I have often noticed that teachers are willing to study their pupils' talk and other behaviour and yet leave themselves out of account, as if what they do and say has no effect upon the pupils. Similarly teachers often talk of pupils' behaviour as if it is *independent of what is being done to them*: "3c's in an awkward mood today". It is as if they delete from conscious awareness the part that they themselves play in classroom interaction' (1976: 33). Part of our developing awareness of group dynamics is our awareness of the part we play and our particular characteristics and way of being. Gender, size, age, accent, attitudes and many other factors influence our interactions. The more we can be aware of how we appear to others the more we will be able to take account of that in our relating.

Enhancing the Teacher's Awareness of Group Dynamics

In the first place the teacher needs to improve her conscious awareness of group dynamics. This knowledge is already possessed by most of us but has not been brought to conscious awareness. It is not difficult to develop what we already know. It would be easy to spend half a day on a training event for teachers to raise awareness. Traditionally this is done by the very scary process of observing the group process in a group of which one is simultaneously a member. This method was invented by Wilfred Bion (1961). However, for most people it is less frightening to consider groups in which one has participated in the past and think about them without actually being in them at the same time.

The Limits of the Teacher's Visual Awareness

The research quoted above on the teacher's focus of attention within the room is interesting because it shows not only the limitations of the teacher's capacity, but the way in which a class where students routinely stand in the same place (as often happens) gets unequal proportions of her attention. In this way the competition and power struggle for the teacher's attention can easily be acted out. What is more, disaffected students can place themselves in the 'unseen' parts of the room and have a negative effect on the functioning of the whole group. Withdrawn or passive students can simply allow the dynamics of the class to happen round them.

Skrinar and Moses report the surprising accompanying finding that 'regardless of position in the room, dancers who stood in a location other than that of their typical location were likely to receive eight times more feedback than those standing in their usual places'. The obvious implication is pointed out. 'Teachers and/or students need to move about the room during class in order to distribute teacher input to students more evenly' (in Clarkson and Skrinar, 1988: 293).

Teaching Styles and Learning Outcomes

Another way of thinking about the problems of whole class teaching is in terms of teaching styles. Clyde Smith (1997, 1998), Lord (1980–82), and Skrinar and Moses (1988) have pointed out that the traditional dance technique class has usually been taught by an authoritarian teacher. But as Skrinar and Moses point out, 'Authoritarian behavior is very important when skill acquisition is the primary focus. When the development of creativity or independent thinking is valued, this form of direct teaching becomes an interference. The art form would flounder without creativity and independent thought. Yet . . . the authoritarian qualities of the dance teacher may be thwarting that growth' (in Clarkson and Skrinar, 1988: 291).

Throughout this book I have stressed the importance to dance training of values other than skill acquisition, particularly those relating to the social and emotional development of the student and to her growth as an artist through her ability to extend her imaginative and intellectual experience. These values demand the establishment of a collaborative learning environment and an interactive teaching style rather than one that is authoritarian (Jaques, 1991). However, it is also my conviction that a collaborative learning environment is better able to harness the energies of the students in a whole group setting and that it will allow issues of group dynamics to be directly addressed.

Targets

Dance psychology (e.g. Taylor and Taylor, 1995) is emphatic that goal-setting is vital to harnessing and focusing the energies of dancers. Yet, by definition, the student cannot set goals if she is in a teaching environment where everything is controlled by the teacher. Goal-setting requires the student to make a judgement about herself and her functioning and set a goal in relation to that. Of course goal-setting can be carried out in the context of the teacher's knowledge and direction of the class and as part of broader goals set by the teacher, but it demands that the student takes responsibility for herself within this broader frame. The model of teaching that is implied is one where teacher and students are understood as contributing their respective strengths and energies to a joint enterprise. In order to maximise the possibilities of this way of teaching, there need to be frequent times when the teacher shares with the students her goals for the medium and short term and where students are invited to discuss these goals and their personal understanding of them (Anne Stannard, interview, 14 September 1998). So, for example, it might be appropriate to have some time at the beginning of each week to discuss the work of the week ahead and for each student to identify her goal within that work. At the beginning of each class a short time might be devoted to stating what the teacher has identified as the content of that particular class and its intended learning outcomes. The student within that framework can clarify her particular goals. Finally at the end of the week's work there might be an opportunity for reviewing the work of the week and for students to evaluate their progress within it. All of this implies a relationship between student and teacher which is governed by an attitude of mutual respect for their partnership and in which the student, as well as the teacher, has a voice.

Group Dynamics

The awareness of group dynamics which I am supposing the dance teacher has by now acquired will be an invaluable tool for identifying what is happening within the class. Students will also benefit enormously from developing some conscious awareness of these processes and thus being better able to take responsibility for themselves. Discussion of issues of group dynamics can be extremely useful, but only if an environment of trust and confidentiality has first of all been established within the group. In my view, the class group has a great deal to offer to the focusing of student energies, but it is, as far as I know, rarely enlisted in the service of the work. Weekly class meetings of half an hour or so could rapidly develop a sense of solidarity and cohesion between students and their teacher and provide a setting within which potentially difficult issues could be dealt with quickly before they became entrenched. It also demands that students and teacher all take responsibility for their own behaviour so that no one gets scapegoated. These are demands for maturity from all concerned.

Group Business

Group discussion time can, in my view, help to deal with pressing anxieties within the group so that it is then more free to get on with the task of learning to dance. Regular group time will provide an opportunity, but real crisis in the life of the group may perhaps need time devoted to it immediately. An obvious example of such a crisis would be some serious event in the life of a group member which means that she will not be able to continue as a member of the group either temporarily or permanently. In general, issues which create tensions within the class, such as assessment, auditions, endings and beginnings, will benefit from a semi-structured opportunity to discuss them. In these strange, new or difficult situations, the group can offer support to each other (Wittenberg, 1983). So, for example, the class teacher may want to name the issue and invite comment ('I wonder how you're feeling about the auditions to the company that are coming up?'). The class is not a therapy group, so the teacher is not expected to explore the meaning of events for individuals in any great depth, but rather to acknowledge that anxieties are around, mobilise the group to offer mutual support ('How are other people feeling? How can you help each other in this situation?'), and, where appropriate, suggest practical responses to them ('I agree it is very scary to take part in auditions. You need some techniques for dealing with your fright so that it doesn't spoil your dancing. Shall we go over the performance psychology programme for getting ready for performance? Shall we structure a few classes as mock auditions?'). Stanley Greben, consultant psychiatrist to the Toronto National Ballet School, has an alternative model for promoting the same ends by the use of health professionals within the school. 'Each consultant psychiatrist does prophylactic work by meeting with a class six to eight times during the academic year to discuss informally matters that trouble, worry or interest the students. Sometimes these discussions lead to referrals for individual guidance or treatment. Every class has such meetings' (Greben, 1990: 277). The costs of such an approach are obviously very high and may be well beyond the resources of the average dance school. What is more, it is possible that the dance teacher may be the preferred person to play this role in that by concerning herself with the emotional welfare of the students she again bridges the all too familiar gap between technique and emotional welfare.

The Use of Pairs and Small Groups

So far in this chapter I have explored how whole class teaching and interaction can be developed to offer the best possible chance for it to facilitate learning and development in students. I now want to turn to the use of pairs and small groups within the dance class. At this point I would like to reiterate that I am not a dancer or a dance teacher, and therefore I cannot explore at any great length the *content* of small group work. That must be a task for dance professionals. What I can do is explore the value of that work in terms of the students' learning and development. Of course there will very likely already be parts of the curriculum that use small groups, for example the choreography class, but I am particularly interested in extending the use of this method into the technique class because it is the most central part of professional dance training.

While I was writing this chapter I did a little informal research with my teenage sons and their friends on their attitudes to the use of small groups in their (mainstream) school. 'I think it's good,' said Barney, 'because it means you have to contribute. You can't just sit there doing nothing.' Exactly! The dance technique class taught as a whole group runs the risk of creating passive learners. Of course they are moving, literally going through the motions, but the small group format requires them to enter actively into the learning process.

These are some of the benefits of having students spend time working in pairs or small groups:

- Looking at another student's work.
- Putting into words thoughts about another's work.
- Peer interaction.

- Communication in 'the language of the subject' (Jaques, 1991: 66).
- Giving and receiving feedback.
- Autonomy in learning/responsibility for learning.
- Collaboration and team-working.
- Acquiring skills appropriate to future professional life.

The first two of these benefits have to do with the student internalising the capacities that have been modelled by the teacher of looking and articulating what she sees in the students' work. These are both very complex skills which require a great deal of practice, but are also likely to be essential to the student's professional life. The requirement to articulate what is seen is itself a part of enabling the student to look more carefully and to see more accurately. The communication is itself a means of learning (Barnes, 1976). What is more, the capacity to use these skills is an achievement that will in itself improve students' self-confidence and motivation. It makes sense to incorporate the learning of these skills into the ordinary routine of the class.

Peer interaction has been stressed throughout this book as an essential aspect of the psychosocial development of the student into a mature adult. Pair and small group work offers an opportunity to incorporate that value into the work of the technique class. Two or three students working together will use each other to learn, and will both support each other in learning and stimulate each other to learn. They will use each other in a way that they cannot and will not use the teacher (Jaques, 1991). Furthermore, this use of each other will promote and enable their personal development towards maturity and autonomy (Saul, in Boyd, 1991). The dynamics of the family that were described above may well be less troubling in small groups because the 'parent' is not dominating the group. Students may therefore have an opportunity (and be required by other students) to find new and more adaptive ways of behaving.

In this interaction, faced with the task assigned to her, the student is given the chance to develop her use of the language of the subject. Professional dance training uses a highly specific vocabulary which is certainly not part of the everyday language of the adolescent, so that it is useful for her to be required to incorporate the technical language within her communication with her peers.

Giving and receiving feedback is a sophisticated skill and one in which students and teachers would benefit from being trained. The outline provided in the panel on pp. 110–11 may be of use as a model for educating students and teachers in these processes. Robbie and Rubin (1999) provide a further dimension to training in giving feedback. They stress the need to distinguish between feedback that is 'critical' and feedback that is 'supportive', and emphasise that we need to be careful in our choice of words. They also point out that the giver of feedback cannot take responsibility for how that feedback will be received. There are plenty of opportunities for misunderstanding by the listener. Their work is particularly relevant for teachers in that it draws attention to the need for us to raise our awareness of the words we use and the possible ways in which they can be (mis)understood.

The whole concept of pair and small group working increases the student's autonomy and responsibility for learning, and fosters maturity. These values, in my view, are at the heart of the need for the development of dance training beyond a traditional format. The student in a small group cannot but take greater charge of her own learning. She will learn skills of self-appraisal simply because her peers do not have the authority of the teacher and their opinions of her dancing will be measured against her own. Obviously these skills take time to learn and will need the teacher's commitment and support, but they are likely to result in higher standards obtained more easily and quickly.

The last two values of collaboration and teamwork, which will be relevant to a future professional career, address areas of functioning that probably do not receive enough attention in dance training. A dance performance is likely to be a highly collaborative venture where there is a great deal of interdependence and teamwork, yet dance technique classes can be conducted as if all dance were a solo performance. The dynamics of dance companies are often described in terms of competition and envy, yet a greater sense of solidarity would modify these dynamics in more creative directions. In more general terms, however, dance training as a liberal education needs to incorporate the development of collaborative working for students as a necessary ingredient in their development towards adult functioning. As Jaques comments, 'An important function of group work . . . is to enable students to know enough about themselves and about others to enable them to work independently and yet co-operatively within a team' (1991: 71).

Improving Skills in Giving and Receiving Feedback

[Teachers might benefit from undergoing this training first themselves before using it with students.]

1. Pretty much everyone has had experience of being given feedback. This exercise aims to use that experience as a way of accessing feelings and opinions about the best way to do it. Ask participants to think back to times when they have been given feedback about their dancing (or if this is not possible, about something else that mattered to them). If the participants are teachers, ask them to remember examples from their own training. Then ask them to see if they can provide memories both of feedback that felt good and helpful and feedback that felt destructive. When participants have finished doing this, ask them then to consider what it was about the content and the way that the feedback was given that made it either useful or destructive. Now ask them to share with one or two other people some of these memories and see what principles about feedback emerge from their experience.

2. Get the whole group back together to discuss these issues and to share their memories. You may well find that people have very powerful and possibly very distressing memories. You can expect that feedback that was felt to be shaming, humiliating or very critical will be very vividly remembered. Ask the group what it was about good feedback that made it useful. You will almost certainly discover that feedback that was felt to be personally insulting or demeaning was damaging, and that specific, limited feedback (whether negative or positive) was felt to be helpful. Draw up lists on a flip chart/ blackboard of useful and damaging ways of giving feedback.

3. Introduce the idea (if it has not so far been mentioned) that positive feedback should be given far more than negative. Most authorities recommend that positive to negative feedback should be given in the ratio of 4:1 or 5:1. Ask the group for their reactions to this. Expect dance teachers to feel that this is ridiculous/impossible/unnecessary. Ask participants to think about how they would feel if this principle were adopted, or had been adopted during their training.

4. Get participants to work in pairs. One person is a dancer who is finding difficulty with a particular movement or exercise. The other is the teacher who sees that she is getting it wrong. Try first of all to use the method of correction that has implicitly been developed in this training session: for each negative statement make four positive statements; make feedback highly specific and limited, with no personal comments. Then ask participants to share how it felt both to give and receive this feedback. Then experiment with old style

insults and negativity as feedback and ask how that felt.

5. Get the whole group back together and discuss the exercise and how it can inform the way that feedback is given. Many teachers find it difficult to be positive, but many students find it difficult to be negative. Depending on who the participants are, try and discuss what seems most difficult and how those difficulties can be overcome. The concept of *useful* feedback is often helpful.

The Teacher's Role in Facilitating Small Group Working

The teacher's role in facilitating the use of small groups within the technique or any other class is of course crucial. Without her it will be impossible. Her first responsibility is to convey her commitment to this way of working. Students have often been so accustomed to giving responsibility to the teacher that they are angry or dismayed at the prospect of taking it themselves (Geeves in Brinson, 1993); the teacher must be able to express her belief in this way of working for the central task of learning to dance.

Secondly, she needs to be able to describe what it is that she wants students to do in their pairs/small groups. The clearer she can be the more likely she is to get good results. So, for example, to set an exercise and then say 'Practise this in pairs' is unlikely to make best use of the opportunity. However, to say something more like, 'You know that our focus this week is on . . . and that today we are particularly going to focus on . . . Now I want you to get into threes and practise . . . paying particular attention to . . . Each of you will have different problems so your task is to help each other identify the difficulties you have and practise trying to correct them.' It will be necessary, especially when students are unfamiliar with working in this kind of way, to specify the structure for the group ('I want you to work in threes and take turns to show the exercise and give feedback to the others. Remember, your job is not to criticise but to identify what is being done right and what needs attention. Your job is to be useful to each other').

The time boundary also needs to be made explicit ('You have fifteen minutes for this task. One of you needs to be time-keeper and you should divide the time equally between you'). Emphasis should be placed on the exercise as a problem-solving activity which requires discussion and sharing, rather than as an opportunity for students to make value judgements on each other ('You're such a good dancer'). The training in giving and receiving feedback which is outlined above is a useful prerequisite for this kind of work. Sometimes it is valuable, once this initial group exercise is complete, to ask students to work with another group, sharing what they have so far discovered and asking each other for further feedback and analysis. Again the task needs to be defined as clearly as possible and the time boundaries indicated. Alternatively the small groups can come back to the whole class group and report their progress and findings.

Teachers accustomed only to whole group teaching and familiar only with being in complete control of the class at all times may find it very challenging to entrust the trainees with this much responsibility and may find committing, let us say, up to half an hour of an hour-and-a-half class to this way of working an alarming proposal. The teacher, however, is not idle during this time; she has her function. Her first task, as has already been described, is to create the environment, the framework, within which the group work can take place at all, and then to maintain it. For example, she should maintain the time boundaries and should be ready to intervene when groups are obviously not engaging with the task.

However, in this setting she is also a major resource. Groups of younger or less confident students may well find themselves in difficulties. Her task is then to intervene in such a way that she strengthens the group process, rather than taking it over, and helps the students towards taking responsibility for the task. For example, if the task has been to identify difficulties with *pirouettes* and the group is having problems, she might want to ask the group what they think is essential to the performance of a *pirouette*. By this device she gets them to use their own energies to think about the work, rather than supplying answers.

The issue of the group of any size within dance training has been very little examined. What I have said in this chapter is necessarily only a beginning. Much more research and development is needed in this whole area. However, I am certain that the better informed about these issues we become in the dance community, the more effective our teaching and training are likely to be.

7

The Student's Responsibility for the Training

> Perhaps more than in any other period of life, the overriding and compelling concern [for the adolescent] is with the nature of the self and its continuity and with the search for integrity and worth. The questions . . . are familiar: 'Who am I?', 'What am I?', 'What am I for?' and 'Am I the same as I was yesterday?' These are private questions, integral to the process of individuation and separation and to adolescents' realisation that they must find and take responsibility for themselves (just as they must care for and take ownership of their own bodies). (Wilson, 1991: 52)

Much of this book focuses on the responsibility of the dance training organisation to the developing adolescent trainee and suggests the principles according to which this responsibility may be exercised. However, in this chapter I want to turn to the trainee's responsibility for her own training and to attempt to define the extent of that responsibility. As I have emphasised earlier, dance training needs, for the welfare of the trainee, to be a collaborative rather than a coercive undertaking; it takes two to collaborate. I have indicated at some length the role of the teacher and the institution in that collaboration. What is the student's part?

Ownership

A crucial issue in the trainee's assumption of responsibility for the training is her need to claim her own motivation. She must be able to come to the point where she is sure that the training is what she wants and is for her benefit, whatever the outcome. '[This is] the question that all dancers have to ask themselves: who am I doing this for? The only answer that will stand the test of time and will enable ordinary emotional growth is ME. I am doing it for myself because I want to' (Buckroyd, 1986d: 890). This process is not one faced only by the dance student; any young person who embarks on a demanding training for whatever profession will face the same necessity (Pruett, 1991; Wheeler and Birtle, 1993; Bell, 1996). However, because dance training typically starts in early adolescence and often implies the sacrifice of an ordinary adolescence, it is particularly necessary for the professional trainee to claim her own motivation.

This may seem an easy task but in fact I think it is more like a process that takes place over time and to which the dance school can contribute. It is very usual for the child and young adolescent to do and perform at least in part to please the significant adults around her. Families usually train their children to like what the parents like (whether vegetarian food or silent movies). We are all familiar with the changes of adolescence when the young person then often rejects emphatically the values and preferences of the family as a way of establishing herself as a separate person and an individual in her own right. The dance student in this respect has a difficult dilemma. Almost inevitably she will have depended on parental approval and support for her early training because as a child without that support she will be unable to engage in training. Most dance training for children in Britain is within the private sector; lessons will have had to be paid for. Even if she has been lucky enough to have dance classes at school these will, with rare exceptions, have had to be supplemented with private classes. Her dance shoes and clothes will also have had to be funded by her family and very likely she will have needed active support to get to and from classes, rehearsals, and so on. As a young dancer she is engaged in an activity of which her family by implication approve and which they support.

How, then, at adolescence is she going to establish difference and individuality? If she rejects dancing as something that is her parents' choice and not hers, she may be making an appropriate decision – and in fact that is what many adolescents do. This is the time when youngsters typically refuse to go on with piano lessons, dancing lessons, or whatever else is experienced as the parents' choice rather than the child's. If she continues, is she doing so to satisfy herself or to satisfy her parents? The answer is probably partly one and partly the other. Many parents influence their children to take opportunities that they themselves never had or want their children to develop talents that are much more evident to the parent than to the child. A recent article on Kiri Te Kanawa describes how her mother's energy was behind Kiri's adolescent development as a singer: '[Kiri's mother] . . . acted, applying for government grants set aside for Maori pupils to enable Kiri to study music full time. She [Kiri] wasn't sure she wanted to, but "for peace's sake, I said yes" she recalled. Nell [Kiri's mother] became even more relentless in her control' (*Sunday Times*, 18 October 1998). We all know that the end of that particular story is a happy one and there can be little doubt that Kiri Ti Kanawa took responsibility for her own motivation and training rather quickly. However, not all such stories end so happily. I have come across a number of trainees, talented enough to train as dancers, who presented themselves to me with depression or eating disorders, who came to the realisation that the reason for their unhappiness was the feeling that the training was not what they wanted to do. With this realisation sometimes came considerable resentment that so much of their adolescence had been spent 'pleasing other people'.

There is no simple answer to this problem. However, the dance school can be instrumental in enabling young dancers to consider this issue as an ongoing process of commitment and recommitment to the training. It is common, when talented students express doubt about whether they wish to continue with the training, for teachers to brush these doubts aside ('Everybody has a bad day sometimes. It would be a terrible pity to waste all your talent. Don't give up now when you're nearly at the end of the training. It would be a shame to throw away all those years of training you've already done'). I think it is much more useful for the student to have these doubts taken seriously and explored ('Tell me what makes you say that? Have you been feeling like this for a while? Do you think you're reacting to something that's happened or is this a more serious worry for you?'). To permit the exploration of fears is to believe that they can be better dealt with once they are voiced: 'The acknowledgment of fears leads us to test them against reality, allows us to bring them within the surveyance of the more mature part of the personality. Instead of being overwhelmed or denying their existence, we can recognise them as a legitimate part of ourselves and utilise our adult capabilities to deal with the situation' (Salzberger-Wittenberg, 1983: 5). What can emerge from such a discussion is a recommitment to the training at a deeper level, or alternatively a process of reassessment of the student's commitment. When this is not done and there are students in the school (as is very likely) who have not yet reached this stage of self-understanding, then their ambivalence is likely to be acted out within and against the school. This is how I think students smoking, or otherwise engaging in behaviour directly detrimental to their training, may be understood. It is the function of the institution to challenge this behaviour, not on the grounds that it contravenes school rules, but because it indicates that the student is not committed to the training and is not taking responsibility for it. As I have said elsewhere in this book, it is unreasonable to expect young people to commit themselves for ever to an activity that they can hardly imagine, but it is reasonable to ask them to consider the meaning of their behaviour for their commitment in the present.

The Limits of the Teacher's Responsibility

The encouragement of this kind of active, conscious assumption of responsibility in the student is not, however, without implications for the training institution, a point made by Peter Brinson, who spoke of the necessity of 'profound changes in school life' (Brinson in Brinson, 1993). Traditionally the dance trainee has been a silent and obedient conformist, doing whatever she is told. It is not likely that adolescents who have been invited to reflect upon themselves and their experience will be so easily subdued. They will have opinions, not only about themselves but about their training, and they will be less willing to undertake the training in a passive and dependent frame of mind. Most teachers will welcome the active engagement of the student with the training and the questioning of the teacher that will go with it. However, the increase in the student's responsibility inevitably implies the decrease in the teacher's; that is a concept that may be hard for teachers to accept. As Brinson understood, these changes have implications for the relationship between teacher and student: 'Question and answer sessions should be integral to training with discussions about training and education, lifestyles, the body, ways of moving, relationships and emotions. These things occur, sure, but often they are seen as extra, a grace-and-favour addition for wet days rather than integral to dance development' (Brinson in Brinson, 1993). At a time when the teacher's responsibility for the student's learning in mainstream education has been subject to considerable revision (e.g. P. Buckroyd, 1988), that of the dance teacher has tended to remain absolute. Within mainstream education students have been increasingly required to set goals, to engage in self-evaluation, to take part in peer organised projects, and so on. In dance training the teacher still often assumes total control and responsibility. I have argued elsewhere in this book that such a role is exhausting and a use of the teacher's competence that is wasteful and debilitating. Nevertheless it involves a perceptual shift to give up the idea that the teacher is the one who is to be held to account for the student's success or failure and that consequently she is the one who should make sure that the student is kept up to the mark in all aspects of her training.

The teacher must instead take a step back, offer what she can to the students and allow them to take the responsibility for what they do with it. This topic needs to be explored by teachers meeting together so that they can examine just what the relinquishing of that control and responsibility might mean in detail within their work. In emotional terms, however, it involves the teacher in a reframing of her function within the training.

Physical Preparation for the Training

The student, in my view, has a number of areas of responsibility within the training. The first is responsibility for her physical preparation for the training. Let us begin with the vexed question of weight, food and nutrition. It is my impression that dance schools these days are trying hard to inform students about appropriate nutrition for dancers. Sometimes I think the information could be presented more effectively, as I describe in the chapter on eating disorders, and could often be sustained, repeated and reinforced throughout the course, more than is usual. However, it is clear that the message of the need for appropriate nutrition has been taken on board by dance training institutions.

It is much less clear that it has been taken on by trainees, who still seem, in my experience, to think that their capacity to sustain the training has nothing to do with what they eat. At the same time both male and female trainees seem on the basis of my contact with them to be end-lessly worried about their weight. Men are struggling to keep their weight up; women are struggling to keep their weight down and seem to be attempting to do so by a combination of fasting and nutritionally defi-cient eating patterns (and sometimes the use of laxatives, diuretics, vom-iting, and so on). I should stress that this information has not been systematically gathered and is an impression only. However, it has been voluntarily shared with me when I have worked with groups of dance students on many occasions. At the very least it is cause for concern. What is clear to me is the degree to which students' use of food is an indication of how far they take responsibility for their own physical well-being. For many students their eating behaviour shows that they do not take that responsibility. There are of course a number of practical prob-lems which make the assumption of responsibility particularly difficult. Students are young and not at an age when in the ordinary way they would be expected to concern themselves very much with food and nutrition. For those living away from home there can be financial prob-lems. The limitations of time and energy are also difficulties which stu-dents raise when I talk to them about these issues. Nevertheless the trainee's nutritional status is such a central issue within the training that responsibility for it cannot just be ignored.

What then happens because the student fails to take responsibility is that the institution attempts to take it. Students may be weighed compul-sorily and teachers may make comments on the student's weight in class. Even if these are intended to be helpful initiatives they play straight into the adolescent drama; the school is seen as taking the role of the restric-tive parent and the student is then free to rebel. From this situation arise attempts to deceive the scales in weighing-in sessions and angry and defiant responses to comments about weight. I am not suggesting that weight is not important, especially as an indication of the student's use of food, but I am suggesting that there is no future in the institution's attempt to assume that responsibility.

The only realistic way to handle this issue is by collaboration between the student and the institution. The institution can and should provide information and support throughout the training with input in as many ways and as creatively as possible. I have sometimes thought that stu-dents would benefit from having these issues raised in discussion with a good role model; perhaps a professional dancer who has learned how to manage food and nutrition well can be asked to talk to students. The responsibility for what a student puts in her mouth must, however, remain with the student. If therefore there are anxieties about a student's weight the institution can offer help, information and support, but it must be spelled out to the student that what she does with that help is her responsibility. In the long run, the trainee must accept that what she does with food, weight and nutrition is an indication of her commitment to the training.

There are a good number of areas where in my view there needs to be a similar collaboration between institution and trainee and where in the long run the student's failure to take responsibility for her behaviour must be taken as a communication about her commitment to the training. One such area is the use of alchohol and drugs. It is highly unlikely that students will present themselves within the school in such a way that they are suspected to be under the influence of either. However, a student who does so is putting both herself and other students at physical risk and in my view should be suspended immediately. Leaving aside the legal issues involved in the use of these substances, a student who cannot control her use of them is clearly in need of some kind of help to explore the meaning of the behaviour in terms of the training. Here is an occasion when the personal tutor or the student counsellor needs to be enrolled to see if the student is reacting to some trauma and distress in the rest of her life, or if the behaviour is indeed a comment upon the training.

Tobacco smoking is another issue. Much has been said in recent years about professional dancers as elite athletes. It is ludicrous to think that the physical expectations of a dancer that can be described in those terms are compatible with cigarette smoking. Nevertheless, Brinson and Dick (1996) report widespread smoking among dancers. This seems to me a very clear example of dancers' failure to take responsibility for themselves. 'Fully 36% of female dancers and 40% of male dancers admitted to smoking, with students being the worst offenders. The actual level is probably higher. Yet many of the health professionals consulted gave this as a major contributing factor to ill-health and injury, contributing to poor cardiovascular efficiency and therefore adversely affecting stamina and fatigue levels, as well as to the more widely recognised health risks' (Brinson and Dick, 1996: 54). Dance schools in which I have worked have had a wide range of responses to student smoking, ranging from permissive (students were aware that there was institutional disapproval of smoking, but it was condoned within the building) to prohibitive

> **Dancers should** pay more attention to their own lifestyles as a cause of injury/illness e.g. less smoking, sensible eating, proper rest.
>
> **A Dancers' Charter** Appendix Three

(students were not allowed to smoke in or near the building). Both of these approaches seem to me to miss the point; a student who is smoking is acting in a way that is directly destructive of the training. She needs to be challenged on this issue; what does her behaviour mean in relation to her commitment to the training?

There is a very nice account of the moment when Martina Navratilova actively took responsibility for herself in relation to cigarette smoking: 'I used to go running on this gravel road under the railroad tracks by the river, and I'd take a cigarette with me. That was really pathetic: here I was, running to get in shape, then sneaking a cigarette and getting myself *out* of shape . . . I gave it up before it could become a habit' (Navratilova, 1986: 136). Trainees need to be challenged to take equivalent responsibility.

Another area that falls into the realm of the student's responsibility is that of lateness. Here there is a reality principle to be understood, since in the professional theatre world lateness for rehearsal or performance will not be tolerated. The dance school has therefore a responsibility to give punctuality the importance that will train students in this particular aspect of their functioning as dancers. Again, however, to have rules and punishments for infringing them does not seem to me to give the student the maximum opportunity to take responsibility for themselves. I would prefer a system in which there may be rules and punishments (such as exclusion from class) but where the persistently late student is engaged in a dialogue to be curious about the reason why she might be threatening her training in this way. I have exactly the same feelings about absence. Clearly, continued absences have an effect on the student's training (and require explanation for those receiving public funds) whatever the reason. In order to enable the student to take responsibility for absence, and thus for the training, the institution can invite the student who seems to be repeatedly absent without adequate cause to consider what her absence means. It may mean that she is struggling with some personal trauma or it may mean that she no longer feels so committed to the training. If she is engaged in a dialogue she may be able to use the institution to support her development to a new clarity about what she wants. If she is simply reprimanded for absence the opportunity for her to take that responsibility is lost.

Finally, the student has the responsibility to ensure that she presents herself for training in such a way that she is not at risk of injury. Recent research has repeatedly stressed the importance of warm-up and warm-down. Students are often taught about these matters when they first come to the school and are then given the responsibility of carrying out these procedures for themselves. Figures provided by Brinson and Dick show very high rates of compliance with warm-up and not quite such high rates for warm-down (1996: 53–4). These figures interest me because they are one of the very few areas where students are explicitly given responsibility for themselves and where there probably are few sanctions for non-compliance. Perhaps this area of functioning can show that students are capable of taking responsibility for themselves, more than is generally supposed.

Collectively these responsibilities are considerably greater than those the ordinary adolescent in mainstream education would be expected to assume. What is more, they demand a lifestyle that is significantly different from that of the average adolescent. I have heard young dancers complain that they feel alienated from their peer group by the endless requirement to concern themselves with their physical well-being. I have also heard complaints that the dance school imposes a way of life upon them that is experienced as restrictive. There is of course a price to be paid for training as a dancer; undoubtedly the training places limits upon the enormous freedoms of the ordinary youngster. However, if the institution can instil pride in its students in their fitness and competence and can repeatedly emphasise the student's own power to choose the training every single day, then the worrying signs of poor self-esteem and lack of self-care that are so frequently seen among trainees will certainly become less common.

Psychological Engagement with the Training

The dance teacher is no different from any other teacher in her hope that her students will take what she has to offer and make it their own, that they will internalise what they get from her, use it, enlarge it and transform it into whatever they need. It is probably the teacher's greatest satisfaction to see what she has taught not slavishly copied but

> **Dancers should** understand more clearly reasons for warm-up and warm-down with adequate preparation before class and take more responsibility for themselves and each other in injury prevention.
>
> A Dancers' Charter Appendix Three

used as the basis for something that is the student's own. The student's physical preparation for the training is only the first step towards this much more complex task of owning what she has been taught. In this section of the chapter I would like to describe what this process might look like at its best so that it can become clearer to the dance school how it can facilitate the student's taking responsibility for this aspect of her growth and development.

I have stressed elsewhere in this book that learning cannot take place in an atmosphere of fear and that the teacher is responsible for providing the safe emotional environment which will maximise the student's capacity to learn. However, the student must also come with a willingness to learn and a openness to what is new. Harsh and authoritarian teaching can easily provide an excuse behind which it is possible for the student to hide and which will conceal the extent to which learning depends on the student's effort and engagement with the task.

Historically, dance teachers have required conformity and passivity from students and have been content to play the role of the one (and the only one) who knows. The result has been either a dependency on the teacher, which means that the student never faces the need to use her own resources, or a rebellion or resentment against conformity and dependency. Neither of these states of mind is likely to enable the student to maximise her potential. However, if the teacher provides a learning environment that is enabling rather than authoritarian the student will be faced with the inevitable discomfort of her own ignorance and the need to be active in her own learning: 'Learning arises in a situation in which we do not as yet know or are as yet unable to achieve what we aim to do. It thus invariably involves uncertainty, some degree of frustration and disappointment. This experience is a painful one' (Salzberger-Wittenberg, 1983: 54). The trainee will need to discover her own curiosity and to use it as a spur to her learning. Yet the impulses of all of us in the learning situation are likely to be less creative: 'We try to avoid having to struggle with uncertainty, yearn for simple answers, become angry when frustrated and easily give up the struggle' (Salzberger- Wittenberg, 1983: 54).

How do these ways of thinking apply to the dance class? Let us consider some examples.

A student has had a slight discomfort in her ankle. She realises that it is worse when she makes certain movements. In the class her teacher notices her discomfort and advises her to work her ankle carefully. However, the student is eager to please and concerned that her teacher will think that she is 'not trying' so she overworks her ankle. The next day it is much more painful and she is unable to do class.

In this example the teacher requires the student to take responsibility for her ankle but the student is not mature enough to do so. Her head is filled with her need to please so that she cannot mobilise her own awareness of her ankle and her curiosity about how she can deal with it. The result is self-harming behaviour which is destructive to her training. The teacher has seen this sequence and has an opportunity to respond to it. She can of course respond along the lines of 'Oh, how stupid', but the student will learn more if the teacher can employ her curiosity: 'I saw that you felt that you had to do everything as if your ankle wasn't sore, even though I had said you should take care of it. I wonder what that was about. Did you think I would be dissatisfied with you if you only did some exercises?' The dialogue with the teacher can enable a shift in the student's response to the training.

In a rehearsal for an end of year performance a student repeatedly makes a mistake in one sequence. Her teacher does not become impatient but asks the student to practise the sequence with another member of the class after the rehearsal is over. Later the student is overheard angrily telling her friends that she was humiliated in front of the whole class for making a mistake.

In this example the teacher tries to weigh up the relative demands of the individual student and the rehearsal group. She asks the student to take responsibility for correcting her mistake. The student is unable to do this without feeling that she has been made to look foolish in front of other students and responds with anger and resentment. If the tutor becomes aware of this incident she might raise it with the student and ask her how else she thought the teacher could have responded. This might well help the student to an awareness of her own responsibility in this situation. It

> Are we aware enough of the mental pressures and stresses on young dancers? How do we instil in them a positive healthy attitude to their bodies and their work so that they are not constantly in fear of injury and more importantly so that they do not work on through the warning signals which often precede the serious injury? We all know of instances in which dancers and dance students almost have to be physically restrained from carrying on even when they risk long term damage to their bodies. Why is this and how do we stop it?
>
> Mason and Bannerman in Brinson (1991: 12)

will be best if the teacher can ask, 'Can you tell me what you would have liked your teacher to say that would have made you less embarrassed?', rather than 'Well what did you expect her to say?'

Over the course of the year, students are being introduced to a variety of contemporary dance techniques. One student has had considerable experience previously of one of these techniques and shines in the classes which are given by a teacher with whom she has studied before. When it comes to the time for the next technique to be introduced she skips classes and is extremely disparaging about it. She tells her tutor that all other techniques are worthless and facile, compared with the one she knows.

In this example the student is clinging to what is known and familiar so that the uncertainty and insecurity of learning something new can be avoided. Her tutor may be tempted to say something like, 'You don't know what you're talking about' but the student will probably be helped more by a response along the lines of, 'It must feel very nice to be able to be good at that technique and feel that you really have understood something.' The hope is that the student will agree with this statement, which will give the tutor the opportunity to say something like, 'I've always been a bit nervous about trying new things too. It's awful to start at the beginning again.' This response may help the student to realise that we all feel anxious about what is unknown and give her a little more courage in future. As Wilson puts it, 'Alongside the [adolescent's] curiosity about what is new and the readiness for new dimensions of experience, there are the opposites and the yearning for the way it was before' (1995: 52).

The unfortunate fact is that it is difficult for all of us to take responsibility for our own learning: 'Participative learning . . . requires that students become more actively involved in and responsible for their own education. The teacher is a guide rather than a source of information . . . This altered focus in teaching and learning . . . has an impact on students who may be anxious and suspicious about the shift in expectations of their teachers. Some express anger and frustration in the face of being required to be more actively involved in directing their own learning' (Wheeler and Birtle, 1993: 12). The alternative, however, means that we remain emotionally undeveloped and immature. The world needs grown-up, thinking dancers (in Anne Stannard's striking phrase, interview, 14 September 1998) and dance schools can be a part of producing them if teachers can expand their role so that they can conceive of themselves as supporting the students in the struggle to learn and to grow, rather than simply conveying information.

Artistic and Imaginative Development

The emphasis on technique in dance training, especially in the ballet world, can lead to an environment that differs little from gymnastics training. It is true that in the current system of funding for professional dance training in Britain, where a three-year post-sixteen or even post-eighteen course is the norm, the demands on the student to reach a technical standard that will lead to employment result in an overcrowded curriculum (Anne Stannard, interview, 14 September 1998). However, I wish to emphasise the importance for the art form, and for the development of the student, of the nurturing of the imaginative and creative potential of trainees. This particular aspect of dance training puts responsibility at the interface between the student and the institution. Clearly the school will demonstrate by the degree of attention that is devoted to these matters how committed it is to the idea of trainees 'as artists in the making. At the same time a considerable responsibility lies with students to receive and use what is offered to them. I have been disappointed by the dismissive attitudes I have encountered among trainees to other art forms, to becoming familiar with a wide range of dance performance and repertoire, and to having a sense of the historical development and varied forms of dance. Too often, it seems to me, trainees are willing to settle for a single focus on technical development. Obviously it is impossible to require anyone to be creative, but in an environment where that identity is fostered and exemplified by teachers it may be possible to induce in students a greater curiosity and respect for their own artistic and creative possibilities.

Responsibility for Learning

Traditionally the dance trainee has depended on those around her, usually her teachers, to tell her how she is doing. It has been as if she said, 'I don't know I'm a good dancer until somebody tells me' (Anne Stannard, interview, 14 September, 1998). Yet if trainees are to take responsibility for their own learning, they must develop the capacity for self-assessment. This capacity is closely related to the development of the ability to feel from the inside how the movement is performed, and to a conscious, active knowledge of what the teacher is asking for. It means that the student must be able to identify targets and goals for herself and so have some means of measuring her progress. In other words, the teacher's total responsibility for these matters is replaced by a collaboration between teacher and student.

The techniques of target-setting and performance enhancement have been used to great effect with athletes and sportsmen. They undoubtedly offer dance trainees methods for focusing on improvement and development. Jim and Ceci Taylor address these issues in *The Psychology of Dance*. Having worked with athletes, they 'witnessed the profound need for a more sophisticated understanding of the psychological aspects of dance instruction' (1995: vii). Their programme is designed to enable the 'highest degree of personal and artistic fulfilment from participation in dance'. They point out, however, that these methods cannot be imposed on the dancer, but will only work with her collaboration.

The detail of these methods is beyond the scope of this book, but using them is one aspect of the way in which trainees can be encouraged to take responsibility for their training. The kind of developmental nurturing that is the basis of this book, and the psychological techniques for enhanced performance referred to above, in my view go hand in hand in the task of maximising the potential of the professional trainee.

Responsibility is a complex concept. It will vary according to age, capacity and circumstances. The institution cannot be free of responsibility; the trainee can only gradually adopt it. There are no simple rules to follow. However, what both student and institution have on their side is the innate push for growth and development within the individual. The dance school can perhaps rely on that inborn drive, to become whatever one is capable of becoming, in the process of facilitating the student to take the training and make it her own.

8

Male Trainees

As the reader will be well aware by now, I have characterised the world of professional dance training as largely female. A majority of both trainees and teachers, in the West, is female. Although, in the performing world, roles of authority such as choreographers and artistic directors tend to be occupied by men, among performers there is still a majority of women, especially in the ballet world (Burt, 1995).

In this chapter I want to present the results of some research that I carried out which began to explore the distinctive qualities of the experience of dance training for boys. There is very little literature of any kind on the psychological aspects of dance training. Schnitt and Schnitt (1991) published a review of what had been done, and were critical of both the quantity and quality of studies. Such literature includes nothing substantial on the emotional experience or needs of the male trainee. As Schnitt and Schnitt remark, 'For dance educators, much is unclear about the special needs of subpopulations among dance students; male dancers, minorities, students of dance disciplines other than ballet, and modern dancers may all be expected to have particular sociological and psychological issues which are not fully elucidated' (1988: 263). Not much has changed as far as male dancers are concerned in the last ten years.

My research was therefore directed at the basic task of trying to identify distinctive issues for boys in professional dance training with the idea of clarifying how dance training could ensure that those needs might be met.

Method

I chose three dance schools in which to carry out this research: London Contemporary Dance School, Central School of Ballet and Elmhurst School. London Contemporary Dance School (LCDS) has a reputation as an unconventional institution, focused on the development of technique and creativity among trainees who start professional training no younger than the age of seventeen or eighteen, usually for a three-year course. There is the possibility of studying for a degree in dance at the school. Their students will never be part of the conventional ballet world, but may go on to join one of the contemporary dance companies or become part of the independent dance world. I expected LCDS to have a high proportion of male trainees because I anticipated that contemporary dance would be a less problematic choice than ballet, but in fact it had the smallest proportion of males, only 18 out of 139 students, approximately 13 per cent.

The second school was Central School of Ballet, also in London, which has earned itself a reputation for effective ballet training and aims to have 80 per cent of graduating students and 100 per cent of male graduates in work within six months of their finishing the course. It is in many ways a conventional ballet school but under the inspiration of its director, Anne Stannard, has been extremely open to new ideas, research and innovation in training. It takes students from the age of sixteen, after they have completed compulsory education, for a three-year course. It has the highest proportion of boys of the three schools, 21 out of 81, approximately 26 per cent.

The third school was Elmhurst, in Camberley in Surrey, a town within commuting distance of London. Elmhurst had its seventy-fifth anniversary in 1998 and is best known for former pupils who have succeeded on the commercial stage. It takes students from the age of eleven, and is a boarding school. Following a recent change of principal, considerable development has been undertaken in the direction of the establishment of the values described in this book. It has the widest range of courses of the three schools and although it is not a stage school in the usual sense of the term, in that its focus is on dance, it offers more scope for specialisation in different kinds of dance. Of the 164 students, 28 are boys, approximately 17 per cent.

Altogether I interviewed 43 boys, 5 from LCDS, 16 from Central and 22 from Elmhurst. Their ages ranged from twelve to twenty-two. They were interviewed in their own schools in focus groups of approximately the same age, of between two and ten members (McLeod, 1999). The schools were provided with the consent forms and the interview schedule a few days ahead of the interviews and asked to distribute them in advance (see Appendix Two for this material). At the beginning of the interview I repeated some of the information that they had already been given. I explained that I was writing a book about the emotional well-being of dance students, that very little was known about the particular needs of male trainees and that I hoped that they would be able to tell me something about their experience. I referred them to the schedule and said that these were the topics that I had imagined might be important to them, but that there might well be other things that they wanted to talk about which they were welcome to do. The interviews varied in length from about 45 minutes to a little over an hour depending on the class schedule of the students involved, and were tape-recorded with the knowledge and consent of the participants.

I also interviewed three male dance teachers: Ronald Emblen, Peter Connell and Lyndon Branaugh, all of whom have had significant experience as professional dancers and of teaching boys. Their views on the training of boys provided an additional perspective on what the boys themselves said.

This was a piece of qualitative research, in the form of semi-structured interviews designed to elicit data that could be used for the generation of hypotheses about the nature of the particular emotional experience of boys in relation to professional dance training. These hypotheses can then be tested further and more systematically by further research. The sample does not include any students from ethnic minorities, whose experience may be different. Nor does it include students from stage schools, whose purpose is to prepare students for the commercial stage. Again, their experience may be different. Further detail of the research method is given in Appendix One.

Results

Pre-training Education and Dance Experience

The routes by which students had come to professional dance training were as varied as they could possibly be. Most had been in state education, a good number, including most of the Central School boys, had been for some time in elite dance boarding schools, and one had been educated at home. Their dance experience also covered a huge range of possibilities besides that of vocational schools. A considerable number of the ballet students had been dancing since early childhood – three, four or five years old – in classes taken after school and at weekends. It was also common for ballet students to have attended Saturday ballet school from the age of nine or ten. However, some had only begun ballet at the age of ten or eleven, even among those students who had then attended Elmhurst from the age of twelve. Among the LCDS students, none had begun to dance before their mid to late teens.

Reactions to Choice of Dance Training

There were no reports of parents who were categorically opposed to the idea of dance training, presumably because parental help is needed, both financially and practically, for the student to be able to undertake the training, with the possible exception of the students at LCDS who were all at least eighteen before they began training. Some parents had been initially doubtful on the grounds of the financial insecurity of a dance career, 'an unstable career in which it is difficult to make a living', or because the student in question had previously had other ideas. One boy, for example, had always intended to go to university to read music; his change of plan was met with initial disappointment. The student's commitment to dance and evident pleasure in it helped to persuade some parents. One boy's parents, themselves both in the arts, had tried to dissuade him because they had experienced how hard that life is, but were eventually persuaded by his commitment. Others were won over by the demonstration of their son's competence in performance. Many described how their parents had not been allowed by *their* parents to follow the career of their choice; they had agreed to their son's choice on the basis that he should do what he felt would make him happy. Quite a number of mothers were said to be very encouraging and supportive. One father, who was described as having been interested in ballet for many years, was the major support for the boy's choice. One father from a military background had initially objected. Another father had said, 'He's going to be gay,' but had been won over when he had seen what his son was capable of as a dancer. Another had initially been told, 'Ballet is for your sister'.

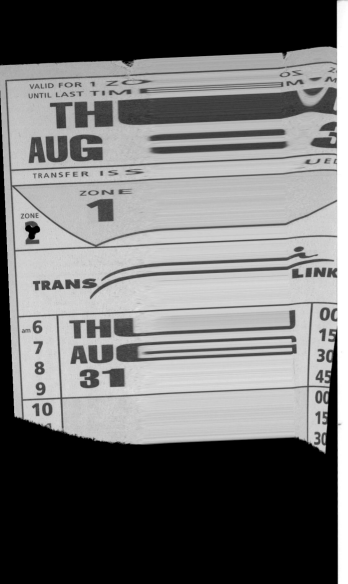

Almost without exception, students reported that their peer group of boys had reacted with mockery or with outright bullying, both verbal and physical, to the knowledge that they were involved in dance. One boy, only, said that his successful audition for the school had been met with congratulations, and one other that his friends had respected his dancing. They described 'hassle', 'a problem', 'comments', 'being given a black eye', being set on by 'gangs', being 'picked on', being excluded from football, not being picked for teams, friends who were 'very cruel', 'being beaten up', 'ridiculed', 'mugged'. Even those who initially said that they had met with 'no hassle' then reported that there had been 'the odd comment', 'a little bit of hassle' and 'the odd spiteful person'.

A great deal of the verbal abuse had been to label the boy as sissy, like a girl, and therefore homosexual. The boys reported that they had been called a 'wuss' [current abusive term in Britain for homosexual male], 'poofs', 'poofter', 'twinkletoes', 'gay'. They quoted explicitly comments such as 'You're a girl, you do ballet'; 'If you do ballet you're a wuss'. One boy said 'They say, "you're gay, you're gay, you're gay" until you wonder if you are'. One said bullying 'made my life complete hell'. Some boys from Elmhurst described some anxiety about meeting an aggressive re-action from off-duty soldiers in the town, or just from other boys: 'Down town other lads recognise us and will give you hassle'. One group of boys at Central, however, felt that this kind of name-calling was typical of boys around the age of thirteen, and that as boys got older and more mature they abandoned that way of talking. They also said, however, they them-selves being eighteen years old, that to call another boy gay was 'ordi-nary banter' among themselves. They felt that 'gay' was no longer a deadly insult since 'people are more open-minded these days'.

Many of them tried to account for the bullying. They made consider-able attempts to understand the frame of mind of their tormentors. They acknowledged that other boys had no idea what was involved in dance training, especially ballet training, and that if they did know, they would both like it and discover how hard it was, which would command re-spect. Even the contemporary dancers said that other males 'don't know what dance is'. Some realised that other boys had no models for male ballet dancers since male dancers were not shown on TV. They thought that other boys were afraid of something that was new to them, and therefore aggressive. Some thought that younger boys could not be ex-pected to understand, since what was unusual was frightening to them. A number of boys identified envy in other boys: 'They don't like the fact you might become famous'. One boy from a depressed area of the country reported being attacked when he said he was a dancer, out of envy of the fact that 'I'm going somewhere and they aren't'. Some boys felt that their posture showed that they were dancers and made them vulnerable to abuse: 'The way you hold yourself makes people think you're gay'.

They described a wide range of ways of dealing with the reactions they met. The commonest had been, and continued to be in some cases, to 'keep it a secret', 'keep it quiet'. One boy described how when it became known at a new school that he did dance, he was subjected to a campaign of mockery and bullying to such an extent that he gave up dance for a number of years and had since been very careful about who he told. Being careful about who you told was a strong theme. Most boys had found a 'mate' or a group of close friends on whom they relied. Sometimes friendships that pre-dated the choice of dance survived. These friends sometimes cautioned the dancer not to tell others that he danced. Many reported that their friends had become those with whom they shared dance or performance arts. Some reported actively concealing what they did now, for example by saying they were doing a performing arts course or that they were a musician. Some older students felt that it was less of a problem for them and that they felt less need now to conceal their dancing. Some reported that their friends now respected them but that 'it had taken a while'. Others reported winning respect by their competence in other sport, especially football, or by the recognition by other boys of their fitness and physical development. A number survived by feeling pride in the knowledge that what they were doing as dancers was hard and 'takes a lot more' than their persecutors put into their activities. The Elmhurst boys managed their worry about other boys in Camberley by feeling proud of what they were doing. This feeling of being proud to be a dancer was voiced by several groups of boys. A number of boys acknowledged that being a dancer made them feel special.

Others again challenged the stereotypes with the argument that professional footballers do some ballet training and manage less well than ballet dancers who do football training. (I was told that Arsenal football team has used ballet training.) A number of boys talked about Eastern Europe and Russia where they felt that the male ballet dancer was part of a chosen and respected elite, rather than one of a despised minority. But the most robust response to the bullying came from one of the youngest boys who reported, 'He called me "tutu-man", so I punched him'.

Students' Accounts of How They Came to Dance Training

Although this was not one of the issues I raised on the interview schedule, many students gave an account of how they came to be dancers. These accounts were based round an identification either as an athlete, or as a performer, and often by naming others in their family in some way involved in dance, performing arts or movement.

One boy had moved into dance from gymnastics, another from rugby. A number had played football for their school or for another team; one had been a swimmer, another a kick-boxer. One had intended to qualify as a PE teacher. A number stressed their need to move, so that during holidays and at weekends they found other ways of exercising. One boy had been a musician; several had spent a good number of years involved in more general performing arts activities before specialising in dance.

Several had friends from whom they had learned about dance; a number had sisters who danced. A good number of boys had been encouraged by their mothers, who had sometimes started them off on ballet lessons before the boy even knew what ballet was. Some had mothers who were dance teachers.

The Effects of Dance Training

Pleasure, pride and satisfaction with the training were striking elements in the responses from the boys. There were many expressions of satisfaction with each of the schools that I visited by the students there, and little criticism or dissatisfaction. One of the youngest boys, however, voiced the feeling, echoed by some of his group, that his 'childhood had been taken away' and that 'you can't run wild'. It was felt as a pressure by the youngest boys to be as analytical as they were required to be about their bodies and the way they looked. They also felt pressured by what they experienced as 'having to be dissatisfied with yourself'. Older boys living away from home could feel that the pressure to be independent was at times a great strain and that financial problems were stressful enough to distract them from the training. Some worried that they were missing out on adolescence and might eventually not be able to continue their self-disciplined way of going on.

On the other hand, many boys felt that dance training had developed their confidence and made them more responsible: 'It's up to you to put to use what you learn, to apply corrections over techniques and over time'. They thought of themselves as more self-motivated, independent and disciplined than their non-dance peer group. They were pleased that dance training meant that 'you have to know what you want' and that they had to be 'focused'. A number took pride in the disciplined lives they led. One or two felt that dance might well have saved them from delinquency. A number commented that they felt that 'you have to be a strong person to make the choice of dance to begin with' and that as a result of the training they felt stronger as people and more articulate. One boy explicitly said, 'I like myself better,' but many expressed the same thought in terms of their increased pride in themselves. One group of boys commented that self-esteem depended on the nature of feedback from classes and felt that they were on a roller coaster of emotions. The same group, however, commented that girls took criticism much more to heart than boys did and that boys maintained their morale better. Some reported the satisfaction of their families with their improved appearance and behaviour. Many observed that they were more mature than their non-dance colleagues. There was general agreement that the training had been good for them.

For many, to be in the company of like-minded people where they were met with 'understanding' had been a huge relief. As one boy said, 'You start realising it's OK'. It had been particularly important for some to be in the company of other boys who danced. Several boys pointed out how much they needed other boys in the dance world to talk to; it had then become more possible to accept that boys are in a minority in the dance world and to come to terms with that reality.

Feelings about Being a Minority Among Girls

The initial response to this area of discussion was that it was 'great' to be a few boys among a lot of girls. Many boys, especially those in their mid- to late teens, expressed their pleasure in 'showing off' to the girls. There was quite a lot of enjoyment of feeling special and different – 'the boys'. One group boasted, 'Everyone knows the names of all the boys'. Some claimed to feel like a privileged minority. Others enjoyed what they felt was special attention; some teachers, both male and female, were thought to like boys more than girls and to favour them accordingly. Many ex-pressed a rather triumphant feeling that the boys proportionately got more attention than the girls, but others hotly denied it and said it was a fiction dreamed up by the girls. At Central, where the proportion of boys was highest (26 per cent), there was one group where there were equal numbers of boys and girls in the class (ten of each). These boys were particularly proud of their specialness and felt that the institution took particularly good care of them, and better care than it did of girls.

Once this had been expressed, however, other less gratifying aspects of their situation were raised. All the boys spent some time being taught with girls. With the exception of LCDS, they also had some ballet classes on their own: five out of six at Central and approximately three out of five at Elmhurst. These were highly valued, but it appeared not only for their technical specificity but also for their confirmation of the boys' male identity. Some boys said, for example, that it was important to be taught as boys, otherwise the exercises were too 'girly'. One boy demonstrated graphically what a 'girly' movement was, to the entertainment of his classmates; it became clear that 'girly' movement was by definition non-male and unacceptable. In class where there was a female teacher demonstrating, boys could feel confused by the female body image. Some also spoke of feeling an excluded minority when female teachers demonstrated to a mixed class.

They were critical of girls' behaviour and attitudes towards their weight, which some boys described as 'silly'. Some boys described the girls as 'immature', like 'sheep' all doing the same thing, thinking the same thing. One girl, whom this group liked, was referred to as an 'honorary boy'. In one group there was a very powerful demand to be recognised as different: 'We are totally different from the girls; we can't just be mixed in'. One boy emphasised how the girls were feminine, and it was agreed in his group that non-dance girls were 'butch'. In two groups at Elmhurst this demand for recognition took the form of a wish to be given extra food without having to ask for it, as a token of difference. The establishment of a boys' boarding house at Elmhurst, with two sporty but non-dance male housemasters who were also on the teaching staff, was greeted with immense satisfaction by all the boys involved in it precisely because in this setting there was 'boy-talk', boy activities (such as football in the park) and a boy-led entertainment for the whole school which had left them with a sense of much strengthened identity and great pride.

In year groups where there were very few boys, the lack of competition with other boys was felt to be a disadvantage, although a few boys were more ambivalent about competition with other boys, which they could feel was threatening. Competition was felt to be a good way of raising the standard. Some boys felt they could compete with the girls – 'You can use the girls for inspiration' – but others found that too difficult and confusing. Others found it distracting. They particularly hated being compared with the girls: 'Come on boys, the girls are jumping higher than you'; 'Look how high the girls have got their legs'. Some boys felt quite lonely for male company and said wistfully that they wanted to be taught by a man with other boys. They found themselves looking for the other boys. One boy from LCDS had ended up the only boy in his group and had felt very lonely and isolated until he had taken matters into his own hands and started attending classes where there were other boys. He commented, 'I see all these girls checking their bums in the mirror, but I can't do that'.

Body Image

Issues of size, weight, shape and food occupied relatively little time in the interviews. There was virtually unanimous agreement on the irrationality of girls' behaviour and opinions around these subjects. Boys, they said, had a much more realistic sense of their size. Many boys expressed some anxiety about the need to maintain their weight. However one boy asserted that bulimia was common among boys, although the others in his group did not seem to agree with him. Only two talked about the danger of being overweight. The younger boys were concerned about growing tall since some of them had not yet started their growth spurt. Many of the older boys were more worried about not being strong enough.

Food was of interest in that many boys wanted to eat well and were concerned to eat enough to maintain their weight. However, they were clear that the subject was not particularly loaded for them. A number of boys in different groups and schools, however, wanted nutritional information that was specifically targeted at boys and their needs. This information had been provided by Central by a distinguished nutritionist, but the boys denied that they took care with their diet.

Social Life

The overwhelming common denominator in response to this question was the complaint that tiredness severely limited the boys' energy to do anything else but their training. The few boys who did energetic things such as cross-country biking were in a small minority. Boys from Central were aware of the danger of injury and were most likely to swim for recreation. Most had an interest in music and listened to it in their spare time. A few played music. Some watched dance performance but were limited financially in how much they could do of this. Younger boys played computer games. Many liked film. Many said they were too tired to do anything but watch TV. Resting, 'vegging out', was their main priority. One group comforted themselves by observing that students who went on tour returned with increased stamina, so that they felt that in due course they would not be so tired.

Their social lives were spent very largely with other dancers. Some boys expressed frustration with the limitations of that social circle, but others wanted to be with people with whom they could easily communicate. A few described keeping in touch with non-dance friends from pre-training days. One or two expressed frustration with the limitations the training imposed on them and felt that the possibilities of adolescence were being very much restricted. The boys at LCDS who had entered training much later were glad that their adolescence had already taken place so that they felt free to concentrate on their training without feeling that they were missing anything.

The Future

There was considerable confidence in all the boys that they would find employment as dancers, although some were anxious that they would not get jobs in companies that they considered really good. Even those at Central who were concerned that they would not get jobs in ballet were sure that they would find jobs in contemporary dance or musical theatre. When pressed to consider what alternatives they might consider if they had to, they mentioned other performance art, for example acting or performing music. One boy mentioned law as an alternative performing profession. Some could imagine other work associated with the arts, for example working backstage, design, direction, choreography. Only a few boys had ideas of a future totally unrelated to the present, for example to train as a vet or a nurse. Boys at Central were particularly aware of the transferable skills that a dance education provided and commented that their discipline and focus had given them better academic exam results than had been anticipated.

Discussion

Considering the wide age range of the students, from twelve to eighteen, and the range of different routes by which they had come to professional dance training, I was surprised by the degree of consensus among the boys about many of the issues I raised across the different institutions and year groups.

Parental support, even if it was won after initial reluctance, was universal. As I have indicated earlier in this book, dance training is virtually impossible without it. However, this may also indicate a degree of parental choice which perhaps contributed to the feeling among some boys, especially those at Elmhurst, the boarding school, that their childhood and adolescence had been taken away. Those boys at Central who had attended an elite boarding school for dance before coming to Central referred to it as a prison. However, these are feelings that may well be common to children of either sex who attend boarding school from an early age.

The tales of mocking and bullying over attending dance class were very widespread and in some cases had plainly been traumatic. Burt states categorically that 'professional dance training during approximately the last hundred and fifty years has not been considered an appropriate activity for white men to engage in'; that 'the male body' (unlike the female) 'should not be a spectacle' (1997: 1, 13). There was apparently immediate association by other boys of dance with homosexuality. It did not seem to me that what was being described in allegations of being 'gay' was, however, sexual orientation, which plainly for primary school children was irrelevant anyway, but rather was an attack on the boys' maleness – they were not really boys.

This issue of whether or not male dancers are gay is not the subject of this chapter; no boy identified himself as gay during these interviews, nor was the question raised by me. The sparse literature on the psychology of boys in dance training does, however, speculate about this issue (e.g. Schnitt and Schnitt, 1988; Schnitt, 1990; Greben, 1990). Burt asserts that in the twentieth century 'gay men, predominantly in the field of ballet . . . have been largely responsible for developing male dancing' (1997: 8). Anecdotal evidence suggests there may be a majority of gay male dancers. Schnitt and Schnitt propose that the situation may be changing anyway: 'Recent changes in societal attitudes about dance have allowed males to enter the dance field in larger numbers and at an earlier age'

(1987 ch. 20; see also Greben, 1990: 276). Lyndon Branaugh also thought that male dance trainees these days were evenly divided between gay and straight.

Much more important in my view, for the purposes of this book, is the disclosure of the challenge to male identity that is posed by the choice of dance training. This was the major theme of the interviews and obviously a very difficult and sensitive issue for many of the boys. This challenge was met in a wide variety of ways as I have described, many of them brave and resourceful. The *need* to answer this challenge was, however, a major preoccupation for many boys. They found themselves having to justify their choice of career in a way that would never be required, for example, of a footballer. This was the reason, I think, that many of them found themselves giving an account of how they came to be dancers, even though I had not raised that issue.

Furthermore, although they found the dance world congenial, the fact of their small numbers compared to the numbers of girls had very strong effects. They talked a great deal of the need for male friends, other boys with whom to identify physically, 'male bonding' (a phrase used a number of times), the need to talk to other boys, and so on. It was particularly interesting that the initial boastful and excited talk about showing off to the girls and being the object of so much female attention was accompanied by a great deal of anxiety about being recognised as male. It is to be expected that adolescent males and females will be preoccupied with questions of identity in an age-appropriate way. However, I felt that the pressure of being in an environment dominated by females demanded that the boys constantly reaffirm, and attempt to get others to affirm, their maleness. It would be very interesting to know if these same preoccupations arise in dance communities like those in Eastern Europe where numbers of males and females seem to be more equal. It was certainly the fantasy of the boys I interviewed that those male dancers were much more confident. Dance schools plainly need to consider this issue and assess whether there are ways in which gender difference, especially for those from thirteen to eighteen or so, might be more routinely confirmed.

The interviews with the male teachers, conducted on the basis of the same interview schedule, provided an interesting counterpoint to these concerns about male identity. Ronald Emblen emphasised the difference he experienced in teaching a class of boys. He described a particular 'positive male energy' which created a healthy competition. This masculine energy, he felt, was the differentiating factor between males and females. He also felt that gender differentiation was essential to the development of the potential of the boys.

Peter Connell, on the other hand, who had many similarities in background to Ronald Emblen in that they had both attended the Royal Ballet School and both been ballet dancers, felt that the task for male trainees was to come to terms with working with a majority of women and learning to deal with their competitive and aggressive feelings sufficiently to be able to relate positively to women and not to alienate them by their behaviour. He also identified the masculine energy of which Ronald Emblen had spoken, but felt that the major task for the male trainee was to focus and direct the energy which could otherwise be unproductive. He felt that in LCDS, where ballet is an auxiliary technique, there was no good reason to teach the boys separately.

Lyndon Branaugh provided a third point of view by emphasising the need for the male dancer to reconcile inside himself his maleness and his identity as a dancer. How can a dancer be male in a world of female sensitivity? Like the other two teachers, however, he emphasised the enormous physical energy of males.

Taken together, these teachers seemed to confirm that maleness within dance training can be problematic both for the boys themselves and for the institution. Obviously more thought is needed on this issue. Plainly, more boys will not train as dancers unless we find some better way of managing the issues.

Another issue that might be appropriate for dance schools to consider is that of adolescence. Many of the boys were aware of the freedoms they had lost by opting for dance training and were concerned, for example, by the limitations of time, by the narrowness of their range of friends, and by the lack of opportunity for ordinary adolescent socialising and activity. Where dance training takes place in an elite boarding environment the normalisation of that environment is clearly a major benefit. The male non-dance housemasters at Elmhurst and their support for ordinary male 'play' was hugely valued. In one of the general interviews with senior dance professionals, Jane Billing, Principal of Arts Educational School at Tring, told me that making the school 'ordinary', 'normal', was one of her guiding themes for its development. On the evidence of this research on boys, her attitude is very helpful for them (interview, 1 February 1999). For those who come to intense dance training in their mid-teens, like the boys at Central, the problem is more acute. Anne Stannard, director of the school, is well aware of this issue and argues that dance training in this way leaves little time for anything other than very intense focus on dance. She argues for dance training to be contained within state education so that it can take place over a much longer period (interview, 15 September 1998). Those who were least affected by this issue were the boys at LCDS, who were pleased that since they had started training at eighteen or older they had already come through much of their adolescence.

Both Lyndon Branaugh and Peter Connell had begun full-time training late (at nineteen and eighteen). Both of them felt that the emotional advantages of having negotiated adolescence before training had been considerable. Peter Connell felt that for some boys the choice of dance training itself constituted their adolescent rebellion.

It was interesting to see that the boys seemed to have relatively good self-esteem and that they seemed able to use the dance training for that purpose. Undoubtedly their confidence in finding dance employment was a factor here. All three of the teachers interviewed felt that this was a significant factor in maintaining their morale. There were indications, however, that their self-esteem might not be quite so secure. Mentions of eating disorders and widespread admission to smoking suggested other-wise. Further research is needed on these issues. Linda Hamilton, one of the very few people who has done research on the personality of the male dancer, did some work that suggests that male dancers are not managing very well in comparison to female dancers. She reports that in the sample of elite dancers that she surveyed, 'the men practised fewer healthy habits, had less stable relationships, and reported more physical symp-toms associated with poor health, fatigue and overuse of alcohol . . . Male dancers . . . experienced strain because of fewer social supports and did not make use of rational/cognitive coping skills as frequently as men in the general population'. She provides other measures of men's poorer functioning in relation to women dancers. Most interesting, for the pur-poses of this study, she hypothesises that men may be suffering from just exactly the same difficulty as the boys in this sample, of how to be male in a female world: 'It is possible that male dancers are reacting to the basic inequalities that exist within the ballet company itself . . . This inequality has widened over the last 50 years . . . Today, classical ballet serves as a showcase for the ballerina, while limiting the male dancer to partnering and occasional moments of technical display. Research on masculine gender-role stress suggests that most men have poorer health habits and demonstrate higher levels of anger and anxiety if they are outperformed at work by women' (Hamilton, 1991: 40).

Conclusion

The suggestion by Schnitt and Schnitt, that there are specific emotional and social issues to be considered in relation to male dancers, does seem to be borne out by this preliminary study of male trainees. In terms of the overall purpose of this book in reconsidering the emotional implications of dance training for trainees, it seems as though our awareness of the particular issues for male trainees does need to be extended so that more care can be taken of their psychological welfare.

9

Dealing with Crisis in the Life of a Dance Student

As the chapter on adolescence indicated, change and crisis are never far away in the life of the dance trainee. In this chapter I would like to begin by exploring what is known about the effects of change and loss on human beings, and what responses may in general be helpful in supporting people in crisis. I then want to discuss the various sorts of crisis likely to face the dance trainee. I will include the ordinary life crises that can affect anyone, and then crises more particular to the dance world, including those of injury and transition.

Bereavement and the Process of Grieving

Death is the major and most significant loss with which most human beings have to cope. Although dance trainees are young, it is not all that unusual for a student to have to deal with the death of someone close to them. In that case it will help if the institution has some idea of the likely emotional effects. The finality of death, especially sudden and unexpected death ('I didn't even have time to say goodbye'), is obviously and evidently difficult to manage. However, there was until about the 1950s a general cultural expectation, at least in the English-speaking Western world, that after a certain amount of time, the bereaved person would 'get over it' (indeed *should* have got over it) and resume normal life. The recent film *Mrs Brown* depicts graphically the incomprehension of the British public at Queen Victoria's failure to 'get over' the death of Prince Albert. From the 1950s, however, researchers began to see that what enabled the bereaved person to recover was not so much time as a psychological process of readjustment which takes place over time. It is the knowledge and understanding of this process that is useful in helping trainees to deal with whatever losses they have to suffer.

Kubler Ross (1969) in America and Parkes (1972) in Britain began to map out a process of grieving through which it seemed bereaved people commonly passed. The process, described slightly differently by different authors, began with numbness and denial of the death ('I don't believe it'; 'There must be some mistake'; 'This isn't happening to me'). Denial gave way, usually within days, to a wide range of feelings including anger, guilt, sadness, depression, pining and longing. This stage of grieving commonly lasted at least months, and often up to the first anniversary of the death if the dead person was of great emotional significance to the bereaved – a spouse or a child, particularly. Usually this phase began to be succeeded by an acceptance of the loss and a reinvestment in life without the person who had died.

Since this process was first described there have been a number of modifications to the theory. Perhaps the most important is that people do not pass through this process in a linear fashion with one stage of grieving neatly succeeding another. The process is perhaps more like a spiral with different feelings being revisited repeatedly, but progressively less intensely. It is also now better understood that the grieving for the loss of very significant people perhaps never quite comes to an end. Another modification has been the recognition that those who mourn may not feel some of the range of feelings that mourning often involves. There has come to be an understanding that people show and express their grief in ways that are particular and individual.

What has survived of the original formulation of the theory is that grief is a process that has a natural and self-limiting progression. If we can allow ourselves and are allowed to grieve, then we will come to the end of it sufficiently to permit us to reinvest in our lives. Equally, where grieving is not allowed, either by the person themselves ('I can't give way to it'; 'I have the children to think of'; 'I can't indulge myself in self-pity'), or by the culture ('You have to be strong for the children'; 'You just have to pull yourself together and get on with it'; 'It's time you were over it by now'), then mourning is likely to become chronic and unresolved and to have limiting effects on how that person is then able to live his life (withdrawal from ordinary social life; emotional remoteness; depression). The obvious implication, if we turn for a moment to the importance of these ideas for those who have the responsibility for the care of dance trainees, is that those who grieve need time and space as well as permission ('I expect that sometimes you must feel very upset about it') and support ('Yes, of course you can talk to me; let's meet later today') from concerned adults.

Loss and Change

At about the same time as theories were being developed about the emotional effects of bereavement and the process of grieving, these ideas were being applied to other kinds of loss. John Bowlby and his colleagues, the Robertsons, researched extensively on the effects on children of separation from their mothers (Holmes, 1993). From this research also springs our relatively recent understanding of the damaging effects on children of the wartime evacuation policy under which children were separated from their mothers and often sent to live with complete strangers.

This widening of the concept of loss and grief, from bereavement to emotional loss of other kinds, has continued. Marris, in a remarkable book entitled *Loss and Change* (1986), used the concept to discuss the effects of forced house moves as a result of slum clearance. Kubler Ross (1969) had already applied it to those who were dying and contemplating the loss of their own lives. Parkes used it to describe reactions by amputees to the loss of a limb (1978). Finally Parkes made the conceptual leap that enabled him to describe all significant change, even change for the better, as loss (1982).

Borrowing concepts from Kurt Lewin, Parkes asserted that all of us have developed our individual expectations of how our life is and how it will be. He called this model our assumptive world. Without necessarily being very conscious of what we take for granted about our world, we are all invested in the continuing of things just as they are. When significant change disrupts these expectations we are forced into a readjustment of our inner world (let alone our outer world) and our assumptions (the ending of a dance career because of injury, for example). This happens even if the change has been planned and is perceived as for the better (for example, being promoted from the school to the company). When major change occurs that is unplanned and perceived to be for the worse, most critically the death of someone close, but also, for example, redundancy or illness, the reorganising of our assumptive world becomes a major task. Dance institutions need to be aware, therefore, of the potentially disastrous emotional effects of the premature end to training, for example.

All these researchers agree that major life changes, of whatever kind, for better or worse, are experienced (at least in part) as losses, to which our reaction is grief. They also agree that if we are to assimilate change so that it does not damage our capacity to function well, then it is necessary for us to undertake the emotional work of grieving for the loss that change implies. Dance schools need to expect, support and allow for these reactions.

Life Crisis and the Dance Trainee

We are now in a better position to begin to consider how the training institution needs to respond to crisis in the life of the trainee. Let us deal first with crisis that occurs outside the context of dance. Most dance trainees are still at an age where they are emotionally very dependent on their families. For this reason, crisis within the family has a very strong effect on them. When parents separate or divorce, when a parent remarries, when a close family member dies, is injured or becomes ill, when there is major conflict within the family, then the effect on the trainee is likely to be considerable. How can the dance school be of use in this situation?

The Pastoral Resources of the Dance School

If some of the values that have been discussed so far in this book are integrated within the dance training organisation then it should be possible for the student to find support immediately from a number of possible sources.

The first is the class group. Adolescents tend to get most support from their peers. If the group has evolved as a cohesive unit, as I described in the chapter on groups, then other class members will be able to support and sustain a group member who is having to deal with a major disruption in her life. It is in this kind of situation when facilitating group development really demonstrates its value.

However, the student or the group may feel that they need the support and understanding of an adult who they may hope will have more experience of major life events than they do. Again, if the relationships between teacher and student have been influenced by the values that are described in this book, then there should be no difficulty in the student approaching one of her teachers.

Tutors, Tutees and Tutorial Groups

One way of creating a more formal first line of pastoral care, which might respond in a situation such as we are describing, is to establish a system of personal tutors. The personal tutor has as her concern the welfare and development of a small group of students. Ideally the tutorial relationship would last throughout the student's career in the school, with provision for change at the student or tutor's request, if the relationship does not work satisfactorily. The student then has a designated adult within the institution who will have a good idea of her history and development and with whom there will be a relationship of trust. How can such a system be established?

The first question is who shall act as tutors. Bearing in mind that for the relationship to have any strength or meaning it will take time and effort from the adult (as well as from the student), then tutors can only deal with a relatively small number of students, say between five and ten. That implies that a good number of tutors will be required, certainly more than just the technique teaching staff. Should everyone who works for the institution (ranging from the principal to the physio to the office manager) then be asked to have a tutor group? There are difficulties with the idea of *requiring* staff to be tutors, when the relationship with the student is expected to be one of care and concern. There is also an issue about the competence of non-dance-trained staff to monitor the training aspects of an individual student's progress.

My preference would be for a voluntary system because it obviously recruits staff who have a commitment to and interest in the work. I would include non-dance-trained staff in the group of those from whom volunteers can be taken, because if they are interested in the students they can refer to other staff members for specialised information and advice on students, if need be, or the student herself can seek the opinion of other members of staff on specialised issues.

But what if dance staff do not want to be among the tutors? Here we have a real problem. The technique teachers are the staff with the highest status within the institution among the students. If they do not want to be involved in the tutorial system, its status and value among both students and staff will be fatally undermined. Pastoral care will be split from the actual business of dancing, as it so often is, so that dance is seen as unconcerned with the welfare and development of the student. This split then perpetuates the system which so bedevils dance training at the moment: the technique teacher teaches a group with whom she need have no emotional connection and therefore can think of herself as having no responsibility for their welfare, other than as technicians.

I think there are comparatively few dance teachers who would be actively unwilling to take on tutorial duties. To those who simply do not see involvement with the student as any concern of theirs, the institution has the option of saying that this dance school asks all staff, especially dance staff, to be concerned for the continuing welfare and development of students and to take part in the systems established to further those values; that if a particular dance teacher does not want to participate in the training in that way, then perhaps this institution is not the right place for them to be teaching.

However, most dance teaching staff are concerned for the student, but may be rather unsure as to how to translate that concern into being a tutor. That anxiety can be very much alleviated by running tutor training sessions. Where a new system is being set up it would probably be worth getting in a trainer; systems that are already operating will benefit from regular training sessions when themes and difficulties relevant to running a tutorial system can be raised and discussed. Such training might also include a basic course in counselling skills (Wheeler and Birtle, 1993).

There seem to me to be four main areas for discussion when a tutorial system is being established: the role of the tutor; the likely needs of the students; difficulties that may arise; the use and structure of tutorial time. Because I have not discovered any published work on this subject in relation to dance schools, I will give an outline of what areas of discussion of these four points might usefully cover. Interested readers should also note that an excellent general text on personal tutors in higher education (Wheeler and Birtle, 1993) gives guidance on many of the relevant issues. Bell (1996) is also useful.

The Role of the Tutor

The tutor's role is principally to create a relationship with the tutee. This relationship is of a particular kind: it is friendly, although it is not a friendship in that it is a relationship within the dance school and for a specific purpose; it is a relationship of oversight and concern, although the tutor does not have responsibility for the student. The tutor is the informed, benign adult who is available to act as a mentor and guide to the student. She is available on a limited basis to offer support, information and advice to the best of her ability. As a result of this relationship the tutor will have a current understanding of the student's welfare and development at any time during her career in the institution. She will monitor her progress and be available to discuss it with the student. If the student becomes ill, starts to do badly in her work, suffers from crisis or appears to be in trouble, then the tutor should be the one who is informed by other members of staff, not to evaluate nor to discipline, but to ensure that the student is aware of how she is seen and has the opportunity to discuss it. In some situations the tutor may feel that she does not possess relevant information – for example, of the best course of action after the student has sustained an injury. In that case the tutor can refer the student to other members of staff who may be better informed, but offer the student the opportunity to return to discuss what she has been told.

The tutor can also act as the link person with the world of work and the adult world outside the dance school. She can use her own experience to understand the student and perhaps to advise her. At the beginning of their time in the school, students are likely to have all the ordinary anxieties involved in any major transition and may value support, information and advice on issues such as housing, transport and money, as well as more psychological issues such as homesickness and loneliness. The tutor can also direct the student towards other sources of information, both inside and outside the dance school, who may be able to help the student with specific needs. She can help the tutor group address issues that are of relevance to all dance trainees, such as diet and nutrition, the problems that a changing body causes the dancer, the way that auditions can be approached, and so on.

The tutor may sometimes want to share some of her own experience and opinions. When she has been a dancer herself, these will very likely be of great interest to the students, who may learn something from them. However, the tutor should be clear that the time is for the students and not for the tutor; the focus is on them and their development. Her satisfaction from this relationship is to be derived from nurturing the development of her tutees.

There may be times when the student brings material to the tutor which she feels unable to cope with adequately. Eating disorders of any severity might be one such example; serious or prolonged emotional upset might be another. Where the tutor feels out of her depth she should be able to say so to the student ('I think that there might be someone else who can help you better than I can in this situation') and refer the student to the student counsellor or equivalent, whose role will be explored in the chapter on eating disorders. The role of tutor does not demand highly specialised skills, but rather the capacity to be interested in and concerned for the development of a young person.

Finally, the tutor also has a role within the school as the link between the individual student and the organisation. When she becomes aware of ways in which the institution could better meet the needs of the students, she is in the position to ask for change. For example, the complaints of one group of tutees that they had no opportunity to eat during the day led the tutor to approach the person responsible for timetabling, and to effect a change in the times of classes.

The Needs of the Student

The principal need of most students will be to discuss their progress in the dance school. The role of the tutor in this situation is to help the student discuss the meaning and importance of what has been said to her by her teachers, rather than to offer her own opinion of the student's progress or to convey opinions that she has heard other staff express of the student's progress, unless those have been conveyed to her as the student's tutor. This degree of clarity about role and self-discipline about passing on overheard comments is not always common in dance schools. If a student is being taught by her tutor there will be the temptation for the tutor to discuss the student's progress in more detail in the tutorial. I think this is inappropriate because it confuses assessment with the tutorial. The tutorial is designed to be the safe place within which assessment can be discussed, rather than a place where assessment may sometimes take place. This distinction may also need to be made clear to the student. If the tutor is in the position of having to give the student an assessment of her progress in her class, this meeting should be separated from and clearly distinguished from the tutorial. The student can then use the tutorial to discuss this assessment if she wishes, but here the teacher is in the role of tutor focusing on the student's reaction to the assessment and helping her consider its meaning and importance.

A further need for the student is likely to be to use the tutorial as a place to complain about the dance school and how it is run. Dance training can be highly stressful, difficult and frustrating (as well as exciting and enjoyable). These feelings often get displaced on to aspects of the dance school such as the teaching, the timetabling, the physical environment, the canteen, and so on. Although the tutor can help by sympathising ('I can see it makes you really fed up'), her job is not usually to act as the student's advocate ('I'll speak to the principal and see if something can be done') but to empower the student to deal with the problems herself ('Do you think you would dare to go and suggest that to the principal? Maybe you could write a note to the principal about it?'). Her job is to contain and hold the student's frustrations, remembering in a way that the student cannot, that they will change and pass, to encourage and support the student when the training seems difficult and to reinforce the student's own capacity to take responsibility for herself.

Another theme for the student will be her hopes and fears for the future. Here the tutor can be useful in helping tutees translate their fantasies into reality: by encouraging them to learn more about companies that they are interested in; by encouraging exploration of where their dance training might lead them if it does not lead to a performance career; by getting them to articulate and develop their interests and talents outside and alongside dance. Tutor groups can together find and exchange information on subjects such as self-employment, auditioning, and so on. The tutor need not necessarily have this information herself; rather, her task is to encourage tutees to find things out for themselves.

Finally, the student may wish to disclose aspects of her personal life which are important to her during the training. These may be joyful events or good news, but are much more likely to be difficult circumstances. The tutor at this point needs to remember her role as mentor and support; she is not called upon to make equivalent disclosure unless she is certain this will be useful to the student. On the whole, her job in this situation is to listen and attempt to understand what the student is feeling. Sometimes this can be difficult, especially if the subject is painful for the tutor (for example, divorce or bereavement). If it is too difficult then the student should be referred to the student counsellor; mostly, however, the simple act of listening with warmth and attention will offer the student the support she needs.

The Difficulties

Assuming that tutorial groups will be formed in the first year, the function of the tutor group, the purposes it is intended to serve, will be unknown to the tutees. The students will also be unknown to each other and to the tutor. The first task, then, is for there to be a group session (more later about group and individual sessions) in which tutees begin to get to know each other and the tutor (probably via an introducing activity). At this first session the work of discussing what the tutorial system is for should also begin. This first meeting is likely to take place soon after students come to the school; the amount that tutees will be able to take in will be limited when their anxiety levels will be high and when everything is new and strange. Understanding the purposes and limitations of the tutorial system and getting to know each other will therefore be a process over time and one essential to its meaningful functioning. However, it will not necessarily be easy to facilitate the development of a strong, cohesive and supportive group. The chapter on groups should be helpful for thinking about this potential problem.

Part of the task of forming the group and making the tutor/tutee relationship is exploring the issue of confidentiality. When a student says something to the group or to the tutor on her own she needs to know who she is talking to. Is she communicating just with those people present or must she reckon with the possibility that what she says will be repeated elsewhere? In groups of this kind, which have an agenda that includes the possibility of sharing personal material, it is usual for there to be a discussion of the boundaries of the group and an agreement about confidentiality. The commonest resolution of the problem is a mutual agreement not to repeat what another person has said within the group to anyone outside it without the knowledge and agreement of the original speaker. What is said in the group (or between tutor and tutee) remains private to those people unless permission is given for it to go further. Such an agreement should if at all possible be a solution arrived at by the group in response to the dilemma put to them by the tutor, rather than a condition imposed on them by the tutor. It then stands a better chance of being observed.

It is, unfortunately, rarely that easy to establish rules of confidentiality because of the real possibility that a student will disclose something which reveals her urgent need of specialist help. If a student comes and discloses to her tutor that she is eating only 500 calories a day, the tutor has the responsibility to refer that student to additional sources of help, even if the student does not wish her to do so ('I think you have been very brave to tell me this because you must know that you can't go on like this. We need to think together of how you can go about getting some proper help. I know you would rather not do that but I don't think you would have told me if you hadn't wanted me to help you get what you need'). The student may feel that the tutor is betraying her, which is of course a very painful accusation. She may also feel that if her situation becomes known she will be asked to leave the dance school. The tutor can then point out that unless the situation changes she certainly *will* be asked to leave, because she will be too ill to continue. Discussion of these kinds of tricky situation is a good subject for tutor training sessions and for evolution of school policy on matters such as eating disorders, drug misuse, HIV infection, and so on.

Even if total confidentiality cannot be promised, the raising of the issue seems to me to be quite essential. If it is not addressed, then the group and the tutor relationship has very little chance of dealing with issues beyond the practical and commonplace. That of course does not make the tutorial system worthless, but it certainly makes it very much less valuable than if it is a trustworthy container of feelings and experiences that trouble students and potentially interfere with their capacity to gain maximum value from the training.

The Use and Structuring of Time

Should tutees meet in a group or individually with the tutor? Group meetings foster the group as a source of support, but make disclosure of personal issues more difficult. Individual meetings permit a more intimate meeting, but do not enable students to make use of each other. The limitations of the tutor's availability may dictate the number of sessions available and whether they are group or individual. However, if the tutorial system is genuinely intended to operate as a first line of pastoral care, there must be at least some opportunity for individual meetings with students on a regular basis. Some of those with whom I have discussed these issues have felt that there should be at least one mandatory individual meeting per term, on the grounds that some students

would not themselves initiate a meeting with their tutor. My own preference would be for a mixture of mandatory group meetings and optional
individual meetings; perhaps monthly group meetings, with an optional
two individual meetings a term at the request of either student or tutor.
Provision on this scale does of course have resource implications. Group
meetings will probably need an hour, while individual meetings can be
given half an hour. With this arrangement, individual meetings will structure themselves since a request to meet by tutor or tutee presumes an
agenda. In crisis, more than the basic two individual meetings may be
required. Group meetings can be structured around themes devised by
the tutor in consultation with the group (food for dancers; responsibility
for training; adolescence in dance training, and so on); they can be
focused on progress reports from individuals; they can be scheduled to
discuss issues that are current in the training (assessment, student performances, auditions, and so on) bearing in mind that the particular
value of the tutor group lies in its freedom to address emotional aspects
of these issues ('How do you feel about . . .?'). So the discussion may
begin with the fact that student performances will soon be staged but can
be focused on how that affects the students and what their feelings are
about it, rather than leaving feelings 'out there' as if performance had no
individual and personal emotional significance.

Ethnic Minority Groups and Overseas Students

Professional dance training is a highly culture-specific activity; forms of
dance and expectations of dancers are closely related to the cultures
in which they emerge. Obvious examples of this truth are manifested in
the almost complete absence of black dancers from ballet and their
strong representation in jazz dance. It is important, then, that when
students from ethnic minorities have been accepted into dance training,
they are supported as much as possible. It is, for example, in my view
unethical to accept a black dancer into ballet training and then discriminate against her for her skin colour or her body shape. Similarly,
students from overseas will be faced with a huge transition, especially
when English is not their first language. If dance schools accept such
students they must also supply the support that a young person will need
to survive in a different culture. In both of these situations the tutor
should be in the position to offer extra time and care. She may also be
able to guide the institution towards developing the best possible struc-

tures for ensuring the welfare of such students (Wheeler and Birtle, 1993; Bell, 1996).

The Student in Crisis

After this rather long diversion, we can again return to the student in crisis. We have discussed how a major life event will elicit a grieving response, and described how an environment of concern for her welfare will enable the dance trainee to have a reasonable expectation of an empathic response from those within the institution. We have outlined how the tutor and the tutor group can provide a system for first line pastoral care. What exactly does the student need from others to enable her to weather the crisis? What she needs above all else is someone who can listen to her with warmth and empathy and attention, but without feeling the need to make it better or find a solution. She needs someone who can bear to listen to the story and witness the tears and distress (or anger and guilt) without feeling overwhelmed herself. She needs someone who can just bear to be with her while she is in pain. These listening skills are often enough in themselves to help a young person go through the process of grieving for the ordinary tragedies of life.

What can also help is the recognition of the feelings that the person who has suffered a loss is expressing ('Oh, I can see how sad you are'; 'Sounds like you feel guilty'; 'You look really depressed'). As I have already said earlier in this book, dance trainees are sometimes not very good at naming feelings; to be able to express *and name* feelings is strengthening to the sense of self. To have feelings accurately recognised and named is to feel validated and acknowledged. In this way the grieving process is permitted and facilitated. These reflective skills can also be taught and, again, would be an appropriate subject for tutor training. Together, listening and reflecting convey acceptance. In an atmosphere of warm acceptance, a young person has an exceedingly good chance of working through grief to resolution.

Losses Relating to Dance

Much earlier in this chapter I divided the losses a student might be likely to experience into two types: those life events which, however tragic or upsetting, do not directly impinge on dance training, and those which do. I am suggesting that those losses which are outside the context of dance may be 'easier' for the institution to deal with because it is not mixed up with them. I certainly do not mean to imply that these 'easier' losses may not be very serious for the student. Obviously the death of a parent or a sibling, for example, for a teenager, will be very hard indeed. However, it is my impression that the dance world is relatively compassionate and understanding in this kind of situation and fairly well able to give support. It can be much more difficult for the institution when the loss has implications for the student's continuing with dance training.

Injury and Physical Unsuitability

Injury is by far the commonest of the crises afflicting the dance student. As I have indicated earlier, all authorities agree on the very high rate of injury among both students and performers (see especially Brinson and Dick, 1996, where much of the recent literature is quoted). A student is almost certain to suffer significant injury during her training. Perhaps because it is so common, there is some excellent literature on how injury can be managed psychologically and how support is essential to the regaining of confidence and motivation (see especially Taylor and Taylor, 1995; Tajet-Foxell and Booth, 1996; Hamilton, 1997). I have little to add to their suggestions. However, I would like to propose that more attention is paid to the emotional circumstances in which the injury takes place. There are, I am sure, many injuries that are the result of physical and material circumstances, but equally there are many where psychological factors have a part to play (Elizabeth Nabarro, LCDS counsellor, interview, 25 January 1999). Some students seem to engage in risk-taking behaviour likely to result in injury in or out of the studio. An inadequate diet and inadequate warm-up are behaviours also likely to lead to injury. Students in distress are vulnerable to injury because of the difficulty in concentrating.

Tutors may be able to engage injured students in reflection upon the background to their injury without blaming them for being injured but rather exploring the emotional meaning of the injury. Some students may be able to see injury as a signal that things are not right with them and seek counselling help. These processes, however, should be an addition to, rather than an alternative to, the support offered to get students back to fitness.

> It needs to be recognised that injury stems often from lack of security, poor self-image, peer group pressure, tyranny of the mirror and the choreographer, fear of injury and losing work. Therefore a more holistic and sympathetic approach to injury is needed, with help from an understanding counsellor.
>
> (Mason and Bannerman in Brinson, 1991: 13)

Most injuries resolve in due course and permit the student to return to training. However, a more difficult situation occurs when a student has to leave the training because of physical unsuitability or injury. Considering all that has been said so far in this book about the identification of adolescents, and in particular dancers, with their bodies, the news that a trainee's body cannot sustain the training is a very difficult piece of information to absorb. As Susan Lee remarks, 'This is the most traumatising entry into transition. Forced immobilisation, the sudden loss of the familiar environment, sudden and total loss of the ability to dance' (quoted Leach, 1997: 47). For some it will be such a devastating blow that it may lead to depression and even suicidal thoughts and feelings. If these persist, then further help should be sought for the student, but they can be understood as the rage that the young person feels and turns against herself when she receives a decision that may very well feel as if it will destroy her. Again, one of the terrible features of such a blow is that she can do nothing about it. No one can do anything about it.

However, what is commoner in my experience, when injury or physical unsuitablity bring training to a premature end, is not a sudden incapacity with which there is no negotiating, but rather chronic discomfort, and eventually, pain. There is likely to follow a series of medical examinations and interventions of various kinds. During what may be an extended period of as long as a year, the student will be successively buoyed up and cast down by the hope of recovery or renewed pain. She may be required to watch class during this time, which will be a difficult and frustrating experience. She may well be asked to do therapeutic exercises of various kinds which are notoriously difficult to sustain, especially for young people, and especially when the student is longing to be in her classes dancing. The emotional result of all this when her condition does not improve is likely to be depression. Eventually someone in the school will have to tell her that nothing more can be done.

The major impact of such news, and its particular meaning to the dance student, means that it needs to be conveyed as carefully and a sensitively as possible, in a place that is private and allows time for questions and reactions. In recent years a lot has been said about the deficiencies of doctors in imparting bad news ('Well of course you realise it's cancer'). Let us learn from what has been understood and use it for the benefit of our trainees. It is now known that bad news shocks people to the point that they do not take in much of what has been said immediately. This implies that if a trainee is being told that because of some physical problem she will be unable to continue to train, then she will need time to take in this information and later opportunities to ask questions. The person who makes the decision needs to be very clear why it is being made and able to convey that reasoning to the student and to her tutor. If the information comes from a health professional then ideally the tutor should also be informed of what the student has been told, in order to be able to support her as effectively as possible. This is the moment when the relationship built up with the tutor really comes into its own and may very well prevent some of the worst effects of receiving such bad news, for instance, drug and alcohol misuse, depression or emotional collapse.

However, for the tutor to be able to contain the student's upset, she must be able to manage her own feelings in relation to the student. It is possible, for example, that she will feel the guilt that belongs to the institution for not noticing something sooner, or for admitting the student to the school in the first place. The tutor may well need to use her own staff support group to help her deal with her own feelings so that she can be emotionally free to support the student.

Financial Problems

Financial problems are difficult for student and institution alike, especially because they often involve circumstances over which neither has any control. The crisis in funding of training in the performance arts in Britain, especially dance, has meant that many students with talent cannot take up places offered to them. That is difficult enough, but it is even more difficult when a student begins her course but is unable to continue. When the student is obliged to leave training in this kind of situation, her grieving is complicated by the rage and frustration that she feels, which may well be directed against the school, however unjustly ('You must be able to do something about it'; 'All you care about is collecting the fees'). The tutor in this situation may be seen as the student's ally against the cruelty of funding bodies, but she may also be seen as a representative of the institution which despite its recognition of her talent will not keep her as a student unless she pays the fees. The task for the tutor is to keep her mind on the student and what she is feeling and to resist any temptation she may have to join with the student in abusing the institution or alternatively to take offence at the student's frustration and anger. This is the moment to remember that anger at the loss is often a part of grieving and that if it can be expressed it will be succeeded by other feelings.

Inadequate Progress

Finally let us turn to the crisis that results from a student being told that she is not doing well enough to be allowed to continue with the training. When a dance school is careful of the welfare of trainees, this judgement is unlikely to come as a shock, since the student will have been given regular assessments which will have been thoroughly discussed between student and tutor. Difficulties with her progress will have been noticed and explored long before the student is thought not good enough to continue. However, that does not mean that she will not be disappointed or angry. It will again be the tutor's job to support her in the emotional work of adjusting to the situation.

The same anguish will be aroused in the student as with other reasons for a premature ending to training, but to be asked to leave because of insufficient progress in the work may well be experienced as a humiliation. A youngster who has made the investment in dance to the point of entering professional training and then is told that she is not good enough not only has to deal with the loss of her dreams and her identification, but at the same time has to accept the fact that her dreams have been to some degree 'wrong' or ill-chosen. Probably there is no way she could have known that, but nevertheless she is likely to feel foolish at best, and at worst completely useless and valueless. It is likely to strike a severe blow to her self-esteem and to lead to depression or even despair. Of course, for some students it will be much worse than others. The relatively mature and well-adjusted youngster will have been aware of her own struggle to keep up and will have been reviewing other possibilities and considering other interests and talents that she might develop. The student who is more narrowly devoted to dance and who has not made much progress with the developmental tasks of adolescence may well be distraught. She is the one who needs to be given immediate, careful and sustained attention. For that reason such decisions should not be conveyed immediately before a holiday, especially not immediately before the summer holiday at the end of the school year, nor immediately before a weekend, nor even, I would argue, at the end of a school day. The student needs to be given the chance to take in what she has been told and begin to react to it, in the environment that can best understand what it means for her. The school has the responsibility for both admitting the student and asking her to leave; it therefore has the moral responsibility for dealing with the effects of those decisions. Of course I am not suggesting that it is particularly agreeable or easy to witness the acute distress of a student who has been asked to leave the school. I do think that it is a support that the school has a duty to offer, if the student wishes to make use of it. Very acutely distressed students, whose upset persists or who become suicidal, should have early access to the student counsellor or equivalent professional help (Greben, 1990).

In all three of the scenarios I have described – injury, physical unsuitability and financial crisis or inadequate progress with the work – there is likely to have been some preparation for the bad news. It is essential that this preparation time is used to help students to consider what other options they have if they cannot continue training, and to do some preliminary mourning. Where there is the opportunity to prepare for loss, the process of grieving is likely to be easier. Conversely, where denial of the possibility of loss has prevented any preparation, bad news will come as a shock and be more difficult to assimilate and process. When each student has a tutor whose stated task is to monitor the progress and welfare of her tutees, it is likely that crisis for the trainee can be managed in such a way that the student is supported and gradually enabled to find her way to another future.

10

Eating Disorders in Trainees

In this chapter I will begin by describing what I mean by eating disorders and review what is currently understood about what lies behind them. I will draw heavily on my own published work for this material (Buckroyd, 1995, 1996) to which the reader is referred for a fuller account. I will then go on to consider eating disorders in the context of dance training. This is the only subject in the whole field of the welfare of dance trainees that has received much attention, so I will use that work to discuss the subject before considering what response the dance school can make in the prevention, early intervention and treatment of them.

Eating disorders are conventionally divided into three broad syndromes: compulsive eating, anorexia and bulimia. Compulsive eating, unaccompanied by the attempts to undo its results that are characteristic of bulimia, leads inexorably to significant weight gain. Since professional dance in the Western world in our times requires a dancer to be less than average weight, both as an aesthetic demand and as a prerequisite for the execution of the technical demands, this chapter will not consider compulsive eating any further but rather focus on anorexia and bulimia.

Anorexia

It is doubtful whether formal definitions of eating disorders are of very much value. They were devised for the use of American insurance companies, so that a diagnosis could be made that would justify payment for treatment (Kutchins and Kirk, 1999). Many sufferers fall outside these parameters and are therefore determined to have sub-clinical symptoms. It seems more important to me to assess how a trainee's functioning is affected. Nevertheless the description creates some kind of base line that is perhaps worth quoting.

The most commonly used definition of anorexia (DSM-IV, 1994) lists the following diagnostic criteria:

1. Refusal to maintain body weight at or above a minimally normal weight for age and height (e.g. weight loss leading to maintenance of body weight less than 85 per cent of that expected; or failure to make expected weight gain during period of growth, leading to body weight less than 85 per cent of that expected).
2. Intense fear of gaining weight or becoming fat, even though underweight.
3. Disturbance in the way in which one's body weight or shape is experienced, undue influence of body weight or shape on self-evaluation, or denial of the seriousness of the current low body weight.
4. In post-menarcheal females, amenorrhoea, i.e., the absence of at least three consecutive menstrual cycles.

In addition, a number of other physical and psychological characteristics may be present such as hair loss, lanugo (fine hair growing all over the body including the face), lowered body temperature and heart rate, low blood pressure, feeling cold, poor circulation, dry skin, brittle nails, reduction in bone density leading to later risk of osteoporosis, insomnia, excessive exercising directed to weight loss, obsessional focus on food and calories, loneliness, social isolation, withdrawn behaviour, loss of the ability to concentrate on anything else, low self-esteem, self-hatred, depressed mood, irritability, diminished interest in sex.

Some anorexics find themselves unable to maintain their regime of starvation, but instead of beginning to eat normally, begin to binge and vomit (and/or purge themselves with laxatives). By this means they maintain a very low weight but at the same time find a way of not having to maintain their severe restriction of food. Since anorexics are proud of their control, bingeing is particularly shameful. Their wish is to return to a food-restricting anorexic state.

The incidence of anorexia is about 1 per cent of the vulnerable population of female adolescents and young adults, and is almost certainly significantly higher among dance trainees. More than 90 per cent of cases are female, although the incidence of the illness in men appears to be increasing.

Clearly, anyone suffering from all of the symptoms that have been described would be immediately recognisable and extremely unwell. No trainee could possibly continue under these circumstances. However, it can take a long time for the illness to progress so far that all these symptoms would be present. Anorexia begins with restriction of food, especially avoidance of 'fattening food'. This is common in our society among women and ordinary among dance trainees. For the developing anorexic, however, the pangs of guilt about eating 'fattening food' and the resolutions to go on a diet and lose weight, that are familiar to the vast majority of women, start to get out of hand. Her anxiety about being 'fat' may start to seem irrational to others ('Of course you're not fat'; 'Don't be ridiculous') and her avoidance of 'fattening food' may start to look like food phobia.

This 'sub-clinical' anorexia (which is certainly much commoner than the developed form of the condition) may stop at this point, be maintained for a while and then gradually fade away. Alternatively it may continue to develop. If so, one way or another, by degrees, the anorexic person will become increasingly preoccupied with food, weight, shape and size, and less and less available for ordinary life or for any kind of education, especially dance training. She will tend to withdraw progressively from social interaction and spend large amounts of time on her own. She will be thinking all day long about how much she has eaten, how much she will eat, how she can limit her intake further, and so on. This preoccupation with food, and the stress and conflict caused by her biological need to eat and her psychological fear of doing so, uses up most of her time and energy.

However, anorexia is not only a system of control and restriction of food (and sometimes of liquid). As the illness progresses, the controls and restrictions often extend to other areas of life. An anorexic may limit her spending severely, especially what she spends on herself; she may limit the length of time she sleeps or rests, irrespective of her need; she may restrict the amount of clothing she wears, without reference to the weather. In fact she will appear to be denying herself the gratification of any ordinary desires. To her it will seem like controlling appetites that seem gross or excessive. Clearly, the further such systems progress the less capable she will be of normal functioning. It can seem as though she is calling a halt to her life; pubertal development and sexual feelings will disappear; social interaction will come to an end; intellectual activity will become impossible since she cannot concentrate, so she will be unable to study or to work; often she will retreat to her family environment even if she is at an age when she would be expected to reduce her dependence on her family. Despite all this, the anorexic feels triumphant so long as she can continue her system. In the end the physical weakness caused by starvation will cause her collapse and bring her, however unwillingly, to medical attention.

Bulimia

In the same way as for anorexia, the standard description of bulimia may be useful as a starting point for recognition and understanding of the condition. The diagnostic criteria for bulimia are listed as follows (DSM-IV, 1994):

1. Recurrent episodes of binge eating. An episode of binge eating is characterised by both of the following:
   (a) eating in a discrete period of time (e.g. within any two-hour period) an amount of food that is definitely larger than most people would eat during a similar period of time and under similar circumstances;
   (b) a sense of lack of control over eating during the eating episode (e.g. a feeling that one cannot stop eating or control what or how much one is eating).
2. Recurrent inappropriate compensatory behaviour in order to prevent weight gain, such as self-induced vomiting; misuse of laxatives, diuretics, enemas, or other medications; fasting, or excessive exercise.
3. The binge eating and inappropriate compensatory behaviours both occur, on average, at least twice a week for three months.
4. Self-evaluation is unduly influenced by body shape and weight.

There is a range of accompanying physical and psychological characteristics that may also occur with bulimia such as damage to tooth enamel (as a result of persistent vomiting), digestive disorders, irritation of the throat and mouth, mineral imbalance leading to water retention or, in severe cases, to heart arrhythmia, loneliness, social isolation, low self-esteem, self-hatred, shame, self-disgust.

The incidence of diagnosed cases of bulimia is about 1 to 3 per cent of the vulnerable population of adolescent and young adult females. Again, the rates are probably much higher in particular populations such as dance trainees. As with anorexia, at least 90 per cent of cases are female.

Also as with anorexia, there are many people who suffer from relatively mild and sub-clinical degrees of bulimia. It seems particularly common among dancers and dance trainees. Occasional bingeing and vomiting are, however, very common among the general population of young females and again may be maintained for a while before fading away. On the other hand, the illness may progress. Like anorexia, bulimia does not only affect food use but extends to other areas of life. Whereas restriction and control are the characteristics of the anorexic's way of life, the bulimic engages in alternating excess and control or restriction. So, extravagant spending may be followed by extremely careful accounting and saving; chaos and untidiness may be followed by obsessional tidiness and order; dirt and squalor may give way to rituals of cleaning both of the self and of living quarters; promiscuous sexual activity may be succeeded by periods without sexual relations; spasms of drug or alcohol misuse may give way to living without drugs or alcohol. Clearly, the further such a pattern of alternating excess and restriction goes, the harder it will be to sustain ordinary life or a dance training, and the more distressed the person will become. Unlike the anorexic, the bulimic has no satisfaction in her illness and will often eventually look for help herself. This is one of the reasons for ensuring that there is some competence to respond to bulimia available within the dance school.

What Causes Anorexia and Bulimia?

A considerable amount of effort has gone into attempts to identify the causes of anorexia and bulimia. Some of this effort has been directed to trying to identify a physical cause. So far there is no conclusive evidence that either condition has other than psychological origins. In both anorexia and bulimia there is an increased incidence among close relatives, which again may suggest a genetic predisposition, but may also suggest a common psychological difficulty. Attempts to link anorexia or bulimia causally with abnormal brain chemistry or brain function have not so far been conclusive.

There appear to be a range of conditions which are necessary for the development of anorexia or bulimia:

1. A culture in which being thin is seen as conferring value, acceptability and desirability.
2. An individual whose sense of self and self-esteem is poor.
3. An individual whose capacity to differentiate, express and name feelings is not well developed.
4. A particular crisis or stress in the life of the individual.

I will discuss these in general terms before applying them to the particular circumstances of the dance school.

Cultural Pressures

It is by now commonplace to notice that the images of women that surround us in advertising, in the media, in films and in public life are overwhelmingly of women who are thin. Estimates of the size of women in the general population in the UK suggest that about half of all women are a size 16 or more. That is to say that half the population of women in Britain are deemed by the culture to be unacceptably big. This situation is new, dating from the 1960s, but shows no sign of changing. Our culture has developed a value system based on body size according to which to be thin is the same as to be good, desirable and acceptable. Unfortunately it is probably impossible for at least half the female population to be thin enough to meet this cultural requirement; the result is an obsessional anxiety in many women about their size. To stand out against this value system requires enormous strength of character and maturity, virtues that few adolescent females possess. Rather, since her sense of self is in any case highly invested in her body self, the adolescent girl is particularly vulnerable to the cultural pressures that she will experience via her peer group as she moves away from the more protected environment of her family (Pipher, 1994).

Self-esteem

Cultural pressures, however, cannot be the whole story, or the incidence of eating disorders would be much higher. It is true, as feminists have argued, that virtually all women have anxieties about food, weight, size and shape, but to argue that all women have eating disorders involves a dilution of the concept that does not seem particularly useful. What else, then, contributes? In order for a young woman to derive her entire sense of value from her degree of thinness, she must feel unusually dependent on what others think of her shape; that is to say, she must have very little sense of her own value. I have argued elsewhere in this book that the child and adolescent *is* very dependent on her body self for her sense of self, but I have also argued that the body self is a capable, active self whose accomplishments can give pleasure and satisfaction and a sense of value. The young woman who has little sense of herself as capable and valuable is vulnerable to a value system imposed from the outside.

Expressing Feelings

Even these two conditions are not enough to account for eating disorders. A poor sense of self is probably endemic in the female population, particularly young females; our society does not prize women and it is extremely difficult to grow up female and confident (Pipher, 1994). A further element in the puzzle is, I think, a difficulty in identifying and expressing feelings. Eating disorders become an emotional language for the expression of distress; why would anyone use them unless they lacked the capacity to express their distress in more direct ways? In Chapter Three I discussed how youngsters are taught to differentiate, name and express feelings and how inadequate many families are to the task of teaching these skills. If a youngster arrives at adolescence without these skills, food and its misuse may well present her with a vehicle for expressing herself.

Crisis

All of these predisposing conditions may exist and yet the youngster not develop an eating disorder. What is also needed is the trigger in the present in the form of crisis which the young person cannot manage. There are many possibilities, for example:

• The death of a parent.

- The illness, mental or physical, of a parent.
- The death of sibling.
- The death of a grandparent who has been close.
- The divorce or separation of parents.
- Sexual abuse.
- Rape or sexual assault.
- Leaving home.
- The ending of a close relationship.
- The loss of a close friendship.
- Examinations.
- Teasing or bullying.

When a vulnerable youngster is faced with crisis and lacks the emotional resources to cope, an eating disorder may be adopted as a way of surviving. Of course to the outside world it doesn't look like coping and its effects can be disastrous, but nevertheless it may be the best option available to that particular young person. If the sufferer is to recover, she must find a better way of managing.

Eating Disorders in Dance Trainees

We are perhaps now in a position to start looking at eating disorders in dance trainees. I would like to begin by reviewing the dance school in relation to the four precipitating factors in eating disorders that I have just described.

If our society exerts a cultural pressure to be thin, then the dance school, as a culture within the culture, certainly intensifies that pressure (Piran, 1999). Pipher, a psychotherapist specialising in working with adolescent girls, remarks of a client of hers, 'She was in a high risk category – women who make a living or have an identity based on being thin. This category includes gymnasts, dancers, actresses and models. Many acquire eating disorders as an occupational hazard' (1994: 168). Although I have argued earlier in this book that to require students to be thin to the point that their welfare is put at risk is unethical, it is certain that many dance schools comply with the perceived demand of current aesthetic and technical fashions and put very great pressure on students to be thin, although the pressures on contemporary and jazz dance students seems to be less extreme (Schnitt and Schnitt, 1986; Schnitt and

Schnitt in Clarkson and Skrinar, 1988; Garner et al., 1988; Schnitt, 1990; Schnitt and Schnitt in Satalott et al., 1991). Failure to meet these standards may well result in the student being asked to leave the school (Lowenkopf et al., 1982; Hamilton et al., 1988) so it will be demonstrated most graphically that her value indeed resides in her being thin. Many schools weigh students frequently; others specify weight loss at a given rate; comments about students' weight are frequent; abusive comments, if a student is thought to be too heavy, are commonplace. The limited amount of evidence that has been collected confirms ordinary observation that professional dance students, especially ballet students, are, by the standards of other non-dance students, very thin. One study declared, 'a ballet dancer's baseline weight may easily be 25% less than the usual estimates of ideal body weight' (Lowenkopf and Vincent, 1982: 55). Another study, this time of ballet students, arrived at a figure of 86.7 per cent of Expected Body Weight (EBW) (Garner and Garfinkel, 1980). A study published five years later arrived at a similar figure for a sample of ballet school students of 87.2 per cent (Szmukler et al., 1985). A further study of ballet dancers found a mean weight for the sample of ballet dancers of 86 per cent (Hamilton et al., 1988). Piran (1999) suggests a figure as low as 75 to 80 per cent.

Since the criteria for anorexia nervosa include weight 15 per cent below EBW, a number of studies have been carried out to try and determine the level of eating disorders in the student dancer population. When are student dancers abnormally thin, and when do they suffer from eating disorders? A review article published in 1986 concluded that it had been established that dance students were at high risk of developing eating disorders (Schnitt and Schnitt, 1986), but a later review by the same authors pointed out numerous problems in the interpretation of the research already conducted (Schnitt and Schnitt, 1991), while still concluding that levels of eating disorders appear to be higher in the dancer and dance student population.

Part of the debate seems to revolve around whether dance students exhibit the full range of symptoms that would 'qualify' them to be diagnosed anorexic or bulimic. Plainly, many do not, although some authors commented upon the range of abnormal eating attitudes and behaviours which, at the severe end, can be diagnosed as eating disorders (Schnitt and Schnitt, 1986). Greben summed up the issue, commenting, 'Certain attitudes and conditions [in the ballet school, including the expectation of low weight] may encourage preoccupations about food and eating, which may predispose a person to eating disorders – anorexia nervosa, bulimia nervosa, or both, in the most severe cases' (1990: 276).

Environment is not, in my understanding, in itself enough to create eating disorders. However, I agree with Pipher, quoted above, that other 'thin professions' also seem to foster eating disorders. Popular report suggests this is so for fashion models; jockeys are reported to keep their weight low by a regime of vomiting and purging which sounds suspiciously like bulimia. A recent report in the *Independent* (25 March 1997) commented, 'Eating disorders are a great problem in many sports involving women, especially gymnastics and ice-skating.' The same picture emerges from women's athletics: 'Of the 35 women who have run for Britain in the junior [World Cross Country] race in the past six years, only four have gone on to run in the senior event. At least half are known to be suffering from eating disorders such as anorexia nervosa or bulimia, which often lead to serious illness or injury'.

What can be done to ensure that dance students do not develop eating disorders as a result of the demand on them to be thin? The most radical solution to the problem has been advanced by Hamilton, whose research suggests that eating disorders in ballet companies are commoner where the genetic inheritance of the dancer means that she will have to make considerable efforts to retain the desired low weight. Dancers who came from families whose members were naturally low in weight developed fewer eating disorders. Her implied proposal, therefore, is that ballet dancers be selected exclusively from those whose genetic inheritance will enable them to be significantly under average expected body weight without stringent dieting (Hamilton et al., 1988).

On the face of it, this research has a sort of logic to it, but for me it illustrates the way 'ballet' can be construed as an impersonal, demanding force which 'requires' dancers to be of abnormally low weight. If 'ballet' demands that only a very small sample of people are genetically suited to its demands, then so be it. All others should be excluded from the profession. But there is no impersonal 'ballet'. There are individuals who have ideas about what ballet can or should be. There are fashions in how a ballet dancer 'should' look that are promoted by particular individuals. These criteria can, do and have changed. The ballet world has the power to choose whether to impose demands for a particular aesthetic that is achievable only by those drawn from a small and highly selected genetic pool. I am suspicious of devotion to 'ballet' where it seems to exclude considerations of expressive talent, in favour of a demand for a body shape that can only be achieved without pathology by a very small number of people. Moreover, I am suspicious of a demand that seems to be more rigorous and more damaging to women than to men, but is very often required by male choreographers, artistic directors, and others, of female dancers (Novack, in Thomas, 1993). It is a great pity that Balanchine's famous requirement of his female dancers, 'I want to see bone', was not met by a robust refusal to engage in the self-destructive behaviours necessary to achieve the results he demanded.

The logic of a situation where demands for low weight produce eating pathologies is, as far as I am concerned, not to sustain the demand by searching ever harder for those who can fulfil it, but rather to moderate the demand. Piran comments, 'Changing the norms of thinness within the ballet world is an essential aspect of successful prevention [of eating disorders] in this field' (1999: 257). As I have said elsewhere in this book, I consider it unethical to require dancers, especially student dancers, to maintain a weight below that at which menstruation can be established and maintained. However, if it is accepted that the *athletic*, rather than aesthetic, demands of ballet (and of other dance forms) require students to be of a weight that is less than average, without compromising their menstrual status, then there are a good number of measures that could be taken which would help avoid the development of eating pathologies. The first is the supply of information. Probably most dance schools now provide some information on food and nutrition, yet my experience of going to dance schools to talk to students about their diet is that the information is learned passively and not sufficiently internalised or applied. Giving students a diet sheet or a lecture about food and nutrition seems to provide them with facts that they do not use. How can this knowledge be made active and personal?

I would like to describe how I go about facilitating this shift from passive to active knowledge when I work with dance students. I begin by trying to establish a framework for the workshop that will convey some of the values that I am trying to encourage. I want to enable participation so I limit group size to about 20, if at all possible. It takes time to win the trust of students sufficiently for them to feel free to be at least somewhat honest about their eating behaviour, so I take an hour and a half, or slightly more, for the workshop. I want to engage the students as responsible people, so I hold the workshops in a room where the students can sit on chairs in a semicircle, rather than on the floor; I try to avoid any suggestion of talking down to them. I ask students to bring pen and paper with them to convey that they will be asked to work and reflect on their own behaviour. I avoid lecturing and adopt an interactive style where students are asked to contribute to the content of the workshop.

I begin by asking students to tell me how we talk about food and to tell me the names of the various food groups (carbohydrate, protein, and so on). This information I write on a flip chart as they are telling me. Because this information is well known to at least a proportion of the students, it gives them confidence and establishes an interactive way of working. I continue by asking them to give me examples of food in each of the groups and again, as they produce this information, I write it on the flip chart. Here again they are well informed. I then ask them what a dancer should eat from the lists they have supplied. There is some mis-information (noted also by Schnitt and Schnitt, 1986) among them – some students, for example, will say dancers should not eat any fat – but on the whole the message about complex carbohydrate, limited protein, lots of fruit and vegetables and limited fat and sugar has been taken in at an earlier point. These principles I also write on the chart. I then ask the students to use the principles to devise lists of the kinds of meals that would be appropriate for dancers to eat for breakfast, lunch and dinner. Here I often add suggestions, especially those that would be appropriate for vegetarians, and, if there are male students present, refer to their need for more food than the female students. By this time I have usually established quite an energetic, interested, confident atmosphere. I then ask the students to work in pairs devising meal plans that they them-selves would be prepared to eat and that conform to the guidelines that we have been discussing. This begins to bring the discussion slightly nearer to the individual and I am often asked at this point to help individuals with particular problems – for instance, problems to do with preferences for particular foods and dislikes of or allergies to others. The process so far takes about 45 minutes to an hour, and on might think that it would be more appropriately be conducted by a nutritionist than by a psychotherapist like myself. (However, Greben (1990) also reports this work being done by a psychologist.) It would be easy to leave at this point and think that some useful principles and information had been rehearsed and the students' nutritional understanding consolidated.

However, my agenda is not the sharing of information, which is very readily available, but the establishment of an emotional environment in which the psychological issues relating to food can be raised. I therefore continue by asking students to write down what they ate the previous day. At this point the group usually laughs because it is immediately apparent to them without going any further that what they know and what they do are not the same thing. I tell them that this information is for them, to show them something, not for me and not for other students unless they wish to share it. What emerges, however, from this exercise and the discussion that follows is that most students are eating in a way that certainly does not conform to the principles they have so enthusiastically shared with me. We spend the rest of the workshop discussing as a group why they do not do what they know they should for their own health and welfare. I begin with practical issues: time, energy, money, circumstances. Together we try and devise strategies for overcoming those problems. Then we move on to more psychological issues: comfort eating; a sense of deprivation created by the need to be thin; alienation from a non-dance peer group who eat what they like; rebellion against an authoritarian regime which is experienced as requiring them to deprive themselves; anger with the dance school or teachers which cannot be expressed directly; loneliness and homesickness (also noted by Greben as a factor, 1990); anxieties about their own abilities and their future as professionals (also Greben, 1990). It takes one brave student to talk more openly about the difficulties inherent in being a trainee dancer, but then others will follow and expand and amplify what has been said. My response is to offer my understanding of the pressures upon them and to ask them how they might deal with those pressures in other ways. I particularly encourage them to share their problems and to use each other for support. Of course in a short time and a fairly large group, students will be unlikely to share real difficulties with me, but my focus is more on directing their attention to the way they use food and trying to get them to generate both a better eating plan for themselves and to identify some of the ways in which they may be misusing food. My hope is that the workshop starts a process of students owning and taking responsibility for the way they use food and moves them on from a passive knowledge of what they should eat which hardly touches what in fact they do eat.

Awareness of the complexity of the issues round food and the problem of maintaining below average weight needs repeated support and reinforcement throughout a student's training if the common problems of poor nutrition, bizarre and compulsive eating patterns and preoccupation with food are to be avoided. These, as has already been said, are the precursors of eating disorders and often in themselves harmful. The

Food

You may feel that cutting down on food will help your budget problems. This is NOT advisable given the physical demands of the training and the importance of nutritional balance for physical growth and repair. It is, of course, possible to eat cheaply if you can take the time to plan carefully. Your classes will begin at 8.45 every morning and so the temptation will be to skip breakfast. A substantial breakfast is necessary to sustain the high level of physical and mental activity required and we encourage students to spread their food intake throughout the day rather than relying on quick-energy snacks from the canteen. This may require a complete rethink of the way you eat and we would like to assist you in reorganising your eating habits. Eating well may not be as expensive as you imagine. For example grains, lentils, pulses and fresh vegetables are relatively cheap, easy to prepare and a good source of energy. Many students, given their financial constraints, find that first class protein (such as meat) is outside their budget and need to obtain the bulk of their protein from vegetarian sources. There are many books available on this and other related topics. We would suggest you spend no less than £20 per week on food. This may seem outside your means, but economise elsewhere before cutting back on food expenses. It is vital that students think carefully about how they eat during their dance training and for their future careers. The terms are long, the timetable is busy and the training is physically hard. If you are not eating properly you will find that you are constantly tired and below par, that you pick up every infection going round the School, that you keep getting injured and do not recover quickly or properly from injury.

If you would like individual advice on the nutritional balance of your diet, please see [the body conditioning tutor] or [the director of student services] who can arrange for you to have a consultation with a dance dietician/sports nutritionist. If you feel you have emotional problems with food or your body image then please do not hesitate to discuss this with someone. You are not alone and many students experience similar struggles during their training and/or careers. We do try to encourage students not to suffer in isolation if they are struggling with food and eating and we welcome approaches from students who wish to resolve their particular problems. Our emphasis is always on the healthier dancer, but we understand that for many young people this is not always a matter of practical information and that emotional factors can get in the way of putting knowledge into practice. Try to find someone to talk to, either someone in the Student Support Department, another student or someone on the staff. If you take the plunge and try to find help you could save yourself years of unhappiness.

London Contemporary Dance School
Induction and Advice Notebook Academic Year 98/99

institution must therefore be involved. The task cannot be left to the occasional visit of the dietician and should not be handed over to the school's medical advisors. The issue can be raised in class group meetings, in group tutorials and in individual meetings with students in tutorials and other settings. The emphasis needs to be on ongoing open discussion of the problems and support for a solution, rather than criticism of a student for gaining or losing weight. (See also Piran (1999) for an extended discussion of a prevention programme.)

Just as students give lip-service to a proper diet, so institutions may give lip-service to a concern for students' welfare in this matter, while pursuing policies that convey another message. One such policy is the compulsory weighing of students. This is a practice which emphasises the authoritarian and objectifying aspects of dance training. It is humiliating for an adolescent to be weighed like a piece of meat and it encourages practices that are harmful, for example the use of diuretics and laxatives or drinking large quantities of water, in order to deceive the scales and the institution. If the institution is genuinely concerned to facilitate the students' ownership of the training, as has been discussed in a previous chapter, then authoritarian functions of this kind must be surrendered. They must be replaced by an interactive and supportive environment which can acknowledge and work with students' problems with their weight.

Similarly, institutions implicitly condone amenorrhoea and anorexia by allowing students with these conditions to continue to dance. As far as I am aware, amenorrhoea is universally tolerated among dance students, despite what is known about its damaging and irreversible effects, but even anorexia is implicitly condoned where students are allowed to continue with classes and performances. Szmukler reported that where the institution insisted that an appropriate weight was maintained and intervened early, the results were good (Szmukler et al., 1985). Greben (1990) also reported that where the institution supports students and validates their seeking help at an early stage, the effects were positive. Conversely, Garner noted that where the institution condoned 'extreme thinness', eating disorders might well be sustained (Garner et al., 1988). Piran comments, 'The decision to temporarily prohibit participation in the dance or training program until significant healing occurs is important not only for the dancer or student but also for the other dancers or students. These decisions reflect the stance of the school towards eating disorders. It reflects the ultimate importance the school or company puts on the medical safety of its dancers or students. It also reflects the importance the school puts on the psychological well-being of students . . . Keeping talented dancers who develop clinical eating disorders in school shows or performances signifies support for eating disorders even if the public says otherwise' (1999: 261).

If the dance world continues to require of adolescent girls that they maintain a weight up to 25 per cent below the norm, then in my view it has a moral responsibility to show them how that result may be accomplished without damage to their health or pathological means of weight control. In practice this means that the dance training institution needs to work hard to develop strategies that create a continuing interactive discussion about this issue with students and to inform and support their efforts.

Self-esteem

Let us now return to our list of predisposing factors to eating disorders in the general population. The second of these factors was poor self-esteem. In earlier chapters, I have already discussed aspects of this issue in relation to dance trainees. Here I would like to add only the comment that self care is a function of self-esteem. If a youngster feels good about herself then she will feel that she is worth taking care of. The dance school cannot of course take entire responsibility for the sense of self of the students it accepts. Some will arrive in the dance school with a much stronger and better idea of who they are than others. However, as I have already suggested, dance training seems to damage rather than support self-esteem in trainees. Schnitt and Schnitt quote a study of students in three ballet schools in New York who 'as a group demonstrated considerable doubt about their capabilities and appearances' (1986: 41); considering that such students are selected from ten times as many applicants for their talent, this does seem remarkable. It is just such a young woman who may feel that she does not need or deserve to eat, may call herself 'greedy' and 'fat' and who will learn to use food as a way of acting out on herself her sense of 'unentitlement' (Orbach, 1989). I would like to challenge dance schools to find ways of supporting trainees to feel proud of their talent and skill and of encouraging them to feel that, as elite athletes and performers, they owe themselves the best possible treatment. Proper nutrition might then be seen as part of the life of a dancer and part of her responsibility to herself as an artist.

Research is currently being carried out at the University of Hertford-shire under the author's direction to establish whether an intervention directed at raising self-esteem will modify pathological attitudes to food in trainee dancers which are risk indicators for eating disorders.

Expressing Feelings

The reader will already have understood from what has gone before that dance students may well be using food to express feelings that they find no other way of expressing. Elsewhere in this book I have commented on the way in which dance training often seems to inhibit and repress the expression of feeling rather than facilitate and encourage it. It follows that students who perhaps have not learned from their families direct ways of expressing feelings and/or those who have become confused about or unaware of their feelings as a result of dance training may well resort to unconscious outlets for what they cannot say. This problem was addressed by Greben in the pastoral care system that he established at the National Ballet School of Canada. Students were provided with readily available psychological help, strongly supported by the director of the school. One of the results was an improvement in the capacity of students to express themselves. The artistic director of the school commented, 'Students are so much better able to express themselves if something troubles them. They are much more articulate. Before it was completely against protocol to express your concerns or feelings; you were expected to swallow them.' The director echoed these sentiments: 'In a profession in which the emphasis is on being seen and not heard, the students are helped to express their feelings, instead of just bowing to authority, the traditional case in ballet.' She goes on, 'The highly motivated "tight" children who are perfectionists are hard on themselves; they may be talented, but they have little expression. As they work with psychiatrists you see enormous changes in their dancing. It helps them as artists. They gain confidence . . . They have a much better sense of self' (Greben, 1990: 278). This particular dance school has put enormous resources into providing a great deal of psychological help for students from health professionals and obviously has reaped very valuable results. For schools that have fewer resources, improvements in the same direction might be made by shifting the way dance students are trained in at least some of the many ways that have been suggested in this book. It is in its way tragic that students of an expres-

> Teachers should include early and regular availability of counselling not only for psycho-
> logical or personal problems but also for advice about alternative dance and related
> careers.
>
> **A Dancers' Charter** Appendix Three

sive art are trained in an environment that is so damaging to their capacity for expression that they must be rescued from it by a battery of mental health professionals.

Crisis

The chapter on crisis in the life of a dance trainee will have given some idea of the kind of response that is needed to enable a youngster to weather crisis without threatening her training, or to survive the necessity to stop training without destroying her equilibrium. Here I wish only to add that if students are required to manage crisis without appropriate help and support within the dance school, they will be at very much greater risk of symbolising their distress by eating disorders.

The Student Counsellor

If some of the strategies suggested above and throughout this book were put into effect there would be fewer students with eating disorders in dance schools. However, even if these changes were to take place there would still be some students with eating disorders and they certainly exist at the moment. In what follows I would like to describe the role of a health professional who can be available to work with students whose difficulties, eating disorders or other, are not adequately managed by the first line pastoral care services that I have described elsewhere, especially the personal tutor. The basic outline that is given here is explored in much greater detail by Bell (1996).

In mainstream education at both secondary and tertiary level it has been increasingly accepted in recent years that a student's capacity to learn may be impaired by emotional difficulties. Consequently, it is now commonplace within tertiary education, and increasingly usual within secondary, to find mental health professionals as part of student welfare provision. Some dance schools have already followed this example. In

> The Student Counsellor . . . is available to assist you with problems you feel may require more in-depth and prolonged assistance. This may include problems you are encountering around eating or relationships or events in your personal history which continue to cause you difficulties, such as sexual abuse. Her office can be found in the same complex as the Student Support Department and the Student Common Room. [She] is in School on Monday, Tuesday, Wednesday and Friday, when she can arrange a regular appointment if necessary. She also runs an injury clinic on Thursdays to help students find a way to manage their injuries emotionally. If you would like to make an appointment to see her about any difficulty which is troubling you, see [the Director of Student Support] or drop a note under [the Student Counsellor's] door, stating your name and free hourly periods for each day of the week. [She] will leave a note on the main notice board for you, confirming the time of your appointment.
>
> If you would rather seek help outside the building rather than through our own support staff, please feel free to ask [the Director of Student Support] for advice about counsellors outside of School. Obviously, as these counsellors work privately, there will be a charge, but it is sometimes possible to find concessionary places. [The Director of Student Support] will treat any such requests in complete confidence. You will also find some contact numbers later in this advice notebook.
>
> London Contemporary Dance School
> Induction and Advice Notebook Academic Year 98/99

what remains of this chapter I would like to discuss the role of counselling and psychotherapy in relation to dance trainees.

In the only published paper that I know of on this subject, other than my own work (Buckroyd, 1995), Stanley Greben, psychiatric consultant to the National Ballet School of Canada, argues strongly for the provision of this kind of help for students, supplied by health professionals who are closely associated with the dance school, are working within the institution and are familiar with staff and students. Greben's justification for professional help of this kind is based on its value to the students for their development as dancers: 'The work has been done on the basis that it is justifiable to use psychotherapy to reduce inner pain and to help ballet students to attain fuller maturity and to achieve more of their potential.' As a health professional, he is aware of the pressure that dance trainees have to endure: 'Beginning early in adolescence the students are under unremitting physical and emotional pressure as they work to master a difficult art, complete their schooling and mature as performers and citizens' (1990: 274).

Individual work with students can, I am certain, be very valuable, but the student counsellor (if we can use that convenient label) can also have a broader role within the institution in developing in both staff and students an environment in which concern for emotional and psychological issues is ordinary and expectable (Piran, 1999). One aspect of this work can be meeting students in groups. I have already described in an earlier chapter how I think that greater use of the class group would enhance the learning environment, and how attention to group dynamics and group concerns would be useful. The student counsellor may be the obvious person to facilitate or perhaps even better, train teachers to facilitate these groups.

In addition, the student counsellor can potentially have a role to play in training and educating staff in issues to do with emotional health. She might well be the person, for example, who trains tutors for their work with students. She can also contribute to the in-service training of staff by running seminars on issues such as adolescence and its various tasks and problems. She can be involved in the evolution of school policy towards such issues as smoking, drug use, eating disorders, and so on.

Some dance schools use external consultants for this work, but this system has the disadvantage that the consultant is not part of the day-to-day provision of the dance school and is unlikely to be closely in touch with what goes on there. If the student counsellor can be integrated within the school there is a much greater chance of the values that she embodies becoming part of the ethos of the school.

Students can sometimes be suspicious of the role played by the student counsellor, so issues of confidentiality need to be carefully thought through. A policy about confidentiality needs to be arrived at and communicated to students who use the service, as well as class groups, etc., with whom the student counsellor may work. Even so, there may be students who are unwilling to use the service because of fears about confidentiality (also found by Greben, 1990). My own experience of this role was that as I became better known and as students discovered and communicated to each other that their confidences were secure with me, so they were more willing to ask me for help.

Where a dance school is conscious of students' problems but anxious and uncertain about the use of health professionals, the student counsellor can be used as a dumping ground for issues that the institution would rather not deal with. This is unfortunate because it perpetuates the split between dance and emotional concern. The student counsellor can best be used in a way which integrates those two areas and which enables the young dancer to benefit from an environment which is focused on maximising her potential. One of the ways in which trainees are prevented from realising that potential is undoubtedly by eating disorders, clinical and sub-clinical. If the counsellor can contribute to developing an environment within the school that is preventative, as well as working with troubled individuals, then the worry that dance schools are breeding grounds for eating disorders may be relieved.

11

Transition and the Dance Trainee

At an age when others are just entering their most productive professional years, the dancer's performing career ends. Years of training and rigorous apprenticeship prepare the dancer for a profession that is relentless in its demands, scarce in its material rewards and fiercely defended by those involved in it. Dancers dance for the love of it, but the performing life is intense, insecure and short. When it comes to an end, either by personal choice, physical limitation or injury, the dancer faces a difficult challenge.

(Promotional brochure, International Organisation
for the Transition of Professional Dancers)

Over the past two decades a growing concern has developed about how professional dancers manage the transition from life as a dancer to another career. The professional life of a dancer is likely to be short, probably no more than ten to fifteen years at the best, with a few magnificent exceptions, and many are much shorter (Greben, 1989; Pickman, 1987; Schnitt, 1990; Leach 1997). Injury is exceedingly common (Brinson and Dick, 1996; Leach, 1997) and leads to many dancers leaving the profession prematurely. There are a few opportunities for older dancers to use their experience and artistry: Netherlands Dance Theatre 3 is a company formed with exactly that purpose (Leach, 1997); individuals such as Merce Cunningham and Jane Dudley have continued to perform into old age. (See *Animated*, Summer 1999, for a discussion of the older dancer.)

However, the vast majority of dancers need to discover another way of earning their living and expressing their talents for what will probably be the majority of their working life. In order to help dancers make this transition, a number of countries – currently (1998) Britain, Canada (Greben, 1989), the United States (Pickman, 1987) and Holland – have set up dancer transition agencies (Leach, 1997), while a number of other countries are in the process of establishing programmes.

Two international conferences, in Lausanne (1995) and The Hague (1998), have consolidated the establishment of an International Organisation for the Transition of Professional Dancers, under the patronage of UNESCO. The proceedings of these conferences (Leach, 1997; Pejovic, 1998) reveal a common concern that professional dancers develop as people so that when the moment comes for transition out of the profession they are as well prepared as possible for finding another direction. Both conferences also concluded that the process of preparing for transition is one that needs to be part of the dancer's training. To wait until a dancer's career is over before considering the next step is to wait too long.

Assuming, then, that the dance trainee will complete her training and find employment as a professional dancer, what measures need to be taken while she is still in training to ensure that she is prepared for what comes next, when her dancing career is over? Perhaps the first and easiest of these measures is the recognition of the skills and qualities developed by dance training. These are not only those physical and artistic skills solely relating to the practice of dance. Stanley Greben, a psychiatrist associated over many years with the National Ballet School of Canada, listed them as follows: 'In order to succeed as a dancer, one must be disciplined, hard-working, persistent, focused and concentrated, able to apply criticism and direction, possess good listening and learning skills and a desire to achieve excellence . . . The abilities to take correction and instruction and to work as a member of a team while taking individual responsibility are features attractive to any employer' (Leach, 1997: 20). A further list of 'adaptive skills' developed by dancers was produced by Suzie Jary, from the American Career Transition for Dancers (Leach, 1997): the ability to work independently and as part of a team; the ability

---

Dancers should understand that performance is one part only of a life career which they should begin to think about and plan from the moment of entering the profession.

A Dancers' Charter Appendix Three

to take direction; the fact that dancers are intelligent, hard-working and disciplined, and also dedicated and persistent; the ability to concentrate and focus; the fact that dancers strive for excellence and are highly motivated to improve and hone their skills; their flexibility and adaptability to change; their ability to think quickly on their feet and under pressure; their energy and physical stamina; an engaging physical presence; their success in one career which predisposes to success in another. As Stephanie Jordan stressed, these are transferable skills (Leach, 1997).

It is remarkable that, despite having these skills, dancers still very often lack confidence, which of course does not help in the process of transition. Dancers' low self-esteem may well be related to the fact that they seem not to be aware of their own qualities (Greben, 1989; Pickman, 1987). This was noted by Andy Evans who asks 'whether the "self-doubt" of the dancer . . . is partly self-ignorance' (Leach, 1997: 21). If we are to give dancers the pride in themselves that will lead to a valuing of what they have gained as people from their training, then these qualities need to be named and recognised in dancers in training. As this book has stressed, young people particularly depend on positive feedback, mirroring and validation for the strengthening of their sense of self. This process needs to extend to the naming and identifying of the qualities inculcated by dance training. When the moment comes to begin to think about transition, a dancer who has internalised a sense of herself as possessing these qualities will have very much more confidence in what she can bring to a new area of development.

In addition to a sense of ownership of the qualities developed by dance training, a trainee needs an academic education. Dance schools which train students who have not yet completed their basic compulsory education are required to provide academic education alongside dance training. Many other schools who admit students after the age of compulsory education provide a supplementary academic programme leading to

Central School strongly encourages students to continue academic study alongside their dance training and these studies are provided within the school building. All students study Dance at A-level . . . all our students can achieve . . . and find that their studies are extremely useful as a means of expanding their knowledge and increasing their personal potential. Besides the A-level work students also study . . . Dance Appreciation and Critical Studies in order to place the art form into its proper historical context.

Central School of Ballet Prospectus

further qualifications and/or provide a programme of study related to dance, for example, music, theatre and dance history, theatre and costume design (Leach, 1997). The way these subjects are presented in school publicity, the way they are timetabled in the school day, the status given to those who teach them, the importance given to them when there is conflict with dance teaching (for example, extra rehearsals) will all reveal whether they are genuinely felt to be important to the trainee, or whether they are a cosmetic and unimportant sideline to the business of technical dance training.

As Leach remarks, 'Unfortunately, academic education has too often been seen by dance teachers and students more as something to be worked around than as an integral and complementary aspect of the dancer's education. Too often, dancers are allowed to limit their academic course load to minimum secondary requirements. As a result, the dance student may fail to meet admission requirements for higher education or retraining programs. Future career alternatives become severely limited' (1997: 29). Dragan Klaic, director of the Theatre Institute in The Netherlands, is forthright on this subject: 'Training programs for future dancers have to pay more attention to the development of the intellectual dimension, the reflective and analytic capacity, and the civic profile of future dancers. This is the prerequisite for dance as an artistic discipline that can develop and remain linked to the changing social and cultural reality, gain and develop new audiences, enjoy respect and recognition. Intellectual development and civic awareness are also prerequisites for a successful career transition' (Klaic in Pejovic, 1998: 11). A student who widens and extends her education during her dance training will not only widen and deepen her personality and thereby enrich her dancing, but will also have a background that will prepare her better for the time when she no longer dances and 'facilitate transition from a professional [dance] career into new fields of work' (Leach, 1997: 29).

Other commentators have noted that dancers often seem to have little grasp of the ordinary practical skills which are usually necessary to the

---

Teachers should give more attention to the educational aspects of training rather than only technique teaching and passing examinations. A broader curriculum will ensure that students are equipped for alternative dance careers or reintegration into the general state education system, if necessary.

A Dancers' Charter Appendix Three

conduct of adult life. Renato Zanella, director of the Vienna State Opera Ballet, remarked at the Lausanne Conference: 'Dancers don't know how to integrate into society, be it such simple things as how to pay taxes, or what their rights are . . . they only want to dance' (Leach, 1997: 31). They 'have led limited lives, so that they are inexperienced in practical matters' (Greben, 1989). Clearly, transition into what Mary Clarke, the editor of *The Dancing Times*, calls 'civilian life' (personal communication) will be made infinitely easier if the dancer has already acquired these skills. It may well be appropriate, therefore, for dance schools to be including these everyday competences in what they offer. Dance students, as has already been noted in this book, are often obsessed with technique so that they have little space for anything else. This phenomenon was described by Richard LeBlond, President of the San Francisco Ballet Association, as 'a kind of almost hysterical concentration on technique that begins at a very, very young age where you stay in that studio and polish your steps and systematically disqualify yourself from learning anything else in the outside world' (LeBlond, quoted Pickman, 1987). Clearly, the student depends on the institution to condone such attitudes; if the dance school can allow itself to remember the long-term need of students to be able to make the transition out of dance, such attitudes can be moderated so that other learning goals are also validated.

In all these practical and concrete ways, dance training institutions can attempt to provide their students with the tools that will be necessary for their eventual transition out of dance. There are, however, a number of additional ways in which students can be prepared psychologically for this change. The first is by a continuing concern for the student's emotional development as an adolescent. This subject has already been explored in some detail in an earlier chapter; here my concern is simply to point out that a dancer who has not experienced the relevant social, emotional and sexual development will be at a terrible disadvantage once she steps outside the confines of the dance world (Leach, 1997).

A related concern, which again has been discussed more fully in an earlier chapter, is for the student's ownership of, and responsibility for, herself and her training. A student who has been educated to make choices for herself and to consider options carefully during her training will have a better chance of considering options and making appropriate choices both as a dancer and once she leaves a dance environment. During The Hague IOTPD conference in 1998, a contributor from the business world pointed out that taking responsibility for oneself is increasingly a feature of the employment world: 'Future employees will increasingly be themselves responsible for their own futures. Self-management is the new buzzword' (IOTPD conference programme, 1998). The dance world is often thought of as 'protecting' (or more pejoratively, 'infantilising') the dancer; increasingly dancers, beginning with dancers in training, need to be required and permitted to take responsibility for themselves.

Above all, dance students can be encouraged from the very beginning of their training to take on board the idea that their dance training is part of a participation in the dance world which will last for only part of their lives (Buckroyd, 1998). The expectation that a young person can give their heart and soul to dance while at the same time thinking that it might not be for all time is one that some commentators find too difficult. Judy Kupersmith thinks it is impossible: 'It is unrealistic to expect a young performer to think about changing a career when everything should be devoted to being the best performer one can be' (Kupersmith, quoted Horosko, 1982: 87; see also Leach, 1997). I am not quite so sure if that is true for trainees. If a trainee is in an environment where there is trust and open discussion between teachers and students, I think these perhaps dangerous and difficult ideas can be addressed and do not have to be defended again so rigidly (Buckroyd, 1998). I also think the concept of changes of career can be more easily grasped now at the beginning of the twenty-first century than in earlier times, since patterns of employment in the Western world are changing so rapidly. Dance training institutions can usefully talk about dance as an initial career choice, rather perhaps as athletes and members of the armed services must do, and foster the notions of change, development and evolution during the course of a lifetime. This is of course a way of thinking diametrically opposed to the 'hysterical concentration on technique' of trainees that was noted by LeBlond, and implies an attempt to foster maturity and self-awareness in the trainee. As Greben comments, 'The profession of dance is highly satisfying to its successful members, but it is always attended by the reality that careers are relatively brief, and the dancer's body is vulnerable to the assaults of injury as well as age' (1989).

So, then, it seems that there are a good number of strategies that dance schools can adopt, both practical and conceptual, which will go some way to preparing a professional dance trainee for the reality that a dance career is short and that career transition will be necessary on the other side of life as a performer. What is much more difficult, and the

In the first year of the course degree students will take the Introduction to Professional Dance Studies course. This course is designed to introduce students to a range of possible career choices, following a professional dance training. It is important for students to consider career options from the first year of the course, so that they have an awareness of the skills and contacts they need to acquire throughout their training and working lives. Practitioners from different fields discuss with students the development and practice of their work. The course covers a range of dance-related employment opportunities, including Dance Film, Integrated Dance, choreographing for different media, setting up a small company, performing and teaching for large and small scale dance companies and dance journalism.

In the second and third years of the course, three days will be set aside for lectures about Arts Administration and finding work . . . These discussions include presentation skills, commercial work, funding structures, personal and company financial management, planning and time management, organisational structures, dance networks, basic word-processing skills, National Dance Agencies, including the Video and The Place Dance Services.

The extensive professional experience of the Faculty provides a resource for companies seeking dancers, and career advice for students and graduates.

London Contemporary Dance School
Induction and Advice Notebook Academic Year 98/99

subject of the rest of this chapter, is to help students survive transition out of dance before their careers have even begun.

By the time a student goes to a professional dance school, she is heavily invested in the idea of herself as a dancer. (Butler (1994) makes the same point about elite music students.) Her lifestyle in every detail will be strongly affected by this orientation. Yet the fact is that many, probably a majority, possibly a large majority (there are no satisfactory figures) will have had to give up this self-concept because their training will have come to an untimely end. The fate of such students has been ignored. As Schnitt remarks, 'What happens to those who drop out of dance prior to, or early in, professional careers is largely unknown' (1990: 34). In what follows I would like to discuss what emotional tasks are imposed upon the student by such a premature transition and how the dance school can facilitate the least painful adaptation to this reality.

The emotional tasks for the student whose training has come to a premature end are in principle no different from those facing the dancer who has had a career and who faces the end of her life as a performer.

These are to mourn what has been lost, to re-establish a sense of identity and to discover a new direction (Pickman, 1987; Horosko, 1982; Greben, 1989; Leach, 1997; Hamilton, 1997). The particular problem that faces the trainee is that in these tasks she cannot look back on what she has accomplished during her career as a way of compensating or soothing herself for the fact that her career has come to an end. The trainee will have had very little real performance experience to confirm her identity as a dancer and probably little opportunity to develop other ideas of what she might do. Her difficulties in transition are likely therefore to be considerable. She will need, and in my view has the right to expect, her training institution to give her as much help and support as possible in this crisis that she faces. My impression is that many dance schools find this work, of supporting the student who is leaving prematurely, very difficult. Teachers may sometimes wish that the failing or unsuccessful student would simply go away and spare them the need to know how painful such a transition can be. However, it seems to me that when a dance school accepts a student it takes on a responsibility for that young person that extends to enabling her to find an alternative to dance training, if that should be necessary and if she wishes it to do so. This is the moment when the pastoral care system established in the school can come into its own and when the quality of the relationships between teacher and student will become evident. Details of how I think the institution can most helpfully respond to crises of different kinds in the life of a dancer have been given in other chapters. Here I would like to discuss in more general terms the emotional tasks listed above: mourning, the re-establishment of identity and the discovery of a new direction.

Mourning

I have already described in the chapter on crisis in the life of a trainee the understanding that loss of any kind provokes a series of emotional reactions in the ordinary person that are usually referred to collectively as mourning or grieving. An initial sense of shock, numbness and disbelief will be succeeded by at least some of a range of emotions which includes anger, guilt, sadness, depression, relief and anxiety, which in turn will give way to acceptance and a renewal of energy. The trainee who has been prepared for the possibility of an end to her training, for example the student who has gradually become aware of some physical problem which cannot be resolved, or who has been aware of the concern of her teachers about her progress over some months, will have had time to accustom herself to the possibility that she might have to leave training. This anticipatory mourning is a well-recognised phenomenon: 'When it occurs before a misfortune it has the effect of focusing the attention on possible dangers and providing an opportunity for appropriate planning. It also enables the individual to begin to alter his view of the world and to give up some of the assumptions and expectations that have been established' (Parkes, 1972: 95–6). Parkes goes on to add, 'This of course is a painful process.' Painful, anticipatory mourning may be, but not nearly as painful as mourning what comes as a shock (see also Hamilton in Leach, 1997). The student who has had an idea for some time that she must make a transition out of dance will have been able to make plans and adjust to new ideas gradually. Her grieving will in all likelihood be relatively easy. For this reason where there is concern about the suitability of the training for the student in question the institution has a moral responsibility to engage the student in discussion at the earliest opportunity, precisely so that the processes of anticipatory mourning are set in motion.

Students also differ greatly in how far dance training is their unequivocal, unambivalent choice. There are at least some students that I have known for whom it has been a relief to be told that they would not be able to continue with the training. We need not assume that a premature end to the training is a disaster for all students. But let us consider a difficult scenario, for example the student who has been injured in such a way that it is clear that she will not be able to have a performance career. This state of affairs could not have been foreseen and no preparation could have been made for it. Let us also assume that this is a promising student who had a good chance of a performance career. What is it exactly that such a student has lost; what is it that she must grieve? She has had no career; what loss has she suffered and why is it so painful to her?

No student gets as far as professional dance training without having spent a great deal of time projecting herself into the future when she will be a performer (hence the continuing popularity of Noel Streatfield's books and other similar more recent stories for children; see also Novack in Thomas, 1993). In order to be able to focus on the training and put up with the many demands it makes on her, the student will repeatedly fantasise about the time when she will actually realise her potential and her dreams will become reality. A very major loss, then, if she is obliged to give up training, will be this imagined future that has been her goal and her dream for many years, probably long before she actually began professional training. Just as the mourning for the miscarried baby can be as painful as for the loss of a living child, so the loss of a career that has not even begun can be as painful as the ending of a career for an established dancer. Maybe it is even harder to grieve for the loss of what you never had, a dream, a hope, an unfulfilled expectation. You have never had the chance to see the down-side of the dream, to become appropriately disillusioned. What you lose is an idealised version of the future, and fantasies are harder to mourn for than ordinary, imperfect realities. But that fantasy is part of you. Susan Lee remarks of transition for dancers who have had a career, 'The core dilemma for the dancer is the level at which dance is part of the personality structure and therefore, unlike a job, it cannot simply be discarded' (Leach, 1997: 54). For some trainees the loss will be as painful.

Along with the loss of the hope goes the loss of the structure that the dream provided for life. For many youngsters who set out to train to be dancers the future is entirely clear. They know what they have to do to realise the dream and they consider no other possibilities. As one student who found herself in the situation we are considering told me, 'I didn't bother going to careers classes because I was going to be a dancer, wasn't I? What did I need with careers classes?' It is a very severe shock to realise that not only is your chosen goal impossible but you have no other alternative that you have ever seriously considered. Life can abruptly seem a trackless void. Research on elite music students revealed that it was the most talented, those for whom the dream was most likely to come true, who had least idea of what alternatives there might be and who were therefore most lost (Butler, 1994). The routine that school provides, the group of people with whom you do class, the teachers that you have got to know, the friends that you have made at the school are all lost and in their place you have nothing.

Perhaps worst of all is the loss of the identity as a dancer that the training has, up to that point, validated and confirmed. Dance students in my experience are often exceedingly proud of their identity as dancers. One student confided to me that she thought that secretly everyone wanted to be a dancer. Certainly the thought revealed that particular student's sense of the prestige and status conveyed by being a dancer. It is generally acknowledged by those working with career professionals that loss of identity is one of the most devastating aspects of transition

(Pickman, 1987; Greben, 1989; Horosko, 1982; Leach, 1997; Hamilton, 1997), yet the dancer who has had a career has at least memories and experience that can never be taken away from her. The trainee has to deal with a very deep disappointment that is unmodified by such compensations (Buckroyd, 1987).

The danger is that the disappointment and despair of the student whose training ends prematurely is so great that she becomes severely depressed or otherwise emotionally disturbed. The responsibility of the school, therefore, which after all was the one which selected and admitted her in the first place, is to allow and accompany the student in the process of mourning. In practical terms this can be done by making sure relevant members of staff, especially the personal tutor, are available for discussion and to listen to the student's grief and distress. This is difficult, of course, because there is not (and nor should there be) an immediate solution. Recovery of a sense of self and finding a new direction will take time and cannot be undertaken while the student is still preoccupied with dealing with the loss. If a youngster's reactions are very severe or prolonged then she may also need to be referred to professional help. Often, however, I think it is not unreasonable to expect that tutors tolerate and accept the painful and difficult feelings that a major trauma of this kind is likely to provoke.

Re-establishing a Sense of Self

Old ideas about mourning used to assume that whatever had been lost had to be left behind and the mourner was faced with the task of constructing life without whatever or whoever had been lost. Recent work has focused more on an idea of integration or incorporation of what has been lost, in another form. This second way of thinking is vital to an understanding of how the identity of a trainee who has lost the possibility of a performance career can be re-established. The loss of identity arises from the thought, 'I will never be a dancer.' How can the identification as a dancer be sustained and integrated even if the youngster in question will never have a performance career? An old response to such a question might have been, 'Well, you'll just have to give up those ideas and find yourself something else to do.' A more sophisticated response might validate the student's central self-concept by saying something like this: 'You will always be a dancer; whatever you do, till the day you die, you will always be a dancer. You will always be someone for whom movement is the most significant mode of expression. You will always be someone in whom the urge to move will be powerful. You will always be someone for whom music and creative expression are important.' Judy Kupersmith has the same idea. She writes, 'Dance will never leave you. You may leave dance, but dance will never leave you' (quoted Horosko, 1982). In speaking like this we recognise, acknowledge and give space to the student's own feeling about herself. After all, her self-concept has not changed just because misfortune has overtaken her. We should not begin a process of healing the wound to her sense of self by asking her to deny or ignore the most important element in that sense of self, but rather by giving weight to it.

Of course it is not clever or kind to deny that there has been a loss, but perhaps the next task can be to define the limits of that loss. In the vast majority of cases what will have been lost is a highly specific and very narrowly defined vision of a future life as a dancer: membership of a particular company; dancing a particular role. One young dancer in this situation said to me, 'I will never dance Giselle.' My answer was something like, 'No, I think you are right. What you have been told is that a career in classical ballet is probably not right for you. It is probably true that you never will dance Giselle. And I can tell by the way you look and your tone of voice that you are terribly disappointed. Maybe it's something you've dreamed of doing for a long time.' The dancer then started to cry and told me between her tears how as a little girl she had gone to see a performance of *Giselle* and had been so transported by it that the thought she might dance that role had been a secret source of inspiration and energy ever since. We talked for some time about the sadness of having to surrender that particular dream, but then she was the one who started to say, 'But it's silly to talk as if there was only one way of dancing. Mrs X didn't say I wasn't any use as a dancer; she said she thought that probably ballet wasn't right for me.' (I silently blessed Mrs X for her sensitivity.) 'I like contemporary and the new jazz teacher has been really encouraging. Maybe I can talk to him about whether he thinks I could be good at that sort of dancing.' In fact this particular student went on to make a sustained and rather successful career as a contemporary dancer.

There are students, however, who will probably never have dance performance careers of any kind. What can usefully be said to them to heal their wounded sense of self? One possible initiative is to ask such a young person what it is that has been important and interesting to her about dance; what is it that she likes about dance; what attracted her to it in the first place. There can be a surprisingly wide range of answers to this question. The obvious answer is, 'I like how it feels in my body when I dance.' Then one can answer something like, 'Could you imagine having that pleasure as something you find for yourself in ways other than as a performer?' Some students can feel reconciled in this way to having dance as part of their lives (via classes, for example) rather than as all of their lives. Some students answer that they like the look of dancing; they like the patterns and the movement as something to watch. Then one might think of choreography or stage and costume design. I have known two male students, both only moderate dancers, who have gone on to careers which were based on their visual appreciation of dance. Another student whose interest in dance turned out to be largely visual, transferred to an art school.

Another initiative one can take in attempting to heal the self-concept is to ask what the student brings to dance. It is a way of asking, 'Who are you?', and can enable the trainee to remember that there was a life before she entered the dance school and that she has done other things than dance. Interestingly, this is a question that will often make youngsters smile as they remember parts of their experience that have been eclipsed by training. One student very surprisingly recalled her great pleasure in mathematics! She eventually decided to return to academic education and in due course joined her former schoolfriends at university. This particular student demonstrates how healing it can be for students obliged to end their training to remember that although dance has undoubtedly been hugely important for them, it is not the sum total of who they are.

There is a group of students, however, for whom none of the above approaches is useful. That is those students described in Chapter Three whose emotional use of dance is as a defence against feelings and against expression. Some such young people have used an identity as a dancer as a total means of identification and as a defence against their great fear of life. To talk to a student like this about how she might modify her self-concept and to try and engage her in an alternative vision of herself is almost impossible. One such student left one full-time training at the end of the course when it became apparent that she would not be given her longed for place in the company and immediately got herself accepted, despite her age and prior training, on another training course. At the end of that she was unable to get a job because of her considerable emotional difficulties and has been unable to find another direction. Her life has become a desert of disappointment, frustration and bitterness. She still describes herself as a dancer. The best hope for this young woman is that she finds psychological help to address her underlying fear, but I tell her story as a reminder that being a dancer means different things to different people and is an identification that cannot always be modified and adapted.

Discovering a New Direction

Alongside the tasks of mourning and re-establishing identity, and overlapping with those tasks, is the work of discovering a new direction. Much of the literature of transition is concerned with this part of the process. In career professionals it often involves retraining, and much effort has gone into providing finance to enable this process. The focus for a student who must find a different direction is obviously rather different. We are trying to explore the role of the dance training organisation in relation to students whose training has come to a premature end. Clearly, the dance school cannot take responsibility for identifying financial resources or for carrying very far the steps required to enable the trainee to take up other training or education. However, the institution does have a responsibility in my view for exploring possible future directions with the trainee so that she does not leave the dance school without any idea of what her options might be or how to explore them further. There has been considerable negative comment in recent years about commercial organisations which virtually evict employers from the building within minutes of their being informed that they are redundant. While dance schools can hardly be accused of such ruthless lack of care, they have sometimes treated those students who cannot complete the training (for whatever reason) as people for whom they have no further responsibility at all. I am eager to develop in the dance training world an attitude of sustained concern which will enable the student in question to have the opportunity to regain her bearings and to begin the process of finding an alternative to her training.

Since the trainee is likely to have been affected by the common narrowing and restricting of experience that dance training tends to impose, it is likely that her awareness of other opportunities open to her is limited. My suggestion, therefore, is that the dance school, in the person

perhaps of the tutor, facilitates and encourages a systematic considera-
tion of alternative possibilities. With the help perhaps of the school
librarian, she can explore what is available in a widening circle starting
from dance training. So she might pursue a series of questions as follows:

- What other dance trainings are available. Are any of them possible,
  suitable, attractive?
- What trainings are available in areas of dance other than performance, such as choreography, teaching, dance administration, dance
  co-ordination?
- What trainings are available in other areas of performance art, such as
  acting, mime, music, singing?
- What trainings are available in visual arts, for example fine arts,
  design, graphic art, film, photography?
- What trainings are available in dance related areas, for example
  stage/costume design, stage management, arts administration, dance
  studies?
- What trainings are available in fitness/body-related subjects, such as
  osteopathy, massage, body control, coaching, fitness instruction,
  physiotherapy?

The point of an exploration conducted like this would be to take seriously
the student's original choice of dance and then to try and deconstruct
that interest. So the task would be to look at dance from as many points
of view as possible (movement, visual, performance, organisation, stag-
ing, history, fitness, and so on) and allow each aspect to lead the student
into a new area of exploration. The value of such an approach is that it
presumes that there may be a number of aspects of dance, other than
having a highly specific performance career, that may be of interest to the
student and that such a search may help to identify them. Obviously the
student will be able to identify areas of greater interest, but she should
also be encouraged to explore subjects of which she knows little.

A second direction for exploration may be to ask the student what,
other than dance, has interested her. Such an inquiry may be difficult.
Young trainees may have had little experience of anything else, so that
other interests or capacities may be embryonic. In addition, as Greben
remarks, 'Often dancers have been directed to ignore, suppress or deny
their own spontaneous feelings or desires.' Consequently, 'It may take
some searching to discover the inner drives or emotions necessary for a

successful transition' (quoted Leach, 1997: 55). As this book has repeat-edly pointed out, the less the trainee is required to 'ignore, suppress or deny', the better adjusted a person and dancer she is likely to be. Cer-tainly, transition will be less traumatic. There are of course plenty of standard questionnaires designed to identify preferences and abilities; dance schools may want to make career counselling of this kind available to those trainees for whom the necessity of transition has been particu-larly difficult.

If a student is very young, then the most obvious course of action will be for her to return to mainstream education. This may feel like a humili-ating defeat, so it is important that the tutor takes the time to validate academic education as an honourable and valuable possibility. It will probably be useful for the student also to identify what subjects she is most interested in, for example as choices for examination courses. How-ever, students of sixteen and over may also gain a great deal from study-ing for A-levels and other qualifications and may find further education colleges a less humiliating possibility than a return to school. It is in my view extremely important that further education or training of some sort is found for students leaving dance training and that tutors endeavour to protect discouraged and depressed youngsters from sliding into menial or unskilled employment.

Finally, it may bring a faint smile to the face of a student engaged in this painful process of readjustment to say to her, 'Dance training isn't just wonderful, and it prevents you from doing a lot of other things. What have you been longing to do during these years that you're going to be able to enjoy with a clear conscience?' The list of answers I have had to this question includes eating cream buns; going to bed very late; going clubbing; eating Sunday dinner with my family; lying in bed on Saturday morning instead of coming in to school. This may seem a trivial question but it is part of the very heart of the notion of successful transition: that there is more to life than dance, that the individual is more than a dancer, and that the world is full of alternative possibilities. I once met a woman in a queue at a check-out who told me that she had trained as a dancer and loved it but wasn't good enough to have a career as a performer. She had gone on to do other things but had good memories of her training. It had been for her a valuable part of her journey and her life experience that she would not have been without. It is just such an incorporation and integration of a valued experience that we are seeking to effect.

12

The Way Forward

> We have to grow up, mature our training methods. We have to look outside the language and atmosphere of dance in which we all live confined. As a profession we need to rethink our philosophy in tune with new times, deciding what we seek to achieve in new circumstances, offering a new . . . vision of dance.
>
> (Brinson, 1993)

The reader who has persevered thus far will realise that what I am proposing for professional dance training is a radical revision of the psychological and educational principles on which it has historically been based. In this final chapter I would like to summarise the argument I have put forward and indicate the implications for dance training of what I have said.

There are a number of areas of study of human development and functioning that are particularly relevant to an exploration of the psychological environment of the professional dance training:

- Adolescence and its importance as a developmental stage which enables mature adult functioning.
- The psychoanalytic concept of containment of negative and destructive feelings.
- Humanistic educational theory and student-centred learning.

- Body-awareness and the sense of self.
- Holistic understanding of the human being.
- The concept of loss and the necessity of grieving.
- A developmental perspective which includes the span.

These intellectual and conceptual tools can be used t
of significant psychological issues in relation t
training.

Self-esteem and the Sense of Self

Physical activity is known to enhance self-estee
to suggest that professional dance trainees may ex
self-esteem as a result of training. This is worrying, especially becau
the lack of self-care which seems to be its common result. Developmental
theory is capable of identifying how the sense of self grows and can be
enhanced in the young person. The processes of emotional holding and
physical handling, together with those of mirroring will, in a good situation, lay the foundations of appropriate self-esteem. Gradually increasing
physical capacity will convey a sense of agency; where this is supported
and valued it will lead to a strengthening of the sense of self. An accompanying growth in the ability to identify and symbolise feelings in words
will enhance a reflexive capacity and thus the sense of self. An awareness
of the crucial importance of self-esteem can lead dance teachers to promote the development of the self by validating and supporting increasing
competence; by finding opportunities within the training for the focused
and conscious expression of feeling; by encouraging the naming and
awareness of feelings so that they can be used in dancing to deepen and
inform the movement; by allowing dialogue and interaction about feelings within the dance class; and by helping students to a heightened
awareness of feelings which can act as guides to self-care during training.

The Creative Use of Dance Training

Ideally, then, professional dance training should strengthen the sense of
self. However, even when the training institution is able to support this
development, the student will have her own agenda; she has the capacity
to use the training for positive and creative purposes or for defensive and

obsessional purposes. Dance schools have considerable scope for encouraging the creative use of dance training; communication between students and staff can be encouraged and facilitated; peer group interaction informally outside class and collaboratively within class can be established; the institution can refuse to condone destructive and self-harming behaviour, such as dancing despite injury, and eating behaviour that ignores nutritional requirements; students can be encouraged to integrate their life experience with their dancing.

The Adolescent

The creative use of the training will be further enhanced by an awareness of and facilitation of the developmental features and tasks of adolescence. A girl's adolescent pubertal development constitutes a major change in physique which will alter her centre of gravity and alignment. The emergence of her genetic inheritance in terms of adult body shape may threaten her continuing training or her sense of herself as a future dancer. At the very least these physical changes will cause some self-consciousness and awkwardness. Dance teachers and other concerned adults, together with the student, have the task of acknowledging, accepting and managing the physical changes of puberty rather than ignoring, denying or attempting to reverse them.

With the physical changes of adolescence goes an intense self-consciousness which is focused on the body. This leads to great sensitivity in the student to what is said about her body. Furthermore, because the student feels that these changes are beyond her control she may well feel despairing about them and is unlikely to have a realistic self-image. The dance teacher working with adolescents needs to be very aware of adolescent anxieties about body shape and size and to ensure that her teaching is respectful of the student's body, supports the student through the changes of puberty and takes account of students' difficulties with achieving a realistic body image.

The psychological tasks of adolescence demand that youngsters separate and differentiate from their families of origin in order to be able to live independent lives. This separation is frequently played out via rebellion against what is expected or required, especially where institutions play a parental role, as dance schools so often do. Dance schools and dance teachers need to promote the development of the trainee as a creative and expressive young person who both can and should take responsibility for herself. They also need to facilitate interaction between students as a means for them of gaining the many skills required in forming friendships and ultimately sexual relationships which are such a vital part of the work of growing up and lead to increasing maturity and self-confidence.

The Dance Teacher as Facilitator of Emotional Development

These ideas and principles lead to the possibility of (re)defining the role of the dance teacher as the one with the expertise in the subject, who also can be guided by an informed concern for the student's development as a person. The widening concept of the dance teacher's role needs to include her awareness of psychological issues relevant to the welfare of the professional dance trainee.

The goals of training so far as psychological purposes are concerned can be expressed as follows:

- The provision of the optimum emotional environment for the facilitation of learning.
- The maximum development of the creative and expressive potential of the student.
- The facilitation of the student's autonomy and responsibility for the training.
- Continuing attention to the enabling of the student's development through adolescence to maturity.

In carrying out these tasks the dance teacher's own welfare needs to be considered. In-service training is essential. A staff support group could also be very helpful.

The teacher also carries out the task of assessment of technique. This task can be facilitated by adopting the principles of assessment methods used in mainstream education which would also enable students to learn more from their assessment. Peer assessment and self-assessment are also valuable tools in enabling students to take responsibility for their learning.

The Use of the Group

Virtually all dance is taught in groups, with the teacher taking the responsibility for all communication in the classroom, in effect teaching a room full of individuals. Very little use appears to be made of the group as a resource for both teacher and student and very little notice is taken of its dynamics. Teachers would benefit from developing their awareness of group processes. They might also find it worthwhile to make use of small group teaching methods. This strategy would also have the function of developing students both as dancers and as mature people. The class group can also be actively developed in such a way that students use it to express concerns and to offer support to each other.

The Student's Responsibility for the Training

Traditionally the dance teacher has given herself the onerous task of the entire responsibility for the student's training and much of what has been said in this book deals with how that responsibility may be discharged. However, the student both can and should have an appropriate share of that responsibility if she is to take ownership of the training. The dance school can help trainees towards an identification of their own motivation for training. This is a ongoing process of commitment and recommitment to the training. It will benefit the student's growth towards maturity to take responsibility for physical preparation for the training in collaboration with the dance school. She is the one who must in the end be responsible for her weight, her nutritional status, her use of drugs, alcohol and tobacco, her punctuality and attendance. Similarly students must take responsibility for their psychological engagement with the training: their willingness to learn; their openness to the enlargement of their artistic and imaginative capacities; their involvement in the group process.

The Welfare of Male Trainees

Virtually nothing has been written about the experience of boys in training. In the Western tradition of professional dance (in former Eastern bloc countries the meaning attached to male dancers appears to be very different) they are often in a minority and a small minority; how does that affect their development as young males; how do they perceive their training; how can dance training organisations best ensure that the learning environment is suitable for boys? The results of a small research project suggest the following answers: The choice of dance training for boys is still met with considerable prejudice and taunts that the student is a 'sissy' or homosexual or unmanly. Dance training organisations need to be particularly careful to protect the male identity of boys by emphasising the athletic demands for strength and endurance and by encouraging pride in their identity as dancers. Boys participating in the study were unanimous and emphatic that a large proportion of their technical training, especially in ballet, should be in classes of boys alone. They felt emasculated by classes that required them to do 'girls' movements' and had difficulty in identifying with girls or female teachers in mixed classes. Boys need to be taught with other boys rather than in mixed classes, at least some of the time, in order to consolidate and validate their male identity as dancers. Anxiety was expressed by the boys in the study about whether their male peer group would understand them or whether they might even be in some danger from other adolescent males. They showed signs of restricting themselves to a very narrow social group of other dancers. This has obvious disadvantages in terms of their needs as adolescents to be exposed to difference and variety of experience. Dance schools can help boys maintain as wide as possible a social circle by facilitating their contact with other young male artists and performers.

Dealing with Loss and Change

Much is now understood about the processes of loss and change and their likely effect on people. It is known that in order for ordinary development to continue it is necessary for people to acknowledge and assimilate psychosocial transitions via a process of grieving. The dance school needs as part of its responsibility to the young people in its charge to concern itself with their reactions to crisis of all kinds. The pastoral care system within the dance school needs to be developed to provide a support system for students in need. The development of a system of personal tutors within the dance school will provide individual dancers with a mentor within the school who can monitor their progress and be available to them in crisis. Staff who undertake this role will need some training in relation to it. Tutors should be available to students suffering from ordinary life crises, such as the illness or divorce of parents. They can also have a very valuable role in helping students deal with crises in relation to their training such as injury, financial crisis or inadequate progress within the training.

Eating Disorders

Anorexia and bulimia appear to be precipitated by a combination of cultural pressures, low self-esteem, difficulty in expressing feelings directly and current trauma or crisis. Although it seems unlikely that dance training 'causes' eating disorders it may very well create an environment in which all four of these predisposing factors are present and where vulnerable youngsters may develop them. The cultural pressure to be thin within dance schools needs to be modified by a requirement that girls establish menstruation and maintain it throughout their training. Support and information to enable students to develop appropriate ways of eating which will avoid the common problems of poor nutrition, bizarre and compulsive eating patterns and preoccupation with food that are the precursors of eating disorders. Particular attention needs to be paid to developing and consolidating the self-esteem of trainees so that they feel proud of their talent and skill and are able to recognise that as elite athletes and performers they owe themselves the best possible treatment. Similarly the dance school needs to encourage students to name and express their feelings in words so that they are less likely to use the indirect vehicles of food and their own bodies as a language in which to code their emotional lives. Greater expressiveness will also promote their development as dancers and as artists. Lastly, the dance trainee needs to have available to her appropriate support from the pastoral care system within the school to help her deal with crisis or trauma that arises during her training. Where the student nevertheless develops eating disorders, the appropriate psychological help needs to be made available to her.

Transition

It is increasingly recognised that preparation for transition out of dance into a post-performance career needs to begin while dancers are still in training. Identification of the transferable skills provided by dance training will help students develop a sense of their capacity to succeed in other fields besides dance. Widening and extending a student's academic background will deepen her personality and thereby enrich her dancing but will also prepare her better for a time when she no longer dances. Ensuring that she has acquired the everyday competences that are needed for ordinary life will also give her confidence in her ability to survive outside the dance world. Most important of all, requiring and facilitating her emotional development into a responsible young adult will give her the emotional tools with which to make appropriate choices for herself in the world outside dance.

It is much more difficult to prepare students for a transition out of the dance world when, for whatever reason, they will never enter on a performance career. Students who end their training prematurely need a great deal of support to weather the crisis. They will need the opportunity to mourn what they have lost, help to re-establish a sense of identity and purpose, and guidance to discover a new direction.

Finally . . . some dance schools will already be familiar with many of these ideas and will have experimented with putting them into practice in various ways that suit their particular circumstances. Others will find many of the ideas new and perhaps strange and unacceptable. My hope is that what I have written can be used not as a blueprint but rather as a resource for all dance schools, whatever their views, to stimulate debate and inspire development in the training of professional dancers.

Appendix 1

Research Methodology

The precise field of interest which this book attempts to address – that is, the emotional welfare of the professional dance trainee – has been given relatively little attention. In writing it, therefore, I have found myself using data from other disciplines to elucidate what may be relevant for dance training. My personal experience as a student counsellor in a dance school has been an important source for the book, as have conversations and interviews with many dance professionals. The research on male trainees provided material for one chapter. In what follows I describe in more detail the research methodology I employed in generating this book. It has been a piece of qualitative research, concerned with meanings and values; the references to research theory and theorists will be found below.

Literature

Jerome and Diana Schnitt have been distinguished members of that small band of researchers who have explored psychological issues relating to dance. In 1988 they came to the conclusion that in order to understand dancers it was necessary to be familiar with 'a widespread theoretical and experimental literature' (240). I have come to the same conclusion. I have drawn my inspiration from three areas: first, from the literature that deals more or less directly with dancers, especially trainees, and their emotional and psychological experience of dance; second, from developmental, psychological and psychotherapeutic studies of individuals and groups; and third, from theorists of learning and education. I have also made use of some of the literature on sports psychology. Some studies of psychological issues in relevant parallel disciplines, for example music and gymnastics, have been used. In what follows I have given an indication of the main fields of work on which I have drawn.

The Dance Literature

Autobiographical Accounts
Schnitt and Schnitt (1987) are dismissive of personal accounts by dancers of their experience as research data: 'It has become fashionable of late to "tell all", as Kirkland has done in her recent book relating her perspectives on some of the realities of the life of the adolescent dancer. This type of account can vividly convey the intensity of some of the challenges dancers encounter. However, no matter how honestly such a work is constructed, it still must be recognised as a subjective recounting of an individual's experiences, which complements but does not replace scientific study.' This comment reveals a belief that there is another kind of knowledge – 'scientific' knowledge – which is superior to 'subjective' knowledge. This assumption has been trenchantly challenged by epistemologists and qualitative researchers (e.g. Reason and Rowan, 1981). Currently many theorists of research in the social sciences are emphasising, rather, the necessary subjectivity of research data, however generated, and emphasising that data without interpretation or application is meaningless (e.g. Moustakis, 1990; Edwards and Talbot, 1994; Toukmanian and Rennie, 1992; Whyte, 1991). In terms of my research interests which privilege meaning and value, these autobiographical accounts, spontaneously created by their authors, rather than in response to any research interview or questionnaire, constitute a valuable source of independent data.

There are a considerable number of such accounts. Some, as Schnitt and Schnitt point out, are stylised, such as those by Judith Jamison (1993) and Makarova (1979) and give relatively little insight into the author's inner world. Others such as those by Kirkland (1987), Gordon (1983) or Brady (1994) are exceedingly rich in their descriptions of the author's emotional life and the ascription of meaning to experience.

There is of course no question of these being *representative* accounts of a dancer's experience. Those that are most interesting are often describing unhappy and difficult experience. Perhaps there is less motivation or likelihood of writing a vivid account if the experience has been more satisfying or more ordinary. In any case, my interest has been in attempting to analyse the problems in dance training, for which purpose these accounts of pain and difficulty have been useful. In addition they highlight central themes in the emotional experience of dance training: for example issues around power and authority; issues of autonomy and self-determination.

The Psychology of Dancers
The literature within this area fall into two fields. The first is an interest in the psychological pitfalls waiting for the dancer, such as those of injury, eating disorders (see below), transition (see below) and competition (e.g. Schnitt and Schnitt, 1987, 1988, 1991; Kyle, 1991). Unfortunately, little of this work, with the exception of that of Greben (1990), has much to say about how these issues can been managed within the dance school or company.

Dance psychology has come from a cognitive behavioural background and has been much influenced by sports psychology (e.g. Wilson 1994; Taylor and Taylor, 1995; Hamilton, 1997; Tajet-Foxell, 1997). It has therefore mostly concerned itself with maximising performance and structuring rehabilitation from injury.

Neither of these groups of writers has focused on issues to do with the provision of an optimum learning environment within dance. There has, however, been some writing on the emotional welfare of dancers and trainees. Horosko (1982) has directly addressed herself to the emotional welfare of young dancers. Brinson's 'Dancer's Charter' (see Appendix Three) also attempted to raise awareness in this area. Brinson and Dick (1996) carried out research into the health of dancers and dance students which included some attention to their emotional welfare. Geeves has addressed many of these issues in *Safedance II* (1997).

Eating Disorders
This is a subject that has generated a significant amount of concern among dance professionals, and consequently has been researched more than many issues relating to the emotional welfare of trainees (e.g. Lowenkopf and Vincent, 1982; Szmukler et al., 1985; Schnitt and Schnitt, 1986; Garner et al., 1987; Hamilton, 1988; Wolman, 1991). However, this

work has mostly been carried out in order to determine prevalence rather than to address prevention or consider therapeutic responses. An exception is recent work by Piran (1999), which describes the establishment of a preventative programme within a dance school.

Transition
There is a very small literature on transition which pre-dates the establishment of the International Organisation for the Transition of Professional Dancers (IOTPD). Pickman (1987) and Greben (1989) described the organisations that had been established in the USA and Canada respectively to help dancers. Otherwise, the subject is mentioned in more general accounts of psychological issues for dancers such as those by Jerome and/or Diana Schnitt. The IOTPD has transformed the literature on the subject by publication of the proceedings of its two conferences in 1994 and 1998 (Leach, 1997; Pejovic, 1998). This material forms an excellent resource for work on the subject. It is mainly concerned with dancers rather than trainees, but much of what it has to say can also be used for trainees.

Dance Education
There is a considerable literature on teacher training in dance. Very little of it is concerned with the process and learning environment; most concerns content. Exceptions to this general rule are most often to do with non-professional dance, for example the work of Davies (1995, 1997), McFee (1994) and Allen and Coley (1995). Skrinar and Moses (1988) were among the few to consider the effect of teaching methods in dance training. Thomas (1993) has been one of those who has tried to suggest positive methods for dance training; Geeves and Gallaher (1993) were among those given a voice by Peter Brinson's Training Tomorrow's Professional Dancers conference in 1993 to urge less coercive and more collaborative methods. Smith (1997, 1998) has been the most trenchant of the critics of old-fashioned methods.

Psychoanalytic, Psychotherapeutic and Psychological Literature

Loss and Grief
Although injury in dancers has inspired a huge medical literature and is the major focus of international conferences, such as those of the International Association for Dance Medicine and Science, there is comparatively

little on the surrounding psychological issues. Some of the dance psychology literature, such as Taylor and Taylor (1995) and Hamilton (1997), does address some of the emotional issues preceding and resulting from injury. However, ideas of loss and grief from the psychotherapeutic literature are helpful in framing these issues in terms of generally understood concepts. The work of Kubler Ross (e.g. 1969), Parkes (e.g. 1972), and Marris (1986). which has been so fundamental to the development of these ideas, is also useful for an understanding of how other losses, especially those relating to transition, may affect dancers and trainees.

The Body and the Mind

The literature on the relationship between body and mind – obviously crucial to any work on the psychology of dancers – is large, and growing fast. From a vast wealth of material I have selected a number of strands.

Exercise psychology is a growing field. The overwhelming conclusion of the literature I consulted on this subject was the creative effects of exercise for participants (Willis and Campbell, 1992; Seraganian, 1993; Raalte and Britton, 1996). It is, therefore, a matter for concern that dance training does not seem to have equivalent benefits. The work of Bakker (1988) confirms this impression, but his pioneering work needs to be extended.

The literature of infant development has focused increasingly on the inseparability of physical care and development with emotional welfare (Spitz, 1945; Bick, 1968; Winnicott, 1960, 1960a, 1962, 1966, 1967, 1970; Symington, 1985; Murray, 1988; Turp, 1999). This work builds on an older tradition within the therapeutic literature of an interest in how emotions are expressed physically (e.g. Lowen, 1958; Keleman, 1985; Kleinman, 1987; McDougall, 1989; Bermudez, 1995; Turp, 1997), and is in turn supported by the recent literature on neuropsychology (e.g. Damasio, 1996; Goleman, 1996). None of this literature is directly related to dance, although it has obvious application and has informed much of my thinking in this book.

Groups

Groups have been of great interest to the therapeutic community over the past fifty years, and an enormous amount of work has been done in developing theories of how people operate within groups. Bion (1961) and Foulkes (1948) are the founding fathers of the subject. Their work has been hugely elaborated and applied since. Yalom's book (1985) has become a modern textbook on the subject. I have used Boyd (1991) for a Jungian perspective on groups, and Jaques (1991) for a modern educational perspective. It is, however, disappointing that this work has not previously been used for dance teaching, since dance is almost always taught in groups.

Education and Learning Theory Literature
There have been huge developments in mainstream education over the past fifty years. From the vast mass of material available, I have used the work of Douglas Barnes (1971, 1976) as an example of the kind of changes in attitude to classroom teaching that are now typical of mainstream teaching. I have also referred to some contemporary teaching materials, such as the work of Dickinson (1996) and Jaques (1991), as examples of the implications for the classroom of changes in philosophy.

I have also consulted the work on the emotional meaning of teaching which has been generated by the therapeutic community. A core text for humanistic understanding is Carl Rogers' *Freedom to Learn* (1969 and later editions), which presents a vision of education as a process of emotional as well as intellectual development; of the learners as capable of self-direction and choice and of taking responsibility for their own learning; and of the teacher as a resource available to learners according to their need. Although revolutionary in their time, these values have been widely adopted by mainstream education.

The psychoanalytic literature on education has been largely concerned with understanding the challenge that learning presents to all of us. The pioneering work of Isca Salzberger-Wittenberg (1983) has been elaborated by a number of authors, including Saul (1991), Wheeler and Birtle (1993) and Coren (1997), commenting on the processes by which the individual may develop in and through education.

Research on Male Trainees

This piece of research was carried out by means of semi-structured interviews with male trainees in focus groups. Details of the research subjects and the practical organisation of the interviews are given in Chapter Eight. The interview schedule and consent form are reproduced in Appendix Two. My intention was to enquire into a fairly limited area of interest, and therefore the schedule attempted to focus the discussion. On the other hand, I was not sure that I could predict all relevant topics, so I stressed that additional subjects could be raised – as, in fact, they were, as the reader can see from Chapter Eight.

In terms of research methodology, this was encouraging. McLeod (1994) points out that power differentials can inhibit open participation in this kind of interview. Certainly, there was a significant power differential of which the subjects could not have failed to be aware: I was much older than even the oldest of them; the interview materials had been distributed to them by the school and consequently must undoubtedly have been associated with it and its authority; I identified myself as someone writing a book about dance training. However, I am very accustomed to working with dance trainees; I am also very experienced in facilitating self-disclosure as a result of my work as therapist with both individuals and groups; I have also taught for many years. In addition, I shared with the students how little was known of the feelings of male trainees about their training, and expressed gratitude for any help the participants could give me. These factors will have reduced the power imbalance

The use of the group, a 'focus group' (McLeod, 1994), was also a device which reduced the power of my presence. I had some hesitations about it because I thought peer pressure might inhibit expression of difficult issues, or create a misleading unanimity. This may, of course, have happened, but there was significant disclosure of difficulties and also expression of differing opinions within the same group. Individual interviews would have been unrealistically time-consuming and certainly would have hugely increased the power differential.

In terms of the ethical issues involved, all students were offered consent forms. Strictly speaking the consent for all those under eighteen could only be given by a responsible adult, in this case the School Principals, who had seen the schedule before the interviews and with whom I had discussed the research and who had given permission for it to be carried out in their schools. However, I wanted each student to have the opportunity of acknowledging that they understood the purpose of the interview, of recognising that the group would be tape-recorded, and of choosing how or whether they wished to be acknowledged in the book. As a result of the form of the research, there was no assurance of confidentiality, which I would expect to further limit self-disclosure.

Interviews with three adult male dance teachers, each of whom had had a significant performing career and had taught boys, provided an additional source of data and point of view for the research.

Experience as a Student Counsellor with Trainees

This book had its origins in my experience of working therapeutically with dance trainees. During the course of that work I produced reports on what I was doing. These reports have now been analysed in the light of my current research interests. During the five years of my employment at LCDS I was also supervised by a senior member of the psychotherapy profession, which also provided me with the opportunity for reflection and analysis of what I was doing. This material has also now been analysed. My book *Eating Your Heart Out* (1989), the articles written for the *Dancing Times* (1986–88) and presented in various other settings since (1990, 1995, 1997, 1998), are also based on this experience and similar psychotherapeutic work with dancers and trainees since I left LCDS. I have, therefore, had a number of ways of reflecting upon my clinical experience in that setting.

Writers on research in counselling and psychotherapy (e.g. Touk-manian and Rennie, 1992; McLeod, 1994; Roth and Fonagy, 1996) have considered the various problems arising from research in this field being carried out by the clinician who also carries out the treatment. Clearly, the distancing of the researcher from the research, the use of randomised controlled trials, and numerous other characteristics of conventional posi-tivist research, are impossible in the psychotherapy situation. In the past, this has been thought to render the clinician's own observations and conclusions valueless. However, scepticism in relation to positivist method, and concern to extend research into clinical work in this way, has led to a reconsideration of the research methodology. It is now generally accepted that research of this kind can generate hypotheses that can then be tested further and produce clinically useful data. The concept of triangulation – that is, that data should, where possible, be tested against knowledge from other fields, for example developmental psychology – helps to validate and contextualise data from the individual clinician's experience. I have followed this procedure in my work for this book, by my use of literature from other disciplines and by gathering data from senior dance professionals.

Interviews with Senior Dance Professionals

Throughout the development and writing of this book I have had many conversations, both formal and informal, with senior members of the dance community. Their assistance is acknowledged in the Preface. These interviews have helped me to bring together the other strands of my research and have validated many of my proposals. They have also provided a further perspective on dance training which has enriched the other material.

Appendix 2

Protocol and Consent Forms for the Research on Boys and for Interviews with Dance Professionals

The data for the chapter on the experience of boys in dance training was collected partly from three focus groups conducted in three separate dance training organisations: London Contemporary Dance School, the Central School of Ballet and Elmhurst School. In each of these institutions the administration invited boys from the second year and above of training to participate in a semi-structured group interview which was recorded. Consent forms and interview questions were made available a few days ahead of the interview date and are reproduced below.

Consent Form

For participation in Julia Buckroyd's research into the experience of male professional dance trainees of their training

I am writing a book about the emotional welfare of professional dance students. As part of it I want to write a chapter on the experience of male trainees. Very little has been written on this subject, so I am hoping that you will help me with some research which I may also publish as a separate article.

I am recruiting groups of male students who are in their second year or later of training in three different dance schools (London Contemporary, Central and Elmhurst) to take part in a one-hour group discussion of the emotional experience of dance training as a male trainee. The discussion will be semi-structured, that is I will be asking for your views on the issues listed on the accompanying sheet. However, if there are other issues you wish to raise, please feel free to do so.

The discussion will be tape recorded. Your contribution will not be individually identified in the text, but unless you wish otherwise, your participation in the research will be acknowledged in the notes to the resulting published work.

If you are willing to participate in this research on these terms, please will you sign the accompanying consent form, which I will collect from you at the interview.

I have read the description of Julia Buckroyd's research and I understand the form and purpose of the group discussion and am willing to participate. I understand that the discussion will be recorded, but my individual contribution will not be identified.

I would/would not like my participation in the group to be acknowledged in her work when it is published.

Name   Signed

Contact number or address   Date

The Experience of Professional Dance Training for Male Trainees

1. How much training had you had before you came to the school? Had you gone to an ordinary mainstream school? How old were you when you entered the school? How old are you now?
2. It is unusual for a boy to enter professional dance training; what were your feelings about it before you came? What did your family feel? How did your friends react?
3. Now that you have been in training for a while, what do you think about its psychological effect on you? Have you changed as a person? Do you feel confident about yourself and your future as a dancer? How good is your self-esteem? Are you proud to be a dancer? Do your friends and family notice any change in you? Do you think the stereotyping of male dancers as effeminate is still around? Has this been an issue for you?
4. What is it like to be a boy among so many girls? Do you think teachers treat you differently from the girls? What effect does your situation in the dance school have on you as a developing adolescent male? Are you different from non-dance male friends?
5. What is it like to be taught with so many girls? Do you compete with the girls, or just with the other boys? Do you think you get more attention than a girl? Do you think you are more visible/vocal in class than the girls? Do male and female teachers react differently to you?
6. How do you think the training could change so that it would be better for your development as an adolescent male?
7. Is weight control an issue? Do you think that male trainees have the same sort of problems with food and weight that the girls do?
8. What do you do apart from your dance training? What kind of a social life do you have in comparison with your non-dance friends? Are your close friends dancers? What sorts of other interests, apart from dance, do you have? How much spare time do you have? What do you do with it? Do you watch dance performance? How much? Have you other artistic interests? Have you other athletic interests?
9. Have you considered what you might do if for any reason you were unable to complete your training or unable to get a paid job as a professional dancer? What kind of standard of living do you hope for as a professional dancer? Have you any ideas for yourself in a life 'after dance'?

Consent Form

for those who have agreed to be interviewed for Julia Buckroyd's book on emotional aspects of the teaching and learning of dance

I am conducting a range of interviews to illustrate good and/or developing practice in professional dance training in relation to the emotional welfare of trainees.

The interview will last about an hour and will be tape-recorded. Extracts from the interview will be printed more or less verbatim in 'boxes' in the main text of the book.

Further extracts may be printed in an appendix.

I would like to be able to acknowledge your contribution beside the text, but if you prefer I will include it only in a general list of acknowledgements.

I have read the description of the purposes of the interview for Julia Buckroyd's research and am willing to participate. I understand that the discussion will be recorded

I am willing for my contribution to be acknowledged by name in the text

I prefer that my contribution is acknowledged only in a general list of acknowledgements

I do not want to be acknowledged by name

Name   Signed

Contact number or address   Date

Appendix 3

A Dancers' Charter

The following document was compiled and edited by Peter Brinson from comments and responses made by participants in the 1990 Dance UK Healthier Dancer Conference and was first published and distributed by Dance UK to the dance community in 1992. It has been repeatedly reprinted and republished and is now in its 7th edition; it will certainly continue to evolve. I have quoted from it throughout this book and thought that it might be useful for the reader to have in a more complete form. It represents a code of good practice for all involved in dance and will be helpful to dance schools who wish to review their current systems.

Dancers should

- Pay more attention to their own lifestyles as a cause of injury/illness e.g. less smoking, sensible eating, proper rest, wearing clothes in class/rehearsal which allow teachers to see the body properly.
- Take more responsibility for themselves and each other in general health and also in injury prevention.
- Understand that performance is one part only of a life career which they should begin to think about and plan from the moment of entering the profession.
- Take a more positive view of injury as a sign that something is wrong which requires consultation, rethinking and acceptance of the fact

that some treatment inevitably is lengthy if it is to be effective.

- Reject peer pressure and emphasis on body image.
- Listen more carefully to corrections and know their own limitations.
- Understand more clearly reasons for warm-up and warm-down with adequate personal preparation before class/rehearsal/performance particularly taking into account stress, fatigue, cold rooms and hard floors.
- Realise the importance of their own attention to nutrition, all-round health, relaxation, general strength and balanced, well structured, felt posture.
- Insist on obligatory classes each working day when this is not written into contracts.
- Be bolder in pointing out to choreographers the physical dangers of some newly-invented movements, excessive repetition and long rehearsals.
- Be careful when consulting general practitioners who lack specialist knowledge of dance work.
- Realise that emotional problems, including depression, often are as urgent as the need to treat physical injury.
- Have a medical examination on joining a professional company, and, if possible, at the beginning of each season.
- Increase their knowledge of anatomy and exercise physiology as a prime means of preventing injury and spoiling careers.

Choreographers should

- Resist the pressure put upon them to innovate and push back the limitations of physical achievement.
- Remember that new choreography is often the cause of injury or psychological stress, therefore, choreographers should avoid this damage to dancers' careers by limiting violent demands on dancers.
- Remember that repetitive work in rehearsal or over-rehearsal can cause injury, so choreographers/managements should plan rehearsals better. At the same time dancers recognise that under-rehearsal also can cause injury. It is a question of balance.
- Understand that the demands of different choreographers involve different styles and even different techniques requiring more time to learn, understand and get used to new movements.

- Pay more care to the differing physiques of second casts with willingness to vary choreography where possible rather than risk strain or injury.

Teachers should

- Rethink teaching to take more account of advances in sports medicine, Olympic athletic experience, nutrition and recent medical knowledge.
- Seek to develop thinking dancers able to respond intelligently to all aspects of their training, including new ideas, rather than dancers who 'react as puppets' with good technique.
- Give more attention to the educational aspects of training rather than only technique teaching and passing examinations. A broader curriculum will ensure that students are equipped for alternative dance careers or reintegration into the general state education system, if necessary.
- Emphasise the need for quality teaching at an early age, including subjects such as anatomy and physiology, as well as openness about physical limitations and personal attributes
- Be more rigorous in selecting students, especially for classical ballet, with no acceptances 'just to keep up the numbers'.
- Include for students accepted on full-time vocational courses a week's induction to help them understand, through talks, seminars and classes, what to expect during training, what is expected of them and their possible career options.
- Provide more and earlier information about how the body works, about anatomy, physiology, the reasons for important aspects of dance such as warm-up, warm-down, the sequences of exercises and the causes and treatment of injury.
- Seek regular in-service/refresher courses to raise standards, update teaching, improve first-aid knowledge and remove old attitudes.
- Demand more education in nutritional, anatomical and injury problems and more knowledge of exercise physiology in teacher training in order to reduce injuries.
- Include more examples of good practice in their teaching.
- Recognise that 'much damage is done at an early age by inexperienced or unqualified private ballet teachers'.

- Recognise a need to rethink teacher training to embrace new know-ledge from within and outside the profession, to extend professional dancer training courses in teaching and 'to destroy the idea that teachers are failed dancers'. Changes in the profession need to start with teacher training to encourage a rounder approach involving personal growth and care for the whole person.
- Include early and regular availability of counselling not only for psychological or personal problems but also for advice about alternative dance and related careers.
- Accept the need to train dancers mentally and psychologically, as well as technically, for today's choreography, so that the emphasis should be placed on versatile interpreters and artists rather than virtuoso gymnasts.
- Develop better liaison between students and teachers and among teachers themselves, including the practice of reports by student groups on their teachers.
- Rcognise that existing training methods are neither infallible nor sacrosanct, that teaching can be wrong and that solutions should be sought more often in consultation with dancers and students.

Administrators should

- Develop more communication between dancers and management.
- Provide adequate financial help, in collaboration with funders, for dancers injured or ill as a result of work, and include this provision as a regular item in annual estimates of expenditure. In particular to:
  (a) continue paying injured or sick dancers where this is not covered in contracts;
  (b) pay for essential treatments, including alternative therapies, where these are not covered by the National Health Service, and they are deemed appropriate;
  (c) safeguard dancers in companies unable to afford treatment themselves;
  (d) institute forms of insurance cover to make these protections possible, learning from, if need be, the help and protections given to top athletes.
- Institute annual health screening of their dancers, since this will save money.

- Maintain a company injury book including the medical recommendations in each case of injury.
- Tour dance floors to limit injury to feet and muscles.
- Make first-aid boxes and first-aid training compulsory in all companies.
- Institute counselling as a regular provision in all companies/schools.
- Rethink the working day to allow:
  (a) proper breaks for meals;
  (b) a shorter working day to allow time for rest and treatment where necessary;
  (c) occasional talks/discussions on injury prevention and treatment, nutrition, lifestyle, exercise physiology and other matters relevant to healthier dancing;
  (d) more time for physiotherapists to treat dancers' problems and more knowledge of exercise physiology in teacher training in order to reduce injuries.
- Encourage closer liaison between artistic and medical staff, e.g. the rehearsal director and the doctor/physiotherapist.
- Adopt a more sympathetic rather than condemnatory approach to injury/illness with a policy emphasis on prevention and help running through all management practice.
- Aim at a team approach in all health policy so that dancers, management and medical staff work together and not in opposition.
- Recognise a need to link more closely with athletes, sports medicine, lessons from Olympic experience, psychological experience and scientific advance in relevant fields.
- Bear in mind that a principal cause of injury and illness is the quality of venues, floors, overloaded schedules, food and living conditions on tour, and take steps to mitigate these causes.
- Give more thought to dancers as individuals and to their personal growth, security, confidence, respect and integrity.
- Recognise that life in community dance or small companies adds to injury risk through additional duties such as stage clearance, wardrobe, management responsibilities and sometimes driving, and therefore take steps to mitigate these risks as far as possible.

Appendix 4

Collaborative Projects between Dance Students and other Arts Students

In this appendix I have given two examples of collaborative projects for dance trainees with other arts students. I am indebted to London Contemporary Dance School for permission to quote the first example, which is a collaboration with music students. The second project is one developed at Central School of Ballet with design students. I am grateful to Sara Matthews of Central School for permission to use this course description.

London Contemporary Dance School

Course: Year 3 BA (Hons), Music Collaboration

Course Outline

The collaborative project is an elective course for experienced student choreographers who have demonstrated an ability to work on an independent basis. Students will investigate issues which arise out of the relationship between dance and music. They will be encouraged to develop those skills which are necessary for a successful collaboration. The course will begin with an intensive two-week workshop for choreography and music students. It will then focus on the work of each collaborative team through the regular presentation of the pieces as they develop throughout the term. The course will culminate in an assessed perform-ance towards the end of March.

Assessment method or criteria for giving credit (attendance alone is not enough)

Process

Workshop 15%
- Consistent attendance
- Active and imaginative participation in the workshop
- Contribution to class discussion

Feedback sessions 20%
- Consistent attendance
- Regular showings of work-in-progress for feedback purposes
- Responsiveness to feedback and growth as a result of that input
- Understanding of and sensitivity to the challenges of the collaborative process
- Active participation in class discussion and an ability to articulate observations clearly about your own work and that of your colleagues

Performed work 65%
- Clear intention: all aspects of production should follow from a central concept agreed by the collaborators.
- Skill in crafting: students should demonstrate an appropriate level of competence in all areas related to the invention, manipulation and organisation of the materials in the piece.
- Invention: work should show a fresh imaginative and distinctive ap-proach to the subject matter.
- Commitment to the collaborative aspects of the work: the work must demonstrate substantive exploration into the relationship between dance and music.

Intended Method of Feedback

There will be regular feedback sessions in class, throughout the term. You are also welcome to make appointments with your tutor to discuss your work.

Central School of Ballet

Design for Dance Project

This project is a collaboration between the Theatre Design Course at Central St Martins and five London-based dance schools. It forms part of the final examinations in the Theatre Design Degree. The performances that result from the project take place at the Cochrane Theatre in London during February and March.

The Central School of Ballet Involvement

Work commences for students during the final week of the 1st year with a series of choreographic workshops.

Students are then given guidelines for putting together a proposal for a piece which is researched and written over the summer holiday. Guidelines include four musical categories from which they should select their piece: ideas for external structure (overall shape); internal structure (how they intend to go about creating movement material); sources of inspiration; notes on colour, mood, design, etc. The resulting proposals take many different forms, ranging from one side of A4 to a six-side project including pictures; some students present scrapbooks of their ideas.

Workshops continue through September and October with all students having an opportunity to make some work. During this period six students are selected to create their full pieces for the project and work starts on these.

The Collaborative Phase

The design students visit the School towards the end of November/ beginning of December. They watch the work which has been created, look at the projects of the selected choreographers and engage in discussion. The design students also bring and share examples of their work. From this meeting the choreographers and designers pair themselves and begin an ongoing dialogue.

From this point the designers come into the School for rehearsals and equivalent meetings take place at Central St Martins. As a result some social contact also takes place.

During production week four days are spent in the theatre putting the work together; there are two performances at the end of the week.

Perceived Benefits

- A valuable opportunity for students to experience the creation of a total dance work.
- Performance experience for dance students (all second-year students participate).
- Rehearsal experience for dance students.
- Development of communication skills between dance students and art students.
- Opportunity to meet other young artists which provides an experience which is valuable both for their artistic development and for its social aspects.

Bibliography

Adair, Christy (1992), *Women and Dance: Sylphs and Sirens*, London: Macmillan

Adams, Stephen (1989), *A Guide to Creative Tutoring*, London: Kogan Page

Allen, A. and Coley, J. (1995), *Dance for All*, London: David Fulton Publishing

Bakal, Donald A. (1999), *Minding the Body: Clinical Uses of Somatic Awareness*, New York: Guildford Press

Bakker, H. (1985), 'Personality Differences Between Young Dancers and Non-Dancers', *Personality and Individual Differences*, 9, 1: 121–31

Balkam, C. (1986), 'Teleology and Fitness: an Aristotelian Analysis', in S. Kleinman (ed.), *Mind and Body: East Meets West*, Champaign, IL: Human Kinetics

Bandy, S.J. (1987), 'A Humanistic Interpretation of the Mind-Body Problem', in S. Kleinman (ed.), *Mind and Body: East meets West*, Champaign, IL: Human Kinetics

Barnes, Douglas (1971), *Language, the Learner and the School*, London: Penguin
——— (1976), *From Communication to Curriculum*, London: Penguin

Belair, Alida (1993), *Out of Step: a Dancer Reflects*, Melbourne: Melbourne University Press

Bell, Elsa (1996), *Counselling in Further and Higher Education*, Oxford: Oxford University Press

Bermudez, J.L., et al. (eds) (1995), *The Body and the Self*, Cambridge, MA: MIT Press

Bick, Esther (1968), 'The Experience of the Skin in Early Object Relations', *International Journal of Psychoanalysis*, 49: 484–6

Bion, Wilfred (1961), *Experiences in Groups*, London: Tavistock
——— (1967), *Second Thoughts*, London: Heinemann

Bowlby, John (1979), *The Making and Breaking of Affectional Bonds*, London: Tavistock

———— (Vol. 1., 2nd edn 1982, Vol. 2 1973, Vol. 3 1980), *Attachment and Loss*, 3 vols., London: Penguin

Bowling, Ann (1991), 'The United Kingdom Story. Injuries to Dancers: Prevalence, Treatment and Perceptions of Causes', in P. Brinson (ed.), *International Papers in Dance Studies, No. 1, The Healthier Dancer*, London: Laban Centre

Boyd, Robert D. (1991), *Personal Transformations in Small Groups: A Jungian Perspective*, London: Routledge

Brady, Joan (rev. edn, 1994), *Prologue: An Unconventional Life*, London: André Deutsch

Brazelton, T. (1982), *Infants and Mothers*, London: Delacourt

Brinson, Peter (ed.) (1991), *The Healthier Dancer*, London: Laban Centre

———— (ed.) (1992), *A Dancers' Charter*, London: Dance UK

———— (ed.) (1993), *Training Tomorrow's Professional Dancers: The Papers of the 1993 Conference*, London: Laban Centre

———— and Dick, F. (1996), *Fit to Dance? The Report of the National Inquiry into Dancers' Health and Injury*, London: Calouste Gulbenkian Foundation

Buckroyd, Julia (1986a), 'Why Do Dancers Dance?', *Dancing Times*, April

———— (1986b), 'Move It Baby', *Dancing Times*, May

———— (1986c), 'Moving Experiences in the Home,' *Dancing Times*, June

———— (1986d), 'My Mother, Myself: Claiming our Motivation', *Dancing Times*, July

———— (1986e), 'One Toe in the Water', *Dancing Times*, August

———— (1986f), 'Feeling like Dancing', *Dancing Times*, September

———— (1986g), 'Step Lively, There!', *Dancing Times*, October

———— (1986h), 'Keeping in Line', *Dancing Times*, November

———— (1986i), 'Leaving the Stage', *Dancing Times*, December

———— (1987a), 'Auditions at London Contemporary Dance School', *Dancing Times*, January

———— (1987b), 'The Pastoral Care of Dancers', *Contact*, 94, 3

———— (1988), 'The Teaching of Dance', *Dancing Times*, April

———— (1991), 'Eating Disorders', in Brinson, Peter (ed.), *The Healthier Dancer*, London: Laban Centre

———— (1994a), 'Eating Disorders as Psychosomatic Illness: the Implications for Treatment', *Psychodynamic Counselling*, 1, 1

———— (1994b), *Eating your Heart Out: Understanding and Overcoming Eating Disorders*, London: Vermilion

———— (1995), 'The Provision of Psychological Care for Dancers', *Performing Arts Medicine News*, 3, 1

———— (1996), *Anorexia and Bulimia: How to Cope*, Shaftesbury: Element

———— (1997), 'Emotional Aspects of the Teaching of Dance', Conference Paper,

International Association for Dance Medicine and Science, Tring, UK

——— (1998), 'Towards a more collaborative learning environment in the studio', in K. Pejovic (ed.), *The Dancer of the XXI Century: Education for Transition in a Changing World*, Theater Institut, Nederland: IOTPD

Buckroyd, Peter (1988), 'Towards Personal Responsibility for Learning', in J. Ogborn (ed.), *O-Level Literature Plain Texts Scheme, 1966–1987*, Cambridge: University of Cambridge, Local Examinations Syndicate

Bull, Deborah (1999), *Dancing Away*, London: Methuen

Burt, Ramsay (1995), *The Male Dancer: Bodies, Spectacle, Sexualities*, London: Routledge

Butler, Catherine (1987), 'Counselling Music Students', *Newsletter for the British Association for Performing Arts Medicine*

——— (1994), 'An Investigation of the Effects of Psychological Stress on the Success and Failure of Music Conservatoire Students', unpublished M.Phil. thesis, University of Keele

Butterworth, G. (1995), 'An Ecological Perspective on the Origins of Self', in J.L. Bermudez, et al. (eds), *The Body and the Self*, Cambridge, MA: MIT Press

Cohen, David (1997), *Carl Rogers: A Critical Biography*, London: Constable

Coren, Alex (1997), *A Psychodynamic Approach to Education*, London: Sheldon Press

Coryndon, Sue (1999), 'Self-esteem and Confidence', Healthier Dance Programme *Newsheet*, 8.

Damasio, Antonio R. (1996), *Descartes' Error: Emotion, Reason and the Human Brain*, London: Papermac

Davies, Mollie (1995), *Helping Children to Learn Through a Movement Perspective*, London: Hodder and Stoughton

Davies, S. (1997), *The Dancing Nation*, London: British Dance Network

Deikman, A. (1990), *The Wrong Way Home: Uncovering the Patterns of Cult Behavior in American Society*, Boston: Beacon Press

Dexter, Joan Blackmer (1989), *Acrobats of the Gods*, Toronto: Inner City Books

Dickinson, Chris (1996), *Effective Learning Activities*, London: Network Educational Press

Eichenbaum, Luise and Orbach, Susie (2nd edn, 1992), *Understanding Women*, London: Penguin

Eilan, N. (1995), 'Consciousness and the Self', in J.L. Bermudez et al. (eds), *The Body and the Self*, Cambridge, MA: MIT Press

Fielding, Helen (1996), *Bridget Jones's Diary*, London: Picador

Foucault, Michel (1979), *Discipline and Punish: The Birth of the Prison*, New York: Vintage Books

Foulkes, S.H. (1948), *Introduction to Group Analytic Psychotherapy: Studies in the Social Integration of Individuals and Groups*, London: Maresfield Reprints

Gallagher, V. (1993) 'What Dance Can Learn from Sports Psychology, Performance Preparation and Enhancement', in P. Brinson (ed.), *Training Tomorrow's Professional Dancers*, London: Laban Centre

Garner, D.M., et al. (1987), 'A Prospective Study of Eating Disturbances in the Ballet', *Psychother. Psychosom.* 48: 170–5

Geeves, T. (1993), 'The Difference between Training and Taming the Dancer', in P. Brinson (ed.), *Training Tomorrow's Professional Dancers*, London: Laban Centre

––––– (1997), *Safedance II Report*, Broddon, Australia: Ausdance

Goffman, Erving (1961), *Asylums: Essays on the Social Situation of Mental Patients and Other Inmates*, London: Penguin

Goleman, Daniel (1996), *Emotional Intelligence*, London: Bloomsbury

Gordon, Suzanne (1983), *Off Balance: The Real World of Ballet*, New York: McGraw Hill

Greben, Stanley E. (1989), 'The Dancer Transition Centre of Canada: Addressing the Stress of Giving Up Professional Dancing', *Medical Problems of Performing Artists*, September: 128–30

––––– (1990), 'Psychotherapy and Other Support Services in a Ballet School', *Humane Medicine*, 6, 4, autumn: 274–9

Hamilton, Linda H., et al. (1988), 'The Role of Selectivity in the Pathogenesis of Eating Problems in Ballet Dancers', *Medicine and Science in Sports and Exercise*

––––– and Hamilton, W.G. (1991), 'Classical Ballet: Balancing the Costs of Artistry and Athleticism', *Medical Problems of Performing Artists*, Philadelphia PA: Hanley and Beyns

––––– (1997), *The Person Behind the Mask: A Guide to Performing Arts Psychology*, New York, NY: JAI Press

HES (Hertfordshire Education Services) (1998), *Framework for the Assessment of Personal and Social Development*, Wheathampstead, Herts: The Education Centre

Hinshelwood, Robert (1994), *Clinical Klein*, London: Free Association Books

Holmes, Jeremy (1993), *John Bowlby and AsJAchment Theory*, London: Routledge

Hopkins, Juliet (1990), 'The Observed Infant of Attachment Theory', *British Journal of Psychotherapy*, 6: 457–69

Horosko, Marian (1984), 'Making Friends with Yourself, Part Five. Handling the Three Big Stress Situations: Loss, Injury, Career Change', *Dance Magazine*, April

Jaques, David (2nd edn, 1991), *Learning in Groups*, Houston, TX: Gulf

Jamison, Judith (1993), *Dancing Spirit: An Autobiography*, New York: Doubleday

Jary, Suzie (1998), *Career Transition for Dancers*, New York: Jaques Organisation

Kahn, Michael (1991), *Between Therapist and Client: The New Relationship*, New York: W.H. Freeman

Keleman, Stanley (1985), *Emotional Anatomy*, Berkeley, CA: Center Press

Kirkland, Gelsey, with Lawrence, Greg (1987), *Dancing on My Grave: An Autobi-ography*, London: Hamish Hamilton

Klein, Melanie (1959), 'Our Adult World and its Roots in Infancy', in *Envy and Gratitude and Other Papers, 1946–63* (1985), London: Hogarth

Kleinman, S. (ed.) (1987), *Mind and Body: East meets West*, Champaign, IL: Human Kinetics

Koutedakis, I. (1993), 'Fitness for Dance – A Dialogue', in P. Brinson (ed.), *Training Tomorrow's Professional Dancers*, London: Laban Centre

Kutchins, Herb and Kirk, Stuart (1999), *Making Us Crazy*, London: Constable

Leach, Barbara (ed.) (1997), *The Dancer's Destiny: Facing the Limits, Realities and Solutions regarding the Dancer in Transition*, Lausanne: IOTPD

Looslie, A.R., et al. (1987), 'Nutrition and the Dancer', in A.J. Ryan and R.E. Stephens, *Dance Medicine: A Comprehensive Guide*, Chicago, IL: Pluribus Press

Lord, Madeleine (1981–82), 'A Characterization of Dance Teacher Behaviors in Technique and Choreography Classes', *Dance Research Journal*, 14, 1 and 2: 15–24

Lowen, Alexander (1958), *The Language of the Body*, New York: Grune and Stratton

Lowenkopf, E.L., and Vincent, L.M. (1982), 'The Student Ballet Dancer and Anorexia', *Hillside Journal of Clinical Psychiatry*, 4: 53–64

Makarova, Natalia (1979), *A Dance Autobiography*, New York: Knopf

Marris, P. (rev. edn, 1986), *Loss and Change*, London: Routledge

Mason, M., and Bannerman, C. (1991), 'The Dancer's Response', in P. Brinson (ed.), *The Healthier Dancer*, London: Laban Centre

McFee, Graham (1994), *The Concept of Dance Education*, London: Routledge

McDougall, Joyce (1989), *Theatres of the Body: A Psychoanalytical Approach to Psychosomatic Illness*, London: Free Association Books

McLeod, John (1999), *Practitioner Research in Counselling*, London: Sage

Mille, Agnes de (1952), *Dance to the Piper*, Boston: Little Brown

—— (1991), *Martha: The Life and Work of Martha Graham*, New York: Random House

Miller, L., Rustin, M., and Shuttleworth, J. (eds) (1989), *Closely Observed Infants*, London: Duckworth

Mitchell, Stewart (1998), *Naturopathy: Understanding the Healing Power of Nature*, Shaftesbury: Element

Murray, L. (1988), 'Effects of Post-natal Depression on Infant Development', in R. Kumar and I. Brockington (eds), *Motherhood and Mental Illness, 2*, London: Wright

Navratilova, Martina (1986), *Being Myself*, London: Grafton Books

Nitsun, M. (1996), *The Anti-Group*, London: Routledge

Novack, C.J. (1993), 'Ballet, Gender and Cultural Power', in H. Thomas (ed.) *Dance, Gender and Culture*, London: MacMillan

Orbach, Susie (1986), *Hunger Strike: The Anorectic's Struggle as a Metaphor for our Age*, London: Faber

——— and Eichenbaum, Luise (1994), *Between Women*, London: Arrow (originally published in 1987 as *Bittersweet*)

Orford, Eileen (1993), *Understanding Your 11 Year Old*, London: Rosendale Press

Parkes, C.M. (1972), *Bereavement: Studies of Grief in Adult Life*, London: Tavistock

Pejovic, Katarina (ed.) (1998), *The Dancer of the XXI Century: Education for Transition in a Changing World*, Nederland: Theater Instituut and IOTPD

Pickman, Alan J. (1987), 'Career Transitions for Dancers: A Counselor's Perspective', *Journal of Counseling and Development*, 66, December: 200–1

Pipher, Mary (1994), *Reviving Ophelia: Saving the Lives of Adolescent Girls*, New York: Ballantine Books

Piran, Niva (1999), 'On the Move from Tertiary to Secondary and Primary Education: Working with an Elite Dance School', in N. Pira, M. P. Levine and C. Steiner-Adair (eds), *Eating Disorders: A Handbook of Interventions and Special Challenges*, Philadelphia, PA: Brunner/Mazel

Pruett, Kyle D. (1991), 'Psychological Aspects of the Development of Exceptional Young Peformers and Prodigies', in R.I. Satalott, et al. (eds), *Textbook of Performing Arts Medicine*, New York: Raven Press

Rejeski, W.J., and Thompson, A. (1993), 'Historical and Conceptual Roots of Exercise Psychology', in P. Seraganian, *Exercise Psychology: The Influence of Physical Exercise on Psychological Processes*, New York: Wiley

Robbie, Eric, and Rubin, Rivca (1999), 'Critical Feedback', *Animated*, spring: 26–8

Rogers, Carl R. (1969, 3rd edn, 1994, with H. J. Freiberg), *Freedom to Learn*, New York: Macmillan

Ross, Elisabeth Kubler (1997), *On Death and Dying*, London: Routledge (1st edn, 1969).

Ryan, A.J., and Stephens, R.E. (1987), 'The Epidemiology of Dance Injuries', in A.J. Ryan and R.E. Stephens (eds), *Dance Medicine: A Comprehensive Guide*, Chicago: Pluribus Press

Ryan, Joan (1996), *Little Girls in Pretty Boxes: The Making and Breaking of Elite Gymnasts and Figure Skaters*, London: Women's Press

Sataloff, R.I., Brandfonbrener, A., and Lederman, R. (eds) (1991), *Textbook of Performing Arts Medicine*, New York: Raven Press

Saul, Jean Rannells (1991), 'A Conceptualization of Individuation in Learning Situations', in Robert D. Boyd (ed.), *Personal Transformation in Small Groups: A Jungian Perspective*, London: Routledge

Schnitt, D. (1990), 'Psychological Issues in Dancers: An Overview', *Journal of Physical Education, Recreation and Dance*, 61, December: 32–4

Schnitt, J.M., and Schnitt, D. (1986), 'Eating Disorders in Dancers', *Medical*

Problems of Performing Artists, 1, 2: 39–44

––––– (1987), 'Psychological Issues in a Dancer's Career', in A.J. Ryan and R.E. Stephens, *Dance Medicine: a Comprehensive Guide*, Chicago: Pluribus

––––– (1988), 'Psychological Aspects of Dance', in P.M. Clarkson and M. Skrinar, *Science of Dance Training*, Champaign, IL: Human Kinetics

––––– (1991), 'Psychological Issues in the Clinical Approach to Dancers', in R.I. Sataloff, et al. (eds), *Textbook of Performing Arts Medicine*, New York: Raven Press

Sidimus, Joysanne (1987), *Exchanges: Life After Dance*, Toronto: Terpsichore

Sime, Wes (1996), 'Guidelines for Clinical Applications of Exercise Therapy for Mental Health', in J.L. van Raalte and W.B. Britton, *Exploring Sport and Exercise Psychology*, Washington DC: American Psychological Association

Skrinar, M. and Moses, N.H. (1988), 'Who's Teaching the Dance Class?', in P.M. Clarkson and M. Skrinar, *Science of Dance Training*, Champaign, IL: Human Kinetics

Skynner, R and Cleese, J. (1983), *Families and How to Survive Them*, London: Methuen

Smail, David (1984), *Illusion and Reality: The Meaning of Anxiety*, London: J.M. Dent

Smith, Clyde (1997), 'The Conservatory as a Greedy Total Institution', 30th Annual CORD Conference. University of Arizona, Tucson, 2 November

––––– (1998), 'Authoritarianism in the Dance Classroom', in S. Shapiro (ed.), *Dance, Power and Difference*, Champaign, IL: Human Kinetics

Spitz, R. (1945), 'Hospitalism: An Enquiry into the Genesis of Psychiatric Conditions in Early Childhood', *The Psychoanalytic Study of the Child*, 1

Stanton-Jones, Kristina (1992), *An Introduction to Dance Movement Therapy*, London: Routledge

Stephens, R.E. (1987), 'The Etiology of Injuries in Ballet', in A.J. Ryan and R.E. Stephens, *Dance Medicine: A Comprehensive Guide*, Chicago: Pluribus

Stern, Daniel (1985), *The Interpersonal World of the Infant*, New York: Basic Books

Storr, Anthony (1972, rev. 1991), *The Dynamics of Creation*, London: Penguin

Symington, Joan (1985), 'The Survival Function of Primitive Omnipotence', *International Journal of Psychoanalysis*, 66: 481–7

Symington, N. (1993), *Narcissism: A New Theory*, London: Karnac

Szmukler, G.I., Eisler, I., et al. (1985), 'The Implications of Anorexia Nervosa in a Ballet School', *Journal of Psychiatric Research*, 19: 177–81

Tajet-Foxell, Britt (1997), 'Appropriate Thoughts', *Dance UK News*: 24

––––– and Rose, F.D. (1995), 'Pain and Pain Tolerance in Professional Ballet Dancers', *British Journal of Sports Medicine* 29, 1: 31–4.

––––– and Booth, Lynn (1996), 'An "Equal Expertise" Approach to Rehabilitation of Athletes', *Physiotherapy* 82, 4: 264–6.

Taylor, Jim, and Taylor, Ceci (1995), *Psychology of Dance*, Champaign, IL: Human Kinetics

Thomas, Brian (1993), 'Psychology and the Art of Positive Thinking', *Bulletin of the Royal Academy of Dancing*, June

——— (1997), 'Learning How to Fly', *Animated*, Autumn: 10–11

Turp, M. (1997), 'The Role of Physical Exercise in Emotional Well-being: A Psychodynamic Perspective', *Psychodynamic Counselling*, 3, 2: 165–77

——— (1998), 'In Sickness and in Health: Psychoanalysis and Psychosomatics', *Psychodynamic Counselling*, 4, 1: 3–16

——— (1999), 'Encountering Self-harm in Psychotherapy and Counselling Practice', *British Journal of Psychotherapy*, 15, 3: 306–21

——— (1999), 'Touch, Enjoyment and Health. (1) In Infancy', *European Journal of Counselling and Health*, Spring: 23–39

Tuson, K.M., and Sinyer, D. (1993), 'On the Affective Benefits of Acute Aerobic Exercise: Taking Stock after Twenty Years of Research', in P. Seraganian, *Exercise Psychology*, New York: Wiley

Tustin, Frances (1986), *Autistic Barriers in Neurotic Patients*, London: Karnac

Weir, Arabella (1997), *Does My Bum Look Big in This? The Diary of an Insecure Woman*, London: Coronet

Wheeler, Sue, and Birtle, Jan (1993), *A Handbook for Personal Tutors*, Society for Research into Higher Education and Open University Press

Willis, J.D., and Campbell, L.F. (1992), *Exercise Psychology*, Champaign, IL: Human Kinetics

Wilson, Glenn, D. (1994), *Psychology for Performing Artists*, London: Jessica Kingsley

Wilson, P. (1991), 'Psychotherapy with Adolescents', in J. Holmes (ed.), *Textbook of Psychotherapy in Psychiatric Practice*, London: Churchill Livingstone

——— (1995), 'Narcissism and Adolescence', in J. Cooper and N. Maxwell (eds), *Narcissistic Wounds: Clinical Perspectives*, London: Whurr

Winnicott, D.W. (1960), 'The Theory of the Parent–Infant Relationship', in *Maturational Processes and the Facilitating Environment* (1965), London: Hogarth

——— (1961), 'Ego Distortion in Terms of True and False Self', in *Maturational Processes and the Facilitating Environment* (1965), London: Hogarth

——— (1962a), 'The Parent–Infant Relationship', in *Maturational Processes and the Facilitating Environment* (1965), London: Hogarth

——— (1962b), 'The Child in Health and Crisis', in *Maturational Processes and the Facilitating Environment* (1965), London: Hogarth

——— (1966), 'Psychosomatic Illness in its Positive and Negative Aspects', *International Journal of Psychoanalysis*, 47: 510–15

——— (1967), 'The Concept of a Healthy Individual', in C. Winnicott et al. (eds), *Home Is Where We Start From* (1986), London: Penguin

———— (1970), 'On the Basis for Self in Body', in C. Winnicott et al. (eds) (1989), *Psychoanalytic Explorations*, Cambridge, MA: Harvard University Press

Wittenberg, Isca Salzberger, et al. (1983), *The Emotional Experience of Learning and Teaching*, London: Routledge and Kegan Paul

Wolman, Roger (1991), 'Amenorrhoea and Osteoporosis in Female Endurance Athletes including Dancers', in P. Brinson (ed.), *The Healthier Dancer*, London: Laban Centre

Yalom, Irvin D. (3rd edn, 1985), *The Theory and Practice of Group Psychotherapy*, USA: Basic Books

Index